Malcolm
LOWRY

a reference guide

A
Reference
Publication
in
Literature

Ronald Gottesman
Editor

Malcolm
LOWRY

a reference guide

WILLIAM H. NEW

G.K.HALL&CO.

70 LINCOLN STREET, BOSTON, MASS.

Library of Congress Cataloging in Publication Data
New, William H
  Malcolm Lowry: a reference guide.

  (A Reference publication in literature)
  Bibliography: p.
  Includes index.
  1. Lowry, Malcolm, 1909-1957 — Bibliography.
I. Series: Reference publications in literature.
Z8522.55.N48   [PR6023.096]   016.813'5'4   77-28579
ISBN 0-8161-7884-4

For Alan and Herbert

Contents

INTRODUCTION ix

TITLE ABBREVIATIONS xxi

MANUSCRIPT COLLECTIONS xxiii

MAJOR WRITINGS BY MALCOLM LOWRY xxv

TRANSLATIONS OF LOWRY'S MAJOR WRITINGS xxvii

WRITINGS ABOUT MALCOLM LOWRY, 1927-1976 1

INDEX 137

Introduction

The first entries in this checklist are brief biographical newspaper accounts that appeared in 1927 and 1929; they record a particularly eventful and troublesome period in Lowry's life--involving a
freighter trip to the Orient and the suicide of a Cambridge classmate
named Paul Fitte. The 1927 reports display a Lowry who was obviously
ill-at-ease, but jaunty at the same time; by contrast, the 1929 reports scarcely hint at the subjective involvement Lowry actually felt,
nor could the various reporters have realized how he would repeatedly
relive these experiences in his own mind and develop them in his
novels, Ultramarine and October Ferry to Gabriola, into themes of intense suffering and debilitating guilt. But the entries that follow,
from 1930 to 1976, trace Lowry's own revelations of his private
trials, the increasing critical sympathy for his life and his writings, and the growth of his international reputation.

The checklist refers not just to books and extended articles, but
also to other citations which might throw a certain light on the kind
of public notice Lowry attracted, and which might facilitate further
commentary and research: substantive reviews, both in English and in
other languages; conference papers wherever these could be located;
comparative allusions which might indicate the critical context in
which Lowry has been perceived; newspaper accounts, particularly from
Lowry's English, Mexican, and Canadian dwelling places; and films.
Other reviews, many of which were nothing more than advertising, have
been omitted. Under the Volcano was widely noticed, by papers like
the Salt Lake City Tribune, the Cleveland Plain Dealer, the Norfolk,
Virginia, Pilot; it was reviewed in 1963 by numerous German newspapers and on German radio; and there have been occasional radio reviews in England and Canada as well. More detailed listing of reviews
and broadcasts--as well as listings of Lowry's own separate publica-
tions--are contained in the bibliography prepared by Earle Birney and
Margerie Lowry for Canadian Literature, nos. 8 and 9 (1961, with sup-
plements in nos. 11, 1962, and 19, 1964), a work to which I am
indebted.

In verifying each of the items to be included in this bibliography, I ran into various difficulties. Some items could not be veri-
fied at all, and have been omitted. A 1961 Europea Romana article
ostensibly by Margerie Lowry, for example, called "Ina[una?] vita

ix

bruciata," could be confirmed neither in North American or European libraries nor by Margerie Lowry herself. Other items, when I located copies of them, carried incomplete data, such as missing page or issue numbers; these have been listed in incomplete form when the missing data could not subsequently be obtained. Still other items demonstrate bibliographic irregularities which require comment. Before it began its unnumbered series, for example, Les lettres nouvelles, because of another editorial change, published two issues numbered 5, in 1957 and 1960 respectively, both containing articles on Lowry by Clarisse Francillon. Some newspapers changed their names: the Liverpool Post and Mercury became the Liverpool Post, and The Vancouver Daily Province became The Province. Other works raised problems of dating. The special Lowry issue of Prairie Schooner (37, no. 4) is dated "Winter 1963-64" and is listed here under the entries for 1964. Similarly, the Winter 1969-70 issue of The Dalhousie Review is listed under 1970. Stephen Slemon's thesis is dated "December 1976" on the title page, and so is listed here as a 1976 publication, but may be considered a 1977 publication if subsequent dating of theses goes by the time of convocation. A fourth problem, in addition to those involving numbering, naming, and dating, is that of classification. Theses devoted wholly to Lowry's work are listed under "Books," as is the 1976 full-length documentary film Volcano; chapters on Lowry, in theses devoted to more general topics, appear under "Shorter Works." Each of the four items which I was not able personally to verify but which still appeared to warrant listing (one dissertation, two articles, and an early newspaper report) is preceded by an asterisk. Anonymous articles are arranged chronologically when possible. Pseudonyms are cross-referenced to writers' actual names when these have been identified.

Any survey of published critical commentary on Malcolm Lowry must take notice of the extraordinary presence which Lowry himself seemed to have. It is not just that many of the books, notes, and articles listed here concern his life, nor that, as several reviewers have asserted, he became almost a kind of cult figure in some critical circles, but also that he possessed a singularity which many of the people who knew him or knew of him attempted in some way to draw on and convey. He appears in various autobiographical memoirs—particularly those of Cambridge in the Thirties, such as Nicholas Monsarrat's, or Gerald Noxon's, or Kathleen Raine's The Land Unknown, which admits with a cheerful candidness how everyone knew Lowry then and how few genuinely recognized his genius—and he appears of course as "Hambo" in Conrad Aiken's memoirs and fiction (Ushant, 1952; A Heart for the Gods of Mexico, 1939). Nor was Aiken alone in appreciating Lowry as raw material for fiction. Charlotte Haldane's 1932 novel I Bring Not Peace draws again on the Cambridge undergraduate she knew; John Sommerfield, in a still unpublished work entitled "The Last Weekend," turns Lowry into a character named David Nordall; and Douglas Day, who in his biography (Malcolm Lowry, 1973) provides further details of these associations, also identifies Lowry with one of the central characters in Jan Gabrial's "Not With a Bang" (Story, 19,

no. 121, 1946, 55-61). In his adoptive Canada, Lowry has become the
subject of poetry rather than fiction: Edward Yeomans' "To Malcolm
Lowry" (Prism, Spring 1967, p. 89) speaks of archetypal tensions and
lost youth; Al Purdy's "About Pablum, Teachers, and Malcolm Lowry"
(The Crafte So Longe to Lerne, Toronto: Ryerson, 1959, pp. 7-8) and
"Malcolm Lowry" (The Cariboo Horses, Toronto: McClelland & Stewart,
1965, p. 9) identify Lowry as a vital person and an enlivening force.
In "Malcolm Lowry," meeting him was a matter of

> bursting from dull green wood
> out to the live green water
> with introductions ...
> on a shore full of driftwood and stones with blue
> boats on a blue horizon
> not seeming to move but moving anyway....

And two Polish-language Canadian poets, Andrzej Busza ("Kohelet" in
Kultura, no. 12 [1975], p. 44) and Bogdan Czaykowski ("Pożegnanie"
in Spór z Granicami, Paris: Instytut Literacki, 1964, p. 50), have
written of Lowry as the symbolic outsider, the immigrant lost in an
immigrant culture, who is at the same time the creator of something
powerful and the perceiver of something true.

   Although these images of what Lowry represented to others suggest
both the kind of man he was and the kind of world he created, neither
is simple. Hence his biographers, like novelists trying to under-
stand the characters they are creating, have been faced with the task
of trying to give credence to the vitality that gave the actual person his character. And in Lowry's case the vitality was often
clearer than the historical details. Even such fundamental matters
as Lowry's given names ("Clarence Malcolm," not "Malcolm Boden" or
"Clement Milton" as some reports have it), his place of birth
(Liscard [now in the township of Wallasey], not Birkenhead or Liverpool), his Cambridge degree (a third, not a first) were repeatedly
identified wrongly in reputable reference works and early commentary.
And he is variously identified as an American (in 1947), a Canadian
writer (1961), a Liverpool writer (1962), a New Brighton writer
(1963), a Sussex writer (1974), as American as he is English (1964),
whose homeland is the USA (1969). Malcolm Bradbury's 1973 attempt,
in Possibilities, to reclaim him as an English writer had first to
confront the critical contradictions that inadequately proclaimed
his public identity. The details of his private life--which Lowry
himself often spoke about and even transformed into his own fictional
world--remained less precise still, for they were complicated by the
intense subjectivity with which he met the world and, in recalling
it, recreated it. For the biographer, approaching from the outside,
inaccurate records, the partiality of friends' memories, and the
inevitably distorted portraits in romans à clef all complicated the
issue further. Lowry's first "official biographer," Conrad Knickerbocker, who died in 1966, produced a number of pioneer essays which
relied heavily on Lowry's own version of events. It is important to

underline the fact that Lowry believed in his own versions, that the
masks he enacted possessed a reality for him none the less powerful
for their often being at some variance from "objective" history.
When Douglas Day took up the challenge Knickerbocker left and began
what was to become a seven-year study, he had to remove the masks to
find the sort of man who needed the masks to be the man he was. Even
at the end of Day's labours, some periods in Lowry's life remain obscure. Subsequent work (Muriel Bradbrook's 1974 book Malcolm Lowry,
for example) has thrown Lowry's early years into clearer perspective;
reviews, occasional memoirs, and sequences of letters to journals as
different as Time and The Times Literary Supplement often contain
points of fact and interpretation that correct or modify earlier
judgments. Certain features of Lowry's contact with Mexico and much
of his experience of Canada remain yet to be elucidated.

The known biographical details establish that Lowry was born on
July 28, 1909, the youngest son of Arthur Osborne and Evelyn Boden
Lowry. A. O. Lowry was a well-to-do Methodist cotton broker, who
sent his son to private schools (Caldicote and The Leys, where--in
The Leys Fortnightly--Lowry published his first stories and essays
and in 1926 received his first critique: some classmates' attack on
his football reporting). In 1927, after an unsuccessful attempt to
launch a song-writing career, he embarked on a four-month job aboard
a freighter, the S. S. Pyrrhus, bound from Liverpool to the East
Coast of Asia, returning via the Suez. The trip gave him raw material for much of his writing: Ultramarine, "Elephant and Colosseum,"
the manuscript entitled "China," and other works. And at Cambridge
University (1929-1932), he studied English, wrote his first novel,
met Charlotte Haldane and mixed in "literary circles," and was
affected by Paul Fitte's death.

At this same time he was deeply influenced by two older writers.
One was the Norwegian novelist Nordahl Grieg (about whom Hallvard
Dahlie and others have written), the influence expressing itself
possibly most strongly in Lowry's lost manuscript called "In Ballast
to the White Sea." The other was the American Conrad Aiken, who in
1929 took Lowry on as a kind of ward. The nature of their acquaint-
ance is told in several ways: in Aiken's own works, in the influence
Aiken exerted on Lowry (R. H. Costa and Geoffrey Durrant have made
particular studies of this relationship), in Clarissa Lorenz's memoir
"Call It Misadventure" (1970) and in the various letters Aiken and
Lowry wrote to and about each other.

Through Aiken, in 1933, Lowry met and married his first wife,
Jan Gabrial, but Lowry's increasing alcoholism, his 1935 sojourn in
Bellevue Psychiatric Hospital (the site of Lunar Caustic), and their
sequence of moves to New York, California, and Mexico caused an es-
trangement that led to divorce in 1940. By this time Lowry had left
Mexico for California, where he met the former starlet and budding
mystery writer, Margerie Bonner, who, in 1940, was to become his
second wife; and probably to renew his visa, in 1938, left the

United States for Canada. With Margerie, Lowry built a cabin on the
foreshore at Dollarton, British Columbia, which--despite fires and
threats of municipal expulsion--was to become for him a kind of
Paradise (the "Eridanus" of his writings), and the place where he
wrote his major works: Under the Volcano (published after several
drafts in 1947), and many of the poems, novels and stories that were
left in manuscript when he died, Hear Us O Lord from Heaven Thy Dwelling Place (1961), Dark as the Grave Wherein My Friend Is Laid (1968),
October Ferry to Gabriola (1970), "La Mordida," "The Ordeal of
Sigbjørn Wilderness," and others. He continued to be an eclectic
reader; he was fascinated by occult systems of all kinds and was
given instruction in cabbala by Charles Stansfeld-Jones, whom he met
in 1941; and he continued to travel: to Mexico again, where he and
his wife were imprisoned in 1946, and to Haiti, New York, and Europe.
When they left Canada in 1954, it was with the intention of returning.
But circumstances intervened, and Lowry died--"by misadventure" ac-
cording to the Eastbourne coroner's report--of barbituritic poisoning
in Ripe, Sussex, on June 27, 1957.

This outline suggests little of the man's psychology: the depth
of his relationships with his parents and the reasons for his feelings
of rejection; his concern about illness; his sense of guilt; his attitudes to women (affecting, perhaps, his ability to create credible
female characters); his wit and the possibly defensive function it
served; his fascination with signs, metaphysics, and coincidences;
and even the reasons for his alcoholism. Yet these aspects of his
character affected both the life he experienced and the lives he
tried to create. Out of daily events scarcely more unusual than
those that many other people encounter--except in the manner in which
he perceived them and in the degree of passion he brought to bear
upon them--he fabricated an intricate and often powerful narrative
world.

The biographical commentaries are important, therefore, not just
for their factual information but also for the insights they provide
into Lowry's published and unpublished work. The truism that writers
write out of their own experience means something in Lowry's case.
He absorbed much that he perceived in the world around him, made it
personal, and wrote it all out into the single ongoing narrative that
he referred to as "The Voyage That Never Ends." But there was more
to it than this. He was struck by an observation Ortega y Gasset
made: to the effect that a writer is "written" by his work. Public
and private identities--in a way that Lowry's characters repeatedly
discover--became perilously enmeshed for him; fiction was an empirical world as well as a metaphysical reflection on the empirical
world, and his changing environment he increasingly saw symbolically,
as though the universe were fatefully stalking him through his daily
life. Many of his letters can be read as meditations on this realization, reflections on the relation between guilt, beauty, suffering,
and joy, and on the certainty of change, which allows him to accept
either no positions or many as "final." As a palliative, and as an

escape from his private torments, he had his friendships, the many happinesses of his second marriage, the wry humour that punctuates his work and that characterizes the way many people remember him. And he had alcohol. Alcohol, however, in time only increased the pressure. Whatever clarity of insight he felt it gave him was counterbalanced by the difficulties it threw in the way of communication. The Consul's problems in <u>Under the Volcano</u>, Llewelyn's problems in <u>October Ferry to Gabriola</u>, Cosnahan's problems in "Elephant and Colosseum" were all versions of Lowry's own. Yet as Hilda Thomas points out in her 1971 account of Lowry's letters, they were <u>versions</u>, and not to be <u>identified</u> with him. To dismiss the works out-of-hand as solipsistic is to risk ignoring what they actually managed to say.

Lowry's alcoholism, though considered seriously by commentators like Art Hill or Max-Pol Fouchet, led to a number of distorted versions of the writer's character and subject. During the 1960's, when a number of Lowry's manuscripts were posthumously edited and published, when his reputation was expanding, and when it became almost <u>de rigeur</u> for reviewers to provide a brief biography as part of their commentary, the fact of the alcoholism often seemed more attractive than the quality or the character of the art. With reviewers, that is, as with those who remembered him from the 1930's, Lowry appears to have exerted a fascination, or to have aroused a passionate response, whether negative or positive, that made ordinary "objectivity" difficult to sustain.

That the fascination with Lowry ultimately goes deeper than simple curiosity shows in the growing body of sophisticated criticism, including that which has appeared in languages other than English. A number of Lowry's works have been translated. <u>Under the Volcano</u> alone has appeared in Norwegian, Swedish, Danish, Finnish, French, German, Dutch, Spanish, Portuguese, Italian, Slovenian, Serbo-Croatian, Polish, Russian, and Japanese. In France, particularly, a distinctive body of critical commentary has appeared, emphasizing as early as the special 1960 issue of <u>Les lettres nouvelles</u> the metaphysical dimensions of Lowry's work. Here the torments of alcoholism are seen as torments of the soul, signs not just of a sensitive writer in psychological distress but even more of a non-sectarian but deeply religious writer seeking a meaning which contemporary life seems recurrently to deny. Much of the Polish criticism adopts a related position, specifying capitalism as the reason for the breakdown of contemporary society but praising Lowry for his ethical concerns in the face of such pressure. Zbigniew Bieńkowski, for example, writing in 1963, explores the problems that Lowry creates for himself because he is a "moral maximalist," but he also goes further, emphasizing how the style of <u>Under the Volcano</u>, and the reliance not on allusion so much as on syncretic structure, contributes to the force of Lowry's message. René Rapin, writing in 1966, echoes this observation when he declares that the stylistic devices contribute to the book's moral atmosphere.

While this repeated concern for the style characterizes the
early commentaries as well as the more recent ones, there have been
marked contrasts in critical receptivity to Lowry's methods. The
earliest reviews of Ultramarine are somewhat confounded by the style,
finding it to be mannered, an impediment to narrative. These early
judgments, moreover, find later support: George Steiner in 1961
talks of Hear Us O Lord from Heaven Thy Dwelling Place being an "incoherent whole"; Christine Brooke-Rose in 1967 finds Under the Volcano
"tedious" and "stylistically wayward"; Jacques Barzun (in 1947) and
Willem Hermans (in 1970) both dismiss Under the Volcano as merely
imitative. But recognitions of Under the Volcano's political and
ethical concerns gradually counter the negative reactions. Though
William Arthur Deacon expressed in 1947 some suspicion of an art that
concerned itself with chaos, the German reviews that appeared in the
late 1950's recurrently voiced their approval of a novel that in-
volved itself with chaos in order to express a chaotic time. The
French review Liens in 1959 asserted what a number of later critics
were to say: that the way into Under the Volcano was by responding
to the language it used rather than with preconceptions about how
language in fiction ought to be used. The Italian reviewer Giuliana
Gramigna in 1961 observed that there was logic underlying the surface
chaos of Under the Volcano. From this position it was a short,
though by no means effortless, step to extended studies of the polarities of the novel (Birgitta Trotzig in 1962), the tensions between
stasis and kinesis (Victor Doyen in 1969, Terence Wright in 1970,
Sherrill Grace in 1973), the balance between tragedy and the idea of
tragedy (Lawrence Raab in 1972), and the explorations of experimental
form (W. H. New in 1971, Muriel Bradbrook in 1974, Matthew Corrigan
in 1975, and others). The quest for Lowry's "tradition" shows a
similar change in emphasis. Comparisons which showed Lowry as an
imitator of Joyce and Aiken gradually became examinations of the
force of Lowry's English education and the range of his reading. The
various parallels that critics have found--with Djuna Barnes, Melville,
Baudelaire, Woolf, Wolfe, Bowen, Lehmann, Conrad, Paul Bowles, Kafka,
Gide, Artaud, Butor, Williams, O'Neill, Green, Greene, Brontë,
Fitzgerald, Faulkner, Coleridge, de Quincey, Wright, White, Durrell,
Beckett, Sargeson, Shelley, Thoreau, Wordsworth, Hesse, Burroughs,
Borges, and Antonioni--describe efforts to locate from the outside a
territory that is recognizably Lowry's own.

Other approaches to Lowry's work emphasize his sources, his ren-
dering of character and landscape, and his political and social views.
The source studies which trace Faustian, Promethean, Dantesque,
Sisyphean, Neoplatonist, Cabbalistic and other symbolic or mythical
motifs--particularly those by Max-Pol Fouchet, A. R. Kilgallin, David
Markson, Perle Epstein, Maurice Nadeau, Geoffrey Durrant, Jim Barnes,
and Carole Slade--throw light at once on technique and on theme. As
recent a study as Kristofer Dorosz's Malcolm Lowry's Infernal Paradise (1976), moreover, stresses the unity of these elements in Under
the Volcano, and tries (developing a point Alfred Kazin made in 1973)
to show how the balances and contrasts which the various patterns

produce constitute in themselves Lowry's articulation of his private
dilemma and his fictional theme.

   Yet there remains substantial critical disagreement. Often what
one critic disparages, another critic praises, and subjective notions
of decorum sometimes distort judgments. Lowry's 1946 letter to
Jonathan Cape, which one observer finds "hysterical," another finds
"eloquent"; the Consul is found to be "tragic" and on another occasion "effete"; the humour that several writers approve of, others
dismiss as "out of place." And though the temptation to stress a
single motif in any one of Lowry's works leads more than once to re-
ductive commentaries, the temptation to praise complexity for itself
sometimes proves equally strong. Lowry's own defence of Under the
Volcano, in his letter to Cape, itself shows something of the critical tension that the novel has aroused. What Cape's reader (and
some reviewers) dismissed as imitation and needless artifice, Lowry
(and other reviewers) praised as constructive pattern. Ursula Brumm
sees the novel as a demonstration of the emptiness of symbolic structure; Alfred Kazin, R. H. Costa, and others see it as a late flower
of a narrative tradition that embraces Joyce, Aiken, Faulkner, and
Mann. The political themes in the novel have caused an even deeper
critical rift, for while much East European criticism praises Lowry's
"socialist" attacks on capitalistic systems, a Marxist-Leninist review in a Canadian journal (Alive) dismisses Lowry's work as "fascist."
But neither of these positions has been developed yet to the point of
there being a critical controversy. Some effort (by Dale Edmonds in
1968, for example, and in the 1964 issue of Revista de la universidad
de Mexico) has been made to trace the Mexican political background of
the time at which Under the Volcano is set, but no study has yet ex-
plored Lowry's political philosophy in depth. As with his metaphysical
concerns, a number of issues still remain unresolved.

   Despite the critical disagreements, Under the Volcano (1947) did
establish Lowry's critical reputation. While extended comment on his
first work, Ultramarine (1933), awaited its revision and republication
in 1962, Under the Volcano won immediate response--enthusiastic in the
United States, disparaging in England, and somewhat puzzled in Canada,
where newspaper reviewers and reporters found the man more interesting than the novel. This was apparently in part a function of setting, for the first work to be widely praised in Canada was the story
set in British Columbia, "The Forest Path to the Spring." Hear Us O
Lord from Heaven Thy Dwelling Place won the Canadian Governor-
General's Award for Fiction in 1961. Canadian critics continued to
be interested in Lowry's short fiction and later work, to anthologize
some of it, and to emphasize Lowry's sense of place, both physical
and mental. The Canadian dramatists Gerald Noxon and Fletcher Markle
did, however, transform Under the Volcano into a radio play in 1947;
George Woodcock wrote the first extended article on the novel (in
Northern Review in 1954); and the National Film Board film on Lowry's
life, released in 1976, went so far as to stress Lowry as a one-book
author. Elsewhere, enthusiasm for the novel brought widespread

reviews in 1947, a number of French commentaries in the 1950's, and various translations. Norwegian and Danish publishers were first, with translations in 1949, and Jöran Mjöberg recognized as early as 1947 the affinity between Lowry and Nordahl Grieg.

A decade later, in 1957, Lowry died, and there were further reflections on his life. But soon these were coupled with anticipations about the unpublished material which in 1961, thanks to the foresight of Earle Birney and Basil Stuart-Stubbs, was in large part lodged at The University of British Columbia in Vancouver. Judith Combs' inventory of these papers appeared in 1973. As much of this work was edited and released during the 1960's (the editors variously praised and attacked for their efforts), interest in Lowry revived, thrived sufficiently for reviews of the later novels to be newsworthy, and seemingly declined again by the time Psalms and Songs, which attracted scarcely any extended notice at all, appeared in 1975. Though there were numerous approving remarks made about them, the late works--Dark as the Grave Wherein My Friend Is Laid, Hear Us O Lord from Heaven Thy Dwelling Place, October Ferry to Gabriola-- seldom lived entirely up to reviewers' expectations, just as they failed to satisfy the publishers to whom Lowry had been sending them in the decade before he died. In a provocative article in Encounter in 1970, Matthew Corrigan chastises the New York publishers for being unreceptive to works that challenged conventional notions about fiction. Many reviewers were caught up in similar quandaries about form. Yet while they were expressing their disappointment that a popular success was not to be repeated (Under the Volcano was, after all, a Book-of-the-Month Club choice and on the American Best Seller list for some time), academic commentaries were starting to appear in larger and larger numbers.

Some of these developed out of Master's and Doctoral dissertations, such as Perle Epstein's analysis of Cabbalism and Under the Volcano, some of Sherrill Grace's essays, Agnes Nyland's work in Psalms and Songs, A. R. Kilgallin's commentary on allusions in Under the Volcano and Ultramarine, and Kristofer Dorosz's Malcolm Lowry's Infernal Paradise. By 1976 at least 53 theses, at various levels, had been completed at universities as distant as British Columbia, Cambridge, Poznan, UCLA and the State University of New York at Buffalo; much of this material--Paul St. Pierre's study of the unity of Hear Us O Lord from Heaven Thy Dwelling Place, for example, or Stephen Slemon's commentary on Lowry's journal forms, or Brian O'Kill's analysis of Lowry's style--contain valuable and as yet still unpublished points of view. In academic journals there appeared studies of sources and parallels, of analogues and mythic patterns, of Lowry's lyrical tone and his experiments with time, his tragic characters and the absence of tragedy, questions of evil, choice, guilt, paradox, love, death, and humour. Suzanne Kim's valuable study of Lowry's juvenilia appeared in Etudes Anglaises in 1965; Daniel Dodson's Malcolm Lowry (1970) and W. H. New's Malcolm Lowry (1971) were the first attempts to chart the directions that Lowry took throughout his career and to assess the totality of his accomplishment; R. H. Costa's and Muriel Bradbrook's longer studies followed in 1972 and 1974; and more detailed analyses of the manuscripts and of the differences between the manuscripts and the published versions are currently underway.

This work establishes a number of critical directions. French critics, drawing on the tradition of Gaston Bachelard, are discovering the virtues of phenomenological approaches to Lowry's writings. Political criticism seems the most articulate in the Russian language work of V. Skorodenko. Brian O'Kill's dissertation is the most sophisticated analysis of Lowry's style. Some of Lowry's stylistic features have warranted special treatment, and Sherrill Grace, Matthew J. Bruccoli, and Paul Tiessen have developed the casually observed idea of "cinematic" techniques, which Stephen Spender alluded to in his 1965 introduction to Under the Volcano, into a serious examination of Lowry's interest in film and of various kinds of influence which film exerted upon him. By contrast, Perle Epstein's exploratory essay on Lowry and jazz (published in Canadian Literature, no. 44 [1970], a special issue which became the basis for George Woodcock's 1971 volume Malcolm Lowry: The Man and His Work) remains one of the few attempts to examine the musical analogies which Lowry's style suggests. And as the studies of Lowry's poetry, which began with Earle Birney's appreciative accounts, continue to grow, there appears to be greater awareness of the interconnection between the poetry and the prose. In a sense, what John Robert Colombo observed in a 1963 review of Lowry's Selected Poems--that readers' judgments of the book will depend on their "willingness to appreciate fragments"--applies as well to their understanding of Lowry's methods in writing fiction.

It is clear that critical attitudes towards Lowry have changed between 1933 and 1976. Some of the change is due to the resolution of various biographical disputes, some to the changes in fictional theory and literary practice that became clearly evident during the 1960's. One of the recent results of the change has been a re-evaluation of Lowry's late works. What Muriel Bradbrook refers to as Lowry's nouveaux romans were experimental when they were written. From a mid-1970's vantage point they seem an early and innovative part of a general movement away from the school of realism towards non-linear narrative forms. The fascination with Lowry's technical versatility and textural density, which showed early in the studies of analogue and symbolic pattern, shows again in the concern for the force of film, journal, and other variations in interrupted form-- criticism of a kind in which Matthew Corrigan (writing in Boundary 2 in 1975, for example) is a skilled and leading exponent. Some of the quarrel about the extent of influence (Joyce, Aiken) upon Lowry and the degree to which he was imitator or innovator remains. But Lowry has also become the influence as well as the influenced, affecting the work of the American writers William Gass and William Styron, for example, and the Dutch writer Bert Shierbeek, and the Guyanese writer

Introduction

Wilson Harris; the range testifies further to the position he now occupies in the history of twentieth-century literature.

This checklist, recording publications only up to 1976, stops short of another burst of publishing. Several studies are underway-- in Canada (where Sherrill Grace, Andrew Pottinger, and Matthew Corrigan are all completing manuscripts), in Australia (where Jennifer Webb is at work on a Jungian study of Lowry's work), in Scotland (where Anne Smith is preparing a collection of essays on Lowry's writing), and in Italy (where Francesco Binni is finishing a work). Others, like Ronald Binns' introductory study of the manuscripts and G. R. Garnett's University of Warwick thesis, are complete. Ronald Walker's "Infernal Paradise" (an examination of Lowry's Mexican settings, his use of underworld archetypes, and his notions about history and time) is due from the University of California Press; and "Voyage au fond de nos abîmes," a guide to the short stories and Under the Volcano by Christine Pagnoulle of the University of Liège, was published in 1977 by Editions L'age d'Homme, La Cité, in Lausanne, Switzerland.

I am indebted to many people for the contributions they have made to this work. My research assistant, Debbie Heintz, patiently searched The University of British Columbia Library holdings of reviews and commentaries. Friends and colleagues generously offered their aid in translating a number of studies in European and Asian languages with which I was not familiar, and I wish to thank them all: Branko Blažičević, Andrew Busza, Jan de Bruyn, R. M. Flores, Michael Futrell, Marilyn Johns, Karl Kobbervig, Gladys Higgins, Teresa Petrala, and Matsuo Soga. When I had assembled nearly all the material for this volume, Brian O'Kill generously donated to The University of British Columbia Library, and made specifically available to me, the card index of an enumerative checklist he had put together, which gave me the invaluable opportunity of objectively double-checking much of my own work and of collating the two bodies of data. Other Lowry scholars--proving the continuing existence of a scholarly community--gave of their time and effort to suggest possible items for inclusion and to track down for me a final two dozen items which proved particularly elusive; again I should like to express my appreciation: to Muriel Bradbrook, Matthew Corrigan, Richard Hauer Costa, Hallvard Dahlie, Sherrill Grace, Hena Maes-Jelinek, Stefan Makowiecki, David Markson, Christine Pagnoulle, Anna Rutherford, Carole Slade, and Ronald G. Walker. Mrs. Margerie Lowry located for me copies of a number of European reviews, and answered all my queries with encouragement and kindness. Various publishers and libraries responded courteously and helpfully to my enquiries about manuscript holdings and reviews. I appreciate, too, the expertise and generous cooperation of Margaret Friesen, Anne Yandle, and the staffs of the Inter-Library Loans and Special Collections Divisions of The University of British Columbia Library, without whose assistance this work would have been far more difficult to assemble. I wish finally to thank Valerie Pusey, who typed the manuscript, and Barbara Garrey, for her editorial guidance.

Title Abbreviations

Dark as the Grave   Dark as the Grave Wherein My Friend Is Laid

Hear Us O Lord   Hear Us O Lord from Heaven Thy Dwelling Place

Manuscript Collections

1   THE UNIVERSITY OF BRITISH COLUMBIA
     VANCOUVER

- drafts of published and unpublished poetry, fiction,
  filmscripts, letters

- letters to Lowry, and various memorabilia

- a portion of Lowry's library

- reviews and copies of most critical and biographical
  commentaries, including theses submitted at insti-
  tutes other than The University of British Columbia

See 1973.A2 for an inventory of these papers.

2   BANCROFT LIBRARY
     UNIVERSITY OF CALIFORNIA
     BERKELEY

- papers connected with the City Lights Press publications
  of Selected Poems, including copies of reviews

3   THE UNIVERSITY OF TEXAS
     AUSTIN

- typescript of Under the Volcano, which is usually cited
  as 4th draft, but may be 1st draft of 4th version

- letters to Gerald and Betty Noxon

- letters to James Stern (15 items)

4   CITY OF LIVERPOOL LIBRARY

- letter to Post Man [identified in a library letter as
  W. D. Cemas] from Joseph Ward

5   THE UNIVERSITY OF VIRGINIA
     CHARLOTTESVILLE

- letter to "Dear Bob" (5 November 1947)
- photograph of Lowry with Catherine Freeman, and Conrad
  Aiken and family

Major Writings by Malcolm Lowry

"Bulls of the Resurrection." Prism International, 5, no. 1
(Summer 1965), 5-11.

China and Kristbjorg's Story In the Black Hills. New York: Aloe
Editions, 1974; "China" and "Kristbjorg's Story: In the Black
Hills" rpt. in Margerie Lowry, ed., Psalms and Songs. New York
and Scarborough, Ont.: New American Library, 1975, pp. 49-54,
250-53 respectively.

Dark as the Grave Wherein My Friend Is Laid, edited by Douglas Day
and Margerie Bonner Lowry. New York: New American Library, 1968;
Toronto: General, 1968; London: Jonathan Cape, 1969; New York:
Meridian, 1969; Harmondsworth: Penguin, 1972.

"Economic Conference, 1934." Arena, 2 (Autumn 1949), 49-57.

"Enter One in Sumptuous Armour." In Psalms and Songs, pp. 228-49.

"Garden of Etla." United Nations World, 4 (June 1950), 45-47.

"Ghostkeeper." American Review, 17 (Spring 1973), 1-34; rpt. in
Psalms and Songs, pp. 202-27.

Hear Us O Lord from Heaven Thy Dwelling Place. Philadelphia:
Lippincott, 1961; London: Jonathan Cape, 1962; New York:
Keystone, 1963; New York: Capricorn, 1969; Harmondsworth:
Penguin, 1969.

"Hotel Room in Chartres." Story, 5 (September 1934), 53-58; rpt. in
Psalms and Songs, pp. 19-24.

"In Le Havre." Life and Letters, 10 (July 1934), 642-66.

"June the 30th, 1934." In Psalms and Songs, pp. 36-48.

"Lunar Caustic." Paris Review, 8 (Winter-Spring 1963), 12-72; rpt.
as Lunar Caustic. London: Jonathan Cape, 1968; New York:
Grossman, 1968; rpt. as "Lunar Caustic" in Psalms and Songs,
pp. 259-306.

Notes on a Screenplay for F. Scott Fitzgerald's "Tender Is the Night" (with Margerie Bonner Lowry). Bloomfield Hills, Mich.: Bruccoli Clark, 1976.

October Ferry to Gabriola, edited by Margerie Lowry. New York and Cleveland: World, 1970; London: Jonathan Cape, 1971; New York: Plume, 1971.

Selected Letters, edited by Harvey Breit and Margerie Bonner Lowry. Philadelphia: Lippincott, 1968; London: Jonathan Cape, 1967; New York: Capricorn, 1969.

Selected Poems, edited by Earle Birney with the assistance of Margerie Bonner Lowry. San Francisco: City Lights Books, 1962.

Ultramarine. London: Jonathan Cape, 1933. Revised edition, Philadelphia: Lippincott, 1962; London: Jonathan Cape, 1963; New York: McGraw-Hill, 1964; London: Four Square, 1965; Harmondsworth: Penguin, 1974.

"Under the Volcano." Prairie Schooner, 37, no. 4 (Winter 1963–64), 284–300; rpt. in Psalms and Songs, pp. 187–201.

Under the Volcano. New York: Reynal and Hitchcock, 1947; London: Jonathan Cape, 1947; New York: Vintage Books, 1958; Harmondsworth: Penguin, 1962; Philadelphia: Lippincott, 1965; London: Jonathan Cape, 1965; New York: Signet, 1966.

"Unpublished Notes from Lowry's Journals." In Perle Epstein, The Private Labyrinth of Malcolm Lowry: Under the Volcano and the Cabbala." New York: Holt, Rinehart and Winston, 1969, pp. 225–28.

Translations of
Lowry's Major Writings

"The Bravest Boat"

"Samaia khrabraia lodka," translated by N. Krolik. In his edition
of Zateriannaia ulitsa: Sovremennaia kanadskaia novella [The
Lost Street: The Contemporary Canadian Novella]. Moscow:
Progress, 1971, pp. 125-37.

Dark as the Grave Wherein My Friend Is Laid

Buio come la tomba dove giace il mio amico, translated by Attilio
Veraldi. Milan: Mondadori, 1971.

Escuro como o túmulo onde jaz o meu amigo, translated by Carmen
González. Lisbon[?]: Colecção Século XX, 1975[?].

Oscuro como la tumba donde yace mi amigo, translated by Alicia
Jurado. Caracas: Monte Avila Editores, 1969.

Sombre comme la tombe où repose mon ami, translated by Clarisse
Francillon. Paris: Les lettres nouvelles, Denoël, 1970.

Hear Us O Lord from Heaven Thy Dwelling Place

Ascoltaci Signore, translated by Attilio Veraldi. Milan:
Feltrinelli, 1969.

Ecoute notre voix ô Seigneur..., translated by Clarisse
Francillon; "Brave petit bateau," translated by Georges
Belmont. Paris: Julliard, 1962.

Escúchanos, oh señor, desde el cielo, tu morada, translated by
Eva Iribarne Dietrich. Caracas: Editorial Tiempo Nuevo, 1971.

Hör uns, o Herr, der Du im Himmel wohnst, translated by Susanna
Rademacher. Reinbeck bei Hamburg: Rowohlt, 1965.

Letters

Choix de lettres, translated and abridged by Suzanne Kim. Paris:
Denoël, 1968.

El volcán, El mezcal, Los Comisarios (Dos Cartas), translated by
Sergio Pitol. Barcelona: Tusquets, 1971.

Lunar Caustic

Caustico Lunare, translated by Vincenzo Mantovani. Milan: Mondadori, 1973.

Lapis, translated by Jacek Laskowski. Literatura na Swiecie, 11 (1973), 56–127.

Lunar Caustic, translated by Clarisse Francillon. Paris: Julliard, 1963.

Lunar Caustic, translated by R. E. Lorente. Montivideo: Editorial Alfa, 1970.

October Ferry to Gabriola

En route vers l'île de Gabriola, translated by Clarisse Francillon. Paris: Les lettres nouvelles, Denoël, 1972.

Il traghetto per Gabriola, translated by Vincenzo Mantovani. Milan: Mondadori, 1974.

Poems

L'urlo del mare e il buio, translated and edited by Francesco Vizioli. Parma: Guanda, 1972.

"Through the Panama"

"Genom Panama," translated by Sonja Bergvall. Bonniers Litterära Magasin, 31 (1962), pp. 285–95.

Por el Canal de Panamá, translated by Salvador Elizondo. México, D.F.: Era, 1969.

Ultramarine

Ultramarina, translated by Valerio Riva. Milan: Feltrinelli, 1963.

Ultramarina, translated by Alfonso Llanos. Caracas: Monte Avila Editores, 1970.

Ultramarine, translated by Clarisse Francillon and Jean-Roger Carroy. Paris: Les lettres nouvelles, Denoël, 1965.

Under the Volcano

Au-dessous du volcan, translated by Stephen Spriel with the help of Clarisse Francillon and Malcolm Lowry. Paris: Editions Corrêa, 1950; Paris: Buchet/Chastel-Corrêa, 1960. Revised edition, Paris: le Club français du livre, 1971; Paris: Gallimard, 1973, la Collection Folio no. 351.

Bajo el volcán, translated by Raúl Ortiz y Ortiz. México, D.F.: Era, 1964; Buenos Aires: Editorial Galerna, 1967.

Debaixo de Vulcão, translated by Virginía Motta. Lisbon:
Livros do Brasil, 1960[?].

Ispod vulkana, translated by Branko Vučičevic. Belgrade: Nolit,
1966, 1975.

Kakkazan no shita, translated by Hideo Kanō. Tokyo: Hakusuisha,
1966.

Onder de vulkaan, translated by John Vandenbergh. Amsterdam:
De Bezige Bij, 1966, 1971.

Pod ognjenikom, translated by Mira Miheličeva. Ljubljana:
Cankarjeva založba, 1965.

Pod wulkanem, translated by Krystyna Tarnowska; poems translated
by Ludmiła Mariańska. Warsaw: Panstwowy Instytut Wydamiczy,
1963, 1966.

Sota el Volcá, translated by Manuel de Pedrolo. Barcelona:
Edicions 62, 1973.

Sotto il vulcano, translated by Giorgio Monicelli. Milan:
Feltrinelli, 1961, 1966.

Tulivuoren juurella, translated by Juhani Jaskari. Porvoo and
Helsinki: Werner Söderström Oy, 1968.

Under vulkanen, translated by Peter Magnus. Oslo: Gyldendal,
1949, 1967.

Under vulkanen, translated by Vibeke Bloch. Copenhagen:
Gyldendals Forlag, 1949; second edition, 1968.

Under Vulkanen, translated by Erik Sandin. Stockholm: Bonnier,
1970.

Unter dem Vulkan, translated by Clemens ten Holder. Stuttgart:
Klett, 1951; Reinbeck bei Hamburg: Rowohlt, 1963, 1974.

U podnozhiya vulkana, Rasskazy, Lesnaya tropa k rodniku,
translated by V. Hinkis, I. Gurova, and O. Soroka. Moscow:
Progress, 1972.

Vulkán Alatt, translated by Árpád Göncz. Budapest: Európa Kiadó,
1973.

Writings about
Malcolm Lowry, 1927–1976

<u>1927 A BOOKS - NONE</u>

<u>1927 B SHORTER WRITINGS</u>

*1   ANON. "Rich Boy as Deck Hand." <u>Evening News</u> (London)
       (14 May), p. 5.
            Interview with Lowry and his mother at the time of his
       sailing on the <u>Pyrrhus</u>. Cited by Day (item 1973.A3,
       p. 91).
            Unlocatable.

 2   ANON. "Once Quite Enough. Cotton Broker's Son as Deckhand."
       <u>The Daily Mail</u> (30 September), p. 9.
            Interview with Lowry after his return on the <u>Pyrrhus</u>.

<u>1929 A BOOKS - NONE</u>

<u>1929 B SHORTER WRITINGS</u>

 1   ANON. "Cambridge Tragedy. Student Found Dead. Gas Filled
       Room." <u>Cambridge Daily News</u> (15 November).
            A report of the death of Paul Fitte.

 2   ANON. "Suicide of Cambridge Freshman." <u>Cambridge Daily News</u>
       (16 November), p. 5.
            An account of the inquest into Paul Fitte's death, in-
       cluding the testimony of Clement Milton Lowry [sic].

<u>1930 A BOOKS - NONE</u>

<u>1930 B SHORTER WRITINGS</u>

 1   LEAVIS, F. R. "Cambridge Poetry." <u>Cambridge Review</u> (16 May),
       pp. 414-15.
            Passing dismissive mention of Lowry's poem "For Nordahl
       Grieg's Fireman" in a review of <u>Cambridge Poetry, 1930</u>.

1930

2   PASCAL, R. "The Venture." <u>Cambridge Review</u> (13 June),
        pp. 509-10.
            Passing mention of Lowry's contribution to <u>Venture</u>.

1933 A BOOKS - NONE

1933 B SHORTER WRITINGS

1   ANON. Review of <u>Ultramarine</u>. <u>The Bookman</u>, 84 (July), 221.
            Compares the novel with poetry, finding it requires
        effort to appreciate the uniqueness of the writer's vision.

2   ANON. Review of <u>Ultramarine</u>. <u>Times Literary Supplement</u>
        (13 July), p. 481.
            A critique of the novel, finding it imitative, as though
        the thoughts and conversations had been unselectively "re-
        produced from a recording machine."

3   ANON. Review of <u>Ultramarine</u>. <u>Life and Letters</u>, 9, no. 50
        (September), 369-70.
            A review of <u>Ultramarine</u>, acknowledging the undisturbing
        simplicity of the autobiographical element in the book,
        finding the scenes vivid, the story "worth reading," the
        problem (of social adjustment) intelligent, and the solu-
        tion unimposed.

4   ARROWSMITH, J. E. S. "Fiction-I." <u>London Mercury</u>, 28,
        no. 166 (August), 361-63.
            Finds the fo'c'sle conversations in <u>Ultramarine</u>
        incomprehensible.

5   P., I. W. Review of <u>Ultramarine</u>. Liverpool <u>Post and Mercury</u>
        (14 June).
            Hopes that in a subsequent work, Lowry will get away
        from unusual treatment and down to narrative.

6   _____. "<u>Ultramarine</u>." Liverpool <u>Post</u> (29 June).
            Finds Lowry's work the result of groundwork laid by
        Joyce and Lawrence, therefore not to be neglected in
        Liverpool.

7   PRITCHETT, V. S. "New Novels." <u>The New Statesman and Nation</u>,
        5, no. 122 (24 June), 850.
            Finds that, despite its strained self-consciousness,
        irrelevant school memories, and broken dialogue, <u>Ultramarine</u>
        contains fine direct descriptions and a quality of urgency.

8   VERSCHOYLE, DEREK. "Fiction." Spectator, 150 (23 June), 920.
        In a review of books about the sea, finds Ultramarine
    "disastrously mannered." Though some scenes are excellent
    and individual episodes satisfactory, the mixing of con-
    ventions produces "no unity of impression."

1945 A BOOKS - NONE

1945 B SHORTER WRITINGS

1   ANON. "A Loss to Cotton." Evening Express (12 February).
        Obituary for Arthur Osborne Lowry.

2   ANON. "Cotton Broker's Death." Liverpool Post (13 February),
        p. 15.
        Obituary for Lowry's father, noting that he "leaves a
    widow and four sons, three of whom are partners in the
    business."
        The Liverpool Echo of 12 February 1945 printed a slightly
    shorter version of the same obituary.

1947 A BOOKS - NONE

1947 B SHORTER WRITINGS

1   ALLEN, WALTER. "New Novels." The New Statesman and Nation,
        34 (6 December), 455–56.
        Considers Under the Volcano a powerful and concentrated
    tragic novel, but finds the associative method of the book
    unsatisfactory. The style is "out of Djuna Barnes by Henry
    James," experimental, skillful, but given to pastiche.

2   ANON. Review of Under the Volcano. The New Yorker, 23
        (22 February), 90.
        Finds the book "turgid"--"a rather good imitation of an
    important novel."

3   ANON. "Man in Eruption." Time (24 February), pp. 114, 116,
        118.
        A review, finding Under the Volcano effective as a
    descriptive work and as a study of the anguish of the soul,
    but not as a portrait of "living human beings."

4   ANON. "The Volcano Inside." Newsweek (24 March), pp. 98–99.
        Finds Under the Volcano difficult and Joycean, but
    rewarding.

1947

5   ANON. "Mortal Distractions." The Times Literary Supplement
       (20 September), p. 477.
           A review of Under the Volcano, praising its passion, its
       preservation of the unities of action, and the originality
       and lucidity of its central character.

6   BARZUN, JACQUES. Review of Under the Volcano. Harper's
       Magazine, 194 (May), 486.
           Dismisses the novel, its language, and its characters as
       "desperately dull," platitudinous--"an anthology held to-
       gether by earnestness."

7   BEATTIE, TODDY. "'He Doesn't Like Who-Dunits But He Thinks
       Mine Are Good.'" The Vancouver Sun (17 April), p. 13.
           A short interview with Margerie Lowry, with comments on
       Malcolm Lowry's life.

8   CLARK, ELEANOR. "Psychology and Symbols." The Nation, 164
       (22 March), 335-36.
           A review of Under the Volcano, along with Rex Warner's
       The Aerodrome, praising the "vitality" of both books--a
       quality considered absent from recent British fiction--and
       the "anarchic brilliance" of the portrait of the Consul.
       Specific failures of vision and subjectivity of treatment
       are noted; the symbols are considered arbitrary and inef-
       fective, the "conception" of the book too "journalistic,"
       and Hugh's innocence is found "boring."

9   CONNOLLY, FRANCIS X. Review of Under the Volcano. Best Sel-
       lers (Scranton, Pa.) (15 June), p. 61.
           Finds textural interest and psychological accuracy
       in the novel, but regards it as "fundamentally a negative
       study of disintegration." Reserves highest praise for a
       positive author.

10 CROSBY, JOHN. "Radio in Review." New York Herald Tribune
       (13 May).
           Mixed review of an hour-long radio adaptation of Under
       the Volcano by Fletcher Markle and Gerald Noxon (CBS,
       29 April).

11 DEACON, WILLIAM ARTHUR. "Drunkards and Insane Interest Jit-
       tery World." The Globe and Mail (Toronto) (22 March),
       p. 23.
           An uncertain review, acknowledging the power of Under
       the Volcano (in part as a "temperance sermon"), yet also
       finding the technique "disorderly," the names unpronounce-
       able, the whole presented with "masterly incoherence"--
       suspicious of an art that depicts chaos.

12   FLINT, R. W. "Weltschmerz Refurbished." The Kenyon Review,
     9, no. 3 (Summer), 474-77.
         A mixed review of Under the Volcano, finding it to be
     energetic and its humour to be its most authentic feature,
     but complaining of its secondhandedness, its "spiritual
     vulgarity," and its lack of control. Finds Shelley to be
     the "strongest spiritual and stylistic influence" upon it.

13   GANNETT, LEWIS. "Books and Things." New York Herald Tribune
     (19 April).
         Praise for Lowry's sophisticated novel; the consul is
     "a symbol of civilization drunk on its own myths, wistful
     for an ever-vanishing vision but fearful of sobering up
     lest soberness mean total death."

14   GAROFFOLO, VINCENT. Review of Under the Volcano. New Mexico
     Quarterly Review, 17, no. 2 (Summer), 264-65.
         A tribute to the novel's intelligence and passion.

15   HALE, LIONEL. "Delirium." Observer (21 September), p. 3.
         A mixed brief review of Under the Volcano.

16   HARDWICK, ELIZABETH. "Fiction Chronicle." Partisan Review,
     14, no. 2 (March-April), 196-200.
         A review, praising the "astonishing and often brilliant
     images" of Under the Volcano and its evocation of the
     deraciné of the 1920s, despite its 1930s setting.

17   HARROP, MONA. "Book Talk." Cincinnati Times-Star (28 April).
         Declares Under the Volcano a work of genius, praising
     the style.

18   HAYS, H. R. "Drunken Nightmare of the Damned." New York
     Times Book Review (23 February), p. 5.
         A review of Under the Volcano, praising its "virile and
     poetic" style, and the "nihilistic" consul's rich, "per-
     versely acute perceptions" and "ramblingly brilliant asso-
     ciations." Finds both the interior anguish and the external
     events effective, though Lowry's "final moral intention is
     somewhat obscure."

19   HEILMAN, ROBERT B. "Four Novels." Sewanee Review, 55, no. 3
     (Summer), 483-92.
         A review of Under the Volcano, noting that its "nexuses
     are imaginative rather than casual, or logical, or chrono-
     logical"; the slight story carries symbolic meanings not
     merely to create mood but as "clues to reality," and its
     sense of "horrifying dissolution" reflects the times.

1947

20   HUMBOLDT, CHARLES. "The Novel of Action." Mainstream, 1,
        no. 4 (Fall), 392-93.
            In a commentary on the need for human realities in fic-
        tion, dismisses Under the Volcano, its symbols, allusions,
        and theology, because of its despair and its reliance on
        irony and unmotivated chance; also quarrels with critics'
        "overestimation" of an imitative book.

21   JACKSON, JOSEPH HENRY. "Year of Books: A Survey of the Prob-
        lems of Publishing and Buying and a Look at the Highlights
        of 1947." San Francisco Chronicle, "This World" supplement,
        11, no. 34 (28 December), 12-14.
            Mentions Under the Volcano in passing as the year's
        second-best novel (superseded by Gerald Warner Brace's
        The Garretson Chronicle).

22   JOHNSON, ELIZABETH. Review of Under the Volcano. Commonweal,
        45 (7 March), 523-24.
            An approving review, criticizing the "preciousness" of
        the main characters' "soul-dives" but praising the "life-
        like feel of Mexico."

23   L[IVESAY], D[OROTHY]. Review of Under the Volcano. The
        Vancouver Daily Province (16 August), p. 4.
            Summarizes the book, explores it briefly as Greek
        tragedy, notes its "unities," and praises the impact of
        its language.

24   MAYBERRY, GEORGE. "Lowry's Inferno." New Republic, 116
        (24 February), 35-36.
            A summary of and a favourable response to Under the
        Volcano, finding it neither realistic nor neatly symbolic,
        yet social and political. The novel is a series of linked
        set pieces, whose view of life lifts it above other con-
        temporary fiction.

25   MJÖBERG, JÖRAN. Nordahl Grieg: Fosterlandsvännen och
        Revolutionären. Lund: C. W. K. Gleerups Förlag, p. 30.
            Passing mention of Grieg's influence on Lowry's Ultra-
        marine, and a novel entitled Benjamin by the Swedish writer
        Ragnar Holmström.

26   MOIR, MYRA. Review of Under the Volcano. The Vancouver Daily
        Province, Saturday Magazine supplement (19 April), p. 4.
            A brief notice, finding "deep significance" in the novel.

27   PRESCOTT, ORVILLE. "Outstanding Novels." The Yale Review,
        n.s. 36 (Summer), 767.

A note on <u>Under the Volcano</u> in the context of a survey; the novel is considered verbally powerful, but pedantic, needlessly obscure, displaying "an arrogance of mind which is a variety of literary decadence."

28 SANDWELL, B. K. "'Under the Volcano' by M. Lowry Shows Style also Symbolism." <u>Saturday Night</u>, 63, no. 9 (1 November), 15.
A summary review, querying Lowry's ability to create women characters.

29 SAVAGE, D. S. "Fiction." <u>The Spectator</u>, 179 (10 October), 474-75.
Review of <u>Under the Volcano</u> along with John O'Hara's <u>Appointment in Samarra</u>, both authors considered "American"; Lowry's book is attacked for being prolix and having "intellectual pretensions," but is claimed as the "most perceptive and the most promising" book to have been reviewed in 1947.

30 SCHORER, MARK. "The Downward Flight of a Soul." <u>New York Herald-Tribune Weekly Book Review</u> (23 February), p. 2.
A review of <u>Under the Volcano</u>, finding it less expansive and mature than Joyce's work, but of the same kind. Mentions the garden imagery and the significance of the scenes involving the Indian peasant, and sees the novel primarily as a story of man's fall from grace.

31 SIMPSON, R. C. Review of <u>Under the Volcano</u>. <u>Northern Review</u>, 1, no. 6 (August-September), 37-38.
A laudatory review of the novel, suggesting its depth of meaning, its stylistic skill, and its political themes. In the tragedy created by free choice, Geoffrey is seen as the happiest character.

32 WEEKS, EDWARD. "Mexico and Moscow." <u>The Atlantic</u>, 179 (May), 144-46.
An approving review of <u>Under the Volcano</u>, pointing to Lowry's powerful style and his "gift of balancing the spoken word and the hidden thought." His handling of time is likened to Conrad's.

33 WILD, ROLAND. "Hollywood Seeks Hit Novel Written Here." <u>The Vancouver News Herald</u> (15 March), p. 2.
A note based on an interview with Lowry, on his intentions for further writing, and a report on Orson Welles' visit to Vancouver in search of film rights for <u>Under the Volcano</u>.

1947

34   WOODBURN, JOHN. "Dazzling Disintegration." <u>Saturday Review</u>,
      30 (22 February), 9-10.
           Finds <u>Under the Volcano</u> a work of genius and Lowry to be
      Joyce's "apt pupil." A biographical note accompanies the
      review.

35   YOUNG, VERNON A. "The Southwest: Truth and Poetry." <u>Arizona</u>
      <u>Quarterly</u>, 3, no. 3 (Autumn), 281-83.
           A review, observing that beneath the stimulating, allu-
      sive, witty surface of <u>Under the Volcano</u> is a thin metaphor
      about life being war--the structure therefore being "need-
      lessly complicated." Finds the Consul "effete."

<u>1948 A BOOKS - NONE</u>

<u>1948 B SHORTER WRITINGS</u>

1   SMITH, A. J. M. "Malcolm Lowry (1909-)" in his <u>The Book of</u>
      <u>Canadian Poetry</u>. Revised edition. Chicago: University of
      Chicago Press; Toronto: Gage, p. 371.
           Headnote to a selection of poems.
           Reprinted: 1957.B8.

2   SR, RE [SPILLER, ROBERT E.] "American Literature." <u>1948</u>
      <u>Britannica Book of the Year</u>. Chicago, London, Toronto:
      Encyclopaedia Britannica, p. 49.
           One sentence, in a summary of the year's fiction, reads
      "But the year produced no new voice as commanding as that
      of the Canadian Malcolm Lowry in <u>Under the Volcano</u> to pre-
      sage a major movement among younger writers of fiction."

3   TINDALL, WILLIAM YORK. "Many-leveled Fiction: Virginia Woolf
      to Ross Lockridge." <u>College English</u>, 10, no. 2 (November),
      66-71.
           In a survey article, alludes to the political implica-
      tions of <u>Under the Volcano</u>, the Consul being symbolic of
      the intellectual who evades his social responsibility. It
      is a visionary rather than propagandistic book, and essen-
      tially tragic.

<u>1949 A BOOKS - NONE</u>

<u>1949 B SHORTER WRITINGS</u>

1   ANON. "A nos amis." <u>Liens</u>, no. 29 (1 October), pp. 1, 6.
           Expects that the publication of <u>Under the Volcano</u> in
      French will cause a great stir in 1950.

2   HALDANE, CHARLOTTE. <u>Truth Will Out</u>. London: Weidenfeld &
      Nicolson, pp. 29-30.
         Mentions that Lowry ("the most romantic undergraduate of
      that period in Cambridge") was the source of the hero of
      her novel <u>I Bring Not Peace</u>.

3   HOEL, SIGURD. "Forord" to Malcolm Lowry, <u>Under Vulkanen</u>.
      Oslo: Gyldendal Norsk Forlag, pp. v-viii.
         After a brief biographical survey and narrative summary,
      defends the opening complexity of the novel. Though influ-
      enced by Joyce (stream-of-consciousness) and Faulkner
      (baroque style and setting, for purposes of showing the
      mind's ability to encompass a range of thoughts and emo-
      tions), Lowry still creates individual characters. The
      author is a Norwegian dramatist.

1950 A BOOKS - NONE

1950 B SHORTER WRITINGS

1   d'ASTORG, BERTRAND. "Un roman de l'ivresse mystique." <u>Esprit</u>,
      no. 173 (November), pp. 702-07.
         A laudatory review of <u>Under the Volcano</u>, summarizing the
      book, then reflecting on the "Anglo-Saxon" exploration of
      lovelessness and anxiety.

2   FOUCHET, MAX-POL. "Postface" to Malcolm Lowry, <u>Au-dessous du</u>
      <u>volcan</u>. Paris: Editions Correâ, Le club français du
      livre, n. p.
         A discussion of the Faustian and Elizabethan sensibil-
      ities of the novel, focussing on Geoffrey's hell, his re-
      lationship with Yvonne, and the hermetic symbolism.
         Reprinted: 1959.B3; 1960.B7.

3   FRÉDÉRIQUE, A. J. "Malcolm Lowry Au-dessous du volcan."
      Liens, no. 33 (1 February), pp. 1, 12.
         Recollections of meeting Lowry a year earlier, with
      comments on the process by which Stephen Spriel and
      Clarisse Francillon translated <u>Under the Volcano</u>. An
      excerpt is reprinted in 1959.B4.

4   GADENNE, PAUL. "Le roman." <u>Cahiers du Sud</u>, 32 (2^e semestre),
      519-22.
         A review of the French translation of <u>Under the Volcano</u>,
      finding it rich and powerful, but querying and examining in
      some detail the apparent disparity between the Consul's
      descent into hell and his love of it.

9

1950

5   HUMBOURG, PIERRE. "'Au-dessous du volcan' aurait pu être
    écrit par Baudelaire." Le Rouge et le Noir (22 August),
    p. 9.
        A review, finding the force of the novel in its mood
    rather than its story. Emphasizes the Consul's alcoholism,
    making a number of references to Poe, Valéry, Verlaine, and
    Baudelaire. Finds the Mexican references obscure.

6   LOWRY, MALCOLM. "Garden of Etla." United Nations World, 4,
    no. 6 (June), 45-47.
        An essay on the beauties and sorrows of Mexico, a memoir
    of visiting Mitla with a friend named Fernando Atonalzin,
    and a reflection on the pressures of time and the past.
    Translated: 1964.B26, B27.

7   _____. "Préface" to Au-dessous du volcan. Translated by
    Stephen Spriel and Clarisse Francillon. Paris: Editions
    Correâ, Le club français du livre, n. p.
        Reprinted: 1959.B6; 1960.B9. Translated: 1961.B41.

8   SIGAUX, GILBERT. "Au-dessous du volcan." La table ronde,
    no. 31 (July), pp. 136-39.
        A review, tracing the novel's themes of despair and
    alcohol, and praising its creation of its own universe and
    language.

1951 A BOOKS - NONE

1951 B SHORTER WRITINGS

1   ASTRE, GEORGES-ALBERT. "Notes." Critique (Paris), 7, no. 46
    (15 March), 271.
        A laudatory review of Under the Volcano, praising its
    symbolic control, and finding its distinguishing character-
    istics to be its ethical concern and its revelation (rather
    than description) of the human condition.

1952 A BOOKS

1   AIKEN, CONRAD. Ushant, An Essay. New York: Duell, Sloan and
    Pearce; Boston: Little Brown, 365 pp.
        An autobiography à clef, in which Lowry figures under
    the name Hambo.
        Reprinted: 1963.A1. Translated in part: 1974.B1.

2   MARKSON, DAVID M. "Malcolm Lowry: A Study of Theme and Symbol in Under the Volcano." Master's thesis, Columbia University, 102 pp.
    An account of the circularity of the novel, the extent
to which the first chapter must be read as an "epilogue,"
the density of the text and its function as part of the
book's meaning.

1952 B SHORTER WRITINGS

1   BAUR, JOSEPH. "Unter dem Vulkan." Das freie Wort (Düsseldorf)
(26 July).
    A summary review of the German translation of Under the
Volcano.

2   HENNECKE, HANS. "Nach zehn Jahren Arbeit ein Meister-
Erstling." Neue Zeitung (27 July).
    A laudatory review of Under the Volcano.

3   HORST, KARL AUGUST. "Ein Höllisches Paradies." Merkur
(Stuttgart), 9, pp. 894-97.
    Examines the influence of the Gothic and the Symbolists
on Under the Volcano, considering leitmotif and myth.

4   LOWRY, MALCOLM. "A Letter." Wake, no. 11, pp. 80-89.
    Concerns Lowry's appreciation of and association with
Conrad Aiken.
    Reprinted: 1965.A1.

5   NEWTON, NORMAN. "Canadian Writing and 'The Great Theme.'"
Impression (Winnipeg), 1, no. 4 (Spring), 74-80.
    Finds that Lowry and A. M. Klein are the only two
writers in Canada with "breadth of vision."

6   PAGNINI, MARCELLO. "The Myth of William Blackstone in a Poem
by Conrad Aiken." Translated from Italian by Janet B.
Morgan. Wake, no. 11, pp. 61-72.
    Passing mention of the dedication to Lowry, in an anal-
ysis of Aiken's The Kid.

7   R., B. "Sturz in die Tiefe: Ein Roman des Rausches."
Frankfurter Rundschau (9 October).
    A summary review of Under the Volcano.

8   THOEL, ROLF. "'Unter dem Vulkan.'" Welt am Sonntag
(24 February).
    Discusses Peter Lorre's film "Der Verlorene" and Under
the Volcano, examining myth and leitmotif.

1952

9   U., S.   "Leiden, Suchen und Hoffen...."   Schwäbische Donau
    Zeitung (Ulm) (24 January).
        A summary review of Under the Volcano.

10 UHLIG, HELMUT.   "Malcolm Lowry: Under the Volcano."
    Neuphilologische Zeitschrift, 4, no. 5 (September), 352-55.
        Summarizes the novel; observes the influence of Joyce,
    Woolf, Aiken, and Svevo; discovers classical unities; and
    examines tensions between nihilism and hope.

1953 A BOOKS - NONE

1953 B SHORTER WRITINGS

1   BIRNEY, EARLE.   "Salmon Drowns Eagle" in his Twentieth Century
    Canadian Poetry: An Anthology with introduction and notes.
    Toronto: Ryerson, pp. 137-38.
        A brief note on the poem as a "beast fable," suggesting
    the presence of irony.

2   EGELAND, KJØLV.   Nordahl Grieg.   Oslo: Gyldendal Norsk Forlag,
    p. 30.
        Passing reference to Grieg's influence upon Ultramarine.

1954 A BOOKS - NONE

1954 B SHORTER WRITINGS

1   WOODCOCK, GEORGE.   "On the Day of the Dead (Some Reflections
    on Malcolm Lowry's 'Under the Volcano')."   Northern Review,
    6, no. 5 (December-January), 15-21.
        Observes that the "meticulous realism" of Lowry's
    descriptions of Mexico is not used for the ends of "natural-
    istic realism." But the way of life of Central Mexico,
    combining the harsh Aztec and Conquistador traditions, has
    led to an obsession with death--manifesting itself contra-
    dictorily in violence and quietism--which the novel captures.
    Despite its reliance on an external Doom rather than on
    human action to lay the trap of the novel, Under the Volcano
    remains important.
        Revised: 1958.B2.

1955 A BOOKS - NONE

1955 B SHORTER WRITINGS

1   FRIEDMAN, MELVIN. Stream of Consciousness: A Study in
     Literary Method. New Haven: Yale University Press, p. 262.
        Sees Lowry, along with Styron and Buechner, as refining
     the lyrical methods developed by Joyce and Barnes, and the
     addition of poetry to fiction as the possible salvation of
     the novel.

2   KLINCK, CARL F. and R. E. WATTERS. "Malcolm Lowry" in their
     Canadian Anthology. Toronto: Gage, p. 409.
        Inexact biographical sketch. Revised 1966.B16; 1974.B54.

3   KUNITZ, STANLEY J. "Lowry, Malcolm" in Twentieth Century
     Authors. First supplement. New York: H. W. Wilson Co.,
     pp. 601–02.
        Brief biographical account, with quotations from reviews
     of Ultramarine and Under the Volcano.

4   TINDALL, WILLIAM YORK. The Literary Symbol. New York:
     Columbia University Press, pp. 98–100.
        At the end of a chapter called "Supreme Fictions,"
     largely concerned with Joyce and Green, briefly summarizes
     Under the Volcano and identifies several of the symbols.
     The intricate composition, weaving inner with outer worlds
     and past with present, follows a tragic course.
        Reprinted: 1960.B18.

1956 A BOOKS – NONE

1956 B SHORTER WRITINGS

1   ALDRIDGE, JOHN W. In Search of Heresy. Port Washington,
     N. Y.: Kennikat Press, pp. 198–99.
        Passing mention of Under the Volcano in a commentary on
     the decline, since the 1940s, of the reading public's
     capacity to respond to language.

2   TINDALL, WILLIAM YORK. Forces in Modern British Literature
     1885–1956. New York: Vintage, p. 292.
        Passing mention of Under the Volcano as a successful
     recent symbolist novel, surpassed in subtlety by Elizabeth
     Bowen's A World of Love.

1957

1957 A BOOKS - NONE

1957 B SHORTER WRITINGS

1   ANON. "She Broke Gin Bottle--Found Husband Dead." <u>Brighton</u>
      <u>Argus</u> (2 July).
          An account of testimony given at the Eastbourne inquest
      into Lowry's death. "Medical evidence showed...acute
      barbituritic poisoning...."

2   BRACHVOGEL, H. H. "Ein mythischer Roman." <u>Telegraf</u> (Berlin)
      (4 November).
          Finds <u>Under the Volcano</u> a chaotic novel to express a
      chaotic time.

3   BRAEM, HELMUT N. "Unter dem Vulkan." <u>Stuttgarter Zeitung</u>
      (29 September).
          Compares Lowry's style and sense of structure with
      Thomas Wolfe's.

4   BREIT, HARVEY. "In and Out of Books: Obituary." <u>The New</u>
      <u>York Times Book Review</u> (14 July), p. 8.
          A memoir, on the occasion of Lowry's death, of a New
      York publication party for <u>Under the Volcano</u>; also a trib-
      ute to <u>Under the Volcano</u>, and an expression of the sense
      that Lowry "had no regard for the instincts of preservation."

5   FRANCILLON, CLARISSE. "Souvenirs sur Malcolm Lowry." <u>Les</u>
      <u>lettres nouvelles</u>, no. 54 (November), pp. 588-603.
          A memoir of first meeting Lowry, and of working with him
      between 1948 and 1950 on the French translation of <u>Under</u>
      <u>the Volcano</u>. Comments on his personal habits, his plans to
      write a Dantesque work, his assertion that he was a
      humourist.

6   McCORMICK, JOHN. <u>Catastrophe and Imagination: An Interpreta-</u>
      <u>tion of the Recent English and American Novel</u>. London and
      New York: Longmans, Green, pp. 65-66, 85-89.
          Compares <u>Under the Volcano</u> with Rosamund Lehmann's <u>The</u>
      <u>Echoing Grove</u>. Novels of ideas about, in part, history,
      space, and time, they succeed in conveying private sensi-
      bilities which have much to say about society. Lowry also
      reveals compassion and humour.

7   SIEDLER, WOLF JOBST. "Gottes einsame Menschen." <u>Die Neue</u>
      <u>Zeitung</u> (Berlin) (16 September).
          Briefly explores the themes of <u>Under the Volcano</u>.

14

8 SMITH, A. J. M. "Malcolm Lowry (1909–)" in his The Book of
   Canadian Poetry. Third edition. Toronto: Gage, p. 371.
      Reprint of 1948.B1.

9 STROMBERG, KYRA. "Von der Weltläufigkeit zur Weltangst."
   Deutsche Zeitung (Stuttgart) (17 November).
      A review of Under the Volcano.

10 VON NOSTITZ, OSWALT. "Aller Seelentag im amerikanischen
   Roman." Das literarische Deutschland (Heidelberg)
   (25 November).
      A summary review of Under the Volcano.

1958 A BOOKS – NONE

1958 B SHORTER WRITINGS

1 BRUMM, URSULA. "Symbolism and the Novel." Translated from
   the German by Willard R. Trask. Partisan Review, 25, no. 3
   (Summer), 341–42.
      Asserts at the end of an article on symbolic meaning that
   Under the Volcano, like Paul Bowles' The Sheltering Sky,
   uses exotic symbols as an escape from reality, thus negat-
   ing and inverting the relation between symbol and meaning.
   Lowry and Bowles therefore represent the empty dead end,
   not the high point, of symbolism.
      Reprinted: 1967.B10.

2 WOODCOCK, GEORGE. "Malcolm Lowry's 'Under the Volcano.'"
   Modern Fiction Studies, 4, no. 1 (Spring), 151–56.
      Revision of 1954.B1. Reprinted: 1970.B36.

1959 A BOOKS – NONE

1959 B SHORTER WRITINGS

1 ANON. "Un sommet de la littérature." Liens, no. 71 (March),
   p. 2.
      Lowry's "terrible world" demands that readers respond
   sensitively to his language and not approach it with preconceptions about fiction.

2 B., J. "Dans un village mexicain brûlé de soleil et de
   passions...'Au-dessous du volcan' ou le testament du génie,
   la grandiose confession du Kafka américain: Malcolm Lowry."
   Liens, no. 71 (March), pp. 4–5.

1959

        Tribute to the novel's strict form and passionate heart.
    Attached are two biographical notes: on Lowry and on
    Clarisse Francillon, Lowry's French translator.

3   FOUCHET, MAX-POL. "Postface" to Malcolm Lowry, <u>Au-dessous du
     volcan</u>. Paris: Le club français du livre, n.p.
         Reprint of 1950.B2.

4   FRÉDÉRIQUE, A. J. "Une rencontre avec Lowry." <u>Liens</u>, no. 71
     (March), p. 5.
         A brief account of a conversation with Lowry, on the
     subject of why Lowry wrote, reprinted from 1950.B3.

5   JEDYNAK, STANLEY L. "<u>Under the Volcano</u>: An Existentialist
     Tragedy." <u>Thoth</u> (Spring), pp. 25-29.
         Asserting the Consul's pessimistic existentialism and
     the spuriousness of Laruelle, Hugh, and Yvonne, finds that
     the Consul chooses death as a manifestation of "ultimate
     reality."

6   LOWRY, MALCOLM. "Préface" to <u>Au-dessous du volcan</u>. Paris:
     Le club français du livre, n. p.
         Reprint of 1950.B7.

7   NADEAU, MAURICE. "Avant-propos" to Malcolm Lowry, <u>Au-dessous
     du volcan</u>. Paris: Le club français du livre, n. p.
         A general introduction to the author, and to the themes
     of the "drunken Divine Comedy": Mexico, alcoholism, re-
     sponsibility, tragic love.
         Reprinted: 1960.B13.

1960 A BOOKS - NONE

1960 B SHORTER WRITINGS

1   ANON. "The Fate of the Consul." <u>The Times Literary Supple-
     ment</u> (28 October), p. 693.
         A commentary on <u>Under the Volcano</u>, rejecting politics
     and cabbala as anything but ornamental in it, and finding
     guilt (alcoholic and sexual) as the "key to the novel."
     A "writer's writer," Lowry finally succumbs to the self-
     defeating temptation to project his own neuroses onto his
     characters.

2   BONNEFOI, GENEVIÈVE. "Souvenir de Quauhnahuac." <u>Les lettres
     nouvelles</u>, 5 n.s. (July-August), pp. 94-108.
         The allusions are important to meaning in <u>Under the
     Volcano</u> (<u>Cuernavaca</u> replacing <u>Quauhnahuac</u>, for example,

16

which means "near the woods"), and the density forces the
reader into an enjoyable process of creative descovery of
meaning. A street map of Cuernavaca appears on pp. 104-05.

3   BREIT, HARVEY. "Malcolm Lowry." Paris Review, 6, no. 23
    (Spring), 84-85.
        A recollection of meeting Lowry in New York serves as a
    preface to "Through the Panama." Lowry is a "dolorous
    guide" through Purgatory; the journal is characteristic of
    his combination of bitterness, wit, irony, and revelation.

4   ____. "A Second Novel." Partisan Review, 27 (Summer),
    561-63.
        A review of William Styron's Lie Down in Darkness, refer-
    ring to Lowry's work as a source.

5   CARROY, JEAN-ROGER. "Obscur présent, le feu...." Les lettres
    nouvelles, 5 n.s. (July-August), pp. 83-88.
        A series of enigmatic but insightful pensées concerning
    Under the Volcano, which is seen as the work of a "tragic
    and visionary" novelist.

6   FOUCHET, MAX-POL. "No se Puede...." Les lettres nouvelles
    5 n.s. (July-August), pp. 21-25.
        A commentary on Chapter I and the good Samaritan scene
    in Under the Volcano, observing in passing that alcohol was
    not a vice but a mode of consciousness which the novel
    explored.
        Reprinted: 1961.B33; expanded 1967.B17.

7   ____. "Postface" to Malcolm Lowry, Au-dessous du volcan.
    Paris: Le club français du livre et Buchet/Chastel-Correâ,
    pp. 429-37.
        Reprint of 1950.B2.

8   FRANCILLON, CLARISSE. "Malcolm, mon ami." Les lettres
    nouvelles, 5 n.s. (July-August), pp. 8-19.
        General biographical account, with some personal
    reminiscence.
        Translated: 1975.B14.

9   LOWRY, MALCOLM. "Préface" to Au-dessous du volcan. Paris:
    Le club français du livre et Buchet/Chastel-Correâ, n.p.
        Reprint of 1950.B7.

10 LOWRY, MARGERIE. "Dans notre courrier...de Mme Vve Malcolm
    Lowry." Les lettres nouvelles, no. 7 (October), p. 200.

1960

Excerpts from a letter to Maurice Nadeau, complimenting the special Lowry issue (no. 5) and commenting on Lowry's complexity, contradictoriness, and nobility.

11   McCONNELL, WILLIAM. "Recollections of Malcolm Lowry." Canadian Literature, no. 6 (Autumn), pp. 24-31.
An anecdotal memoir by a Vancouver friend, stressing Lowry's physical presence, Rabelaisian sense of humour, childlike innocence, literary enthusiasms, and gift of total recall.
Reprinted: 1961.B43; 1975.A3.

12   MYRER, ANTON. "Le monde au-dessous du volcan." Translated by Clarisse Francillon. Les lettres nouvelles, 5 n.s. (July-August), pp. 59-66.
Puts Under the Volcano among the great Russian and French accomplishments. Praises its evocative language, fine style; compares it with Moby Dick for its Elizabethan rhythms; refers to the desert and barranca metaphors, and the Tarot and Promethean allusions.

13   NADEAU, MAURICE. "Avant-propos" to Malcolm Lowry, Au-dessous du volcan. Paris: Le club français du livre et Buchet/Chastel-Correâ, n.p.
Reprint of 1959.B7.

14   ____. "Lowry." Les lettres nouvelles, 5 n.s. (July-August), pp. 3-7.
Refers to various critical approaches to Under the Volcano (the jealousy theme, secret science studies, the allegory of Redemption, Faustian motifs). Referring to Lowry's mention of Cabbala and Schopenhauer, he traces the Faust theme further and refers to the Voyage cycle.

15   SIGAUX, GILBERT. "Au-dessous du volcan." La table ronde, no. 31 (July), 136-39.
Summarizes Under the Volcano; compares it with Ulysses; finds it original and unclassifiable, its creative style the voice of the alcoholic, of a man with an intense relationship with externals in search of a lost world and afraid of finding himself alone.

16   ____. "Avec Malcolm Lowry (1909-1957)." Le Figaro littéraire (27 August), p. 2.
A survey of Lowry's life, and a commentary (mainly on Lunar Caustic, Under the Volcano, and French criticism of these works) which explores Lowry's alcoholism and his concern for making a lasting form out of his life.

16   SPRIEL, STÉPHEN. "Le cryptogramme Lowry." Les lettres
        nouvelles, 5 n.s. (July-August), pp. 67-81.
            Praises Lowry's fine ironies and comments on both the
        importance of method to meaning in Under the Volcano and
        the problems involved in translating the work (the number
        of references, etc.). Provides a clinical description of
        the Consul and claims "deliverance from the self" as the
        key to the novel.

18   TINDALL, WILLIAM YORK. The Literary Symbol. Bloomington:
        Indiana University Press, Midland, pp. 98-100.
            Reprint of 1955.B4.

19   WILD, ROLAND. "Dollarton Had a Wild Genius." The Province
        (Vancouver) (30 September), p. 4.
            Reflections on visiting Lowry--a non-conformist who
        acted on spur-of-the-moment enthusiasms--in 1948.

20   WOODCOCK, GEORGE. "French Thoughts on Lowry." Canadian
        Literature, no. 6 (Autumn), pp. 79-80.
            A notice and summary of the articles in the special
        Lowry issue of Les lettres nouvelles (n.s. 5, 1960).

21   _____. "Malcolm Lowry 'Greatest Since Joyce.'" The Vancouver
        Sun (24 September), p. 5.
            Hopes that international tributes to Lowry--e.g. that in
        Les lettres nouvelles--will stimulate more serious Canadian
        recognition of his work.

1961 A BOOKS - NONE

1961 B SHORTER WRITINGS

 1   ADAMS, PHOEBE. "Neurotic Limbo." The Atlantic, 208 (August),
        96.
            A review of Hear Us O Lord which finds the episodes not
        "stories" but revelations of "the author's disintegrating
        mind," of "debatable relevance" to "humanity in general."

 2   AIKEN, CONRAD. "Malcolm Lowry: A Note." Canadian Literature,
        no. 8 (Spring), pp. 29-30.
            A memoir of their initial encounter.
            Reprinted: 1971.A5; 1975.A3.

 3   _____. "Not Too Lost." Time, 77, no. 25 (16 June), 7-8.
            A letter to the editor, asserting that the manuscript
        of Ultramarine was never totally lost, because copies did

1961

exist. Mentions the relationship between the book and
Blue Voyage.

4   ANON. "UBC Buys Works of Late Writer-Poet." The Vancouver
     Sun (27 February), p. 15.
          An account of The University of British Columbia's
     manuscript purchase.

5   ANON. "University Buys Work of Late Dollarton Poet." The
     Province (Vancouver) (27 February), p. 3.
          An account of The University of British Columbia's
     manuscript purchase.

6   ANON. "Unpublished Manuscripts Purchased." U.B.C. Reports,
     6 (March–April), 3–4.
          An account of The University of British Columbia manu-
     script collection, including an interview with Earle Birney.

7   ANON. "Answer to the Sphinx." Times Literary Supplement
     (19 April), pp. 257–58.
          A review of several works on and by Conrad Aiken, which
     makes passing reference to Lowry.

8   ANON. "The Squatter's Plato." Time (Canadian edition), 77,
     no. 19 (5 May), 14.
          An account of Lowry, observing that October Ferry to
     Gabriola is "about an alcoholic haunted by guilt after in-
     fluencing a man to commit suicide."

9   ANON. "Voyage That Never Ended." Time, 77, no. 23 (2 June),
     72.
          Distinguishing between "writers who shoot" (Hemingway)
     and "writers who encircle," places Lowry in the latter cate-
     gory, but finds that Hear Us O Lord is a series of "anarchic
     fragments of autobiography" rather than stories. Against
     the sterility of existence Lowry had only a "Forest Pri-
     meval Complex" as a weapon, and his sick romanticism turned
     a quest for solitude into a fascination with oblivion.

10   ANON. "Writer's Memorial Site Asked." The Vancouver Sun
     (15 June), p. 10.
          A report of a North Vancouver district Council meeting
     at which "Park Lane" is changed to "Lowry Lane" and a site
     for a plaque in Cates Park is requested.

11   ANON. "A Legend a Little After His Own Time." Maclean's.
     74 (15 July), 19.

A brief biographical sketch to accompany a reprint of a shortened version of Lowry's love story "of his hope," "The Forest Path to the Spring" (pp. 18-19, 32-34).

12   ANON. "Cates Park Plaque to Honor Writer." The Vancouver Sun (26 July), p. 12.
        A report of a North Vancouver Municipal Council meeting, approving of a site for a plaque.

13   ANON. "'To the Volcano': The Life and Work of Malcolm Lowry." CBC Times, 12, no. 20 (18-24 November), 3, 7.
        A biographical background to a CBC television programme ("Explorations," 22 and 29 November) on Lowry's life and works, interviewing a number of people who knew him.

14   ANON. "Publisher's Notes" in Malcolm Lowry, Hear Us O Lord from Heaven Thy Dwelling Place. Philadelphia and New York: J. B. Lippincott, pp. 7-8.
        Comments on Lowry's plans for the stories in this volume.
        Reprinted: 1962.B5; 1963.B6; 1969.B1-B2.

15   BARO, GENE. "Lowry: Posthumous, Personal." New York Herald Tribune Book Review, 37 (4 June), 27.
        The personal element in Hear Us O Lord is both a strength and a weakness, but the irony saves the work from the charge of sentimentalism.

16   BARUCCA, PRIMO. "Il libro dell'ebrietà." La Fiera Letteraria (Rome) (28 May).
        A laudatory review of Under the Volcano, emphasizing its political contemporaneity, and the tension between human hope and human failings.

17   BIRNEY, EARLE. "Glimpses into the Life of Malcolm Lowry." The Tamarack Review, no. 19 (Spring), pp. 35-41.
        Conscious of the dangerous speculation involved in dis- tinguishing between fiction and autobiography in Lowry's works, draws attention to certain parallels between his life and that of his characters. Details of his early life--some of them later disputed--are based on information from Margerie Lowry.

18   _____. "Malcolm Lowry's Poetry." Contact (San Francisco), 2, no. 7 (February), 81-82.
        Recounts his own association with Lowry's verse, and observes that the poems contain "the prototypal symbols of his prose."

1961

19   . "Notes." The Dalhousie Review, 41, no. 3 (Autumn), 385.
    Brief end-notes on four poems.

20   . Preface to Nine Poems. Canadian Literature, no. 8 (Spring), pp. 17-19.
    Commentary on the editorial tasks involved in dating the poems, together with explanatory notes on some of their allusions.
    Reprinted: 1971.A5.

21   . "The Unknown Poetry of Malcolm Lowry." B.C. Library Quarterly, 24, no. 4 (April), 33-40.
    Traces the publication of Lowry's poems. The intense poetic vision expressed itself in prose, though the uneven poems (unsuccessful attempts at exorcism) do have a "strange success." His writings constituted fragments of a "spiritual autobiography." His wry utterances and his preoccupation with death reflect modern man's uneasiness. The unfinished "Be Patient for the Wolf" came closest to subduing (by identifying with) Lowry's horrors.
    Translated: 1962.B10.

22   and Margerie Lowry, comps. "Malcolm Lowry (1909-1957): A Bibliography. Part I: Works by Malcolm Lowry." Canadian Literature, no. 8 (Spring), pp. 81-88.
    A preface (p. 81) explains the organization of the two-part bibliography. This section is divided into seven categories (Short Stories and Novellas, Novels, Poetry, Articles and Reviews, Letters, Radio Adaptations, Unpublished Material).

23   . "Malcolm Lowry (1909-1957): A Bibliography. Part II: Works about Malcolm Lowry." Canadian Literature, no. 9 (Summer), pp. 80-84.
    There are three sections (Critical, Biographical, Bibliographical), the first being further subdivided by subject. Like its supplements (See 1962.B11 and 1964.B9), it contains an excellent (though the compilers say incomplete) list of reviews, both in English and in other languages.

24 CASTELNAU, MARIE-PIERRE. "Malcolm Lowry: un écrivain 'inclassable.'" La gazette littéraire (Lausanne), 53 (4-5 March), 13, 17.
    Lowry himself is likened to Dylan Thomas; his work said to be influenced by Melville, Aiken, Gide, and others; his technique compared to that of Kafka, Joyce, and Faulkner. The visible themes of Under the Volcano are said to be love,

Mexico, and alcohol, and the text declared full of references to Jewish Cabbala.

25 CATHELIN, JEAN. "Dans une chambre forte de Vancouver un
    romancier déchiffre les inédits de Malcolm Lowry." Arts
    (Paris), no. 817 (12–18 April), p. 3.
        An interview with Earle Birney, in which Birney com-
    pliments French critics' exploration of Lowry's metaphysics,
    discusses the editing of Lowry's manuscripts, and shows
    Cathelin around the Lowry collection at The University of
    British Columbia.

26 CHAVARDÈS, MAURICE. "Un monument romanesque sans précédent."
    Le monde (12 January), p. 9.
        A review of the "definitive" translation of Under the
    Volcano, finding it an even more impressive account of the
    sickness of the soul than it had seemed in 1950.

27 CURLEY, THOMAS. "Unpopular Virtues." Commonweal, 75
    (20 October), 102–03.
        A general review of Hear Us O Lord from Heaven They
    Dwelling Place [sic], singling out "Through the Panama" for
    special praise.

28 DAVENPORT, JOHN. "Malcolm Lowry." Spectator, 207
    (1 September), 287, 290.
        A letter correcting errors in Tuohy's article (See
    1961.B56) concerning Lowry's stay with Davenport in Holly-
    wood in October 1936. A brief biography, with an attack on
    English reviews of Under the Volcano.

29 DOBBS, KILDARE. "Engines Sing Frere Jacques." Saturday Night,
    76, no. 13 (24 June), 29–30.
        A reflection on the growing reputation of Under the
    Volcano becomes a review of Hear Us O Lord. "Through the
    Panama" (summarized) is the most powerful realization of
    the recurrent theme of life-as-a-voyage, with a haven fol-
    lowing the torments. The lyric pitch of his work conveys
    an intense impression of reality, and "The Forest Path to
    the Spring" contains the "confession of a heroic
    temperament."

30 EDELSTEIN, J. M. "The Legacy of Malcolm Lowry." New Republic,
    144 (5 June), 24–25.
        Finds that Lowry's "virile and poetic," "rich, profound
    and moving" prose conveys many levels of meaning. Inven-
    tion and reportage intertwine in the impressive story
    "Through the Panama." "The Forest Path to the Spring" is
    also singled out for comment.

1961

31   E.[LEKTOROWICZ, LESZEK]. "Malcolm Lowry." Życie Literackie,
     no. 25, p. 15.
        A brief note explaining who Lowry is, saying that like
     other great modern writers he will have to wait for his
     work to be appreciated.

32   ESTANG, LUC. "Au-dessous du volcan." Le Figaro littéraire
     (14 January), p. 14.
        A review, disputing the claims of several French critics
     and praising the novel for its drama rather than for any
     esoteric symbolic meaning.

33   FOUCHET, MAX-POL. "No se Puede...." Canadian Literature,
     no. 8 (Spring), pp. 25-28.
        Reprint of 1960.B6.

34   FULFORD, ROBERT. "Revival for Lowry." Toronto Daily Star
     (11 April), p. 20.
        An account of recent and forthcoming Lowry publications.

35   GRAMIGNA, GIULIANO. "Un nuovo Ulisse sotto il vulcano di
     Lowry." Settimo Giorno (Milan) (9 May), p. 69.
        Reviews Lowry's connections with and publication in
     Italy, particularly Giorgio Monicelli's translation of
     Under the Volcano. Emphasizes the book's Joycean connec-
     tions, the logic that underlies its surface chaos and its
     Christian understanding of the concept of damnation.

36   HEILMAN, ROBERT B. "The Possessed Artist and the Ailing Soul."
     Canadian Literature, no. 8 (Spring), pp. 7-16.
        Observes that the quality allowing the survival of Under
     the Volcano is the "spiritual burden" which the "intensity
     accompanies." Lowry was a "possessed artist"-- his mate-
     rials using him as a channel to expression. Compares the
     novel with Mann's Doctor Faustus, then proceeds with an ex-
     plication of its themes, motifs, and allegorical impulses,
     singling out the Good Samaritan scene for comment.
        Reprinted: 1971.A5.

37   HUTCHINSON, JACK. "'After the Volcano....'" CBC Times, 11,
     no. 50 (17-23 June), 2, 4, 8.
        A brief biography, providing background to a CBC
     "Wednesday Night" radio programme (21 June) of readings
     from Lowry's works.

38   JANEWAY, ELIZABETH. "A Legacy, A Man and A Legend." The New
     York Times Book Review (21 May), pp. 1, 16.

24

A review of Lowry's accomplishment, perceiving reflections and connections which join the stories of <u>Hear Us O
Lord</u> into a humorous, visionary, and celebratory whole.

39   KIRK, DOWNIE. "More Than Music: Glimpses of Malcolm Lowry."
     <u>Canadian Literature</u>, no. 8 (Spring), pp. 31-38.
        Surveys the letters he received from Lowry, isolates
     their comments on Ortega, Pirandello, film, politics, and
     voodoo, and comments on his friendship with the man.
        Reprinted: 1971.A5; 1975.A3.

40   _____ "'Under the Volcano.'" <u>The Times Literary Supplement</u>
     (23 March), p. 137.
        A letter to the editor responding to the 28 October 1960
     editorial, quoting from one of Lowry's letters re his plans
     for a Dantesque trilogy.

41   LOWRY, MALCOLM. "Preface to a Novel." <u>Canadian Literature</u>,
     no. 9 (Summer), pp. 23-29. Translated from French by George
     Woodcock.
        Translation of 1950.B7. Refers to Lowry's letter to
     Cape, commenting on various images in <u>Under the Volcano</u>,
     the rhythm of the first chapter, subjectivity and Cabbala.
     In a letter to Markson [<u>See</u> 1971.A5], Lowry claims to have
     written this preface in Haiti, though Clarisse Francillon
     observed to Woodcock that she wrote the French version
     after Lowry had told her orally what he wanted said.

42   LOWRY, MARGERIE BONNER. "Biographical Note on Malcolm Lowry"
     in <u>Presenting Lippincott Authors</u>. Philadelphia: J. B.
     Lippincott, pp. 1-3.
        An account of Lowry's life, recording a number of anec-
     dotes later disputed. Contains details on the writing of
     the stories in <u>Hear Us O Lord</u>.

43   McCONNELL, WILLIAM. "Recollections of Malcolm Lowry" in <u>Masks
     of Fiction: Canadian Critics on Canadian Prose</u>. Edited
     by A. J. M. Smith. Toronto: McClelland & Stewart, New
     Canadian Library No. O 2, pp. 141-50.
        Reprint of 1960.B11, with a brief headnote concerning
     McConnell and Lowry.

44   MARKSON, DAVID. "A Posthumous Publication from Author of
     <u>Under the Volcano</u>." <u>The News</u> (Mexico City) (21 May), p. 6A.
        A brief review, praising the "texture" of Lowry's work,
     and the incomparable qualities of the short stories in <u>Hear
     Us O Lord</u>.

1961

45 NICHOLS, LEWIS. "In and Out of Books: Lowry." The New York
    Times Book Review (9 April), p. 8.
        An inaccurate account of Lowry's Canadian sojourn, con-
    fusing Dollarton with Gabriola Island.

46 PACEY, DESMOND. Creative Writing in Canada. Second edition.
    Toronto: Ryerson, pp. 227–29.
        Observes that if Lowry is a Canadian writer, his works
    would redeem the period 1920–1950 from dullness.

47 PORZIO, DOMENICO. "Il Vulcano di Lowry." Oggi (Milan), 17,
    no. 20 (18 May), 62.
        A commentary on Under the Volcano, its mythic sensibil-
    ities, critical reception, and poetic power.

48 READ, FORREST. Review of Hear Us O Lord. Epoch, 11, no. 3
    (Fall), 190–92.
        A favourable review, tracing the shift from detached
    point of view to interior monologue, from seriousness to
    comedy, from artifice to life.

49 SCOTT, JACK. "Jack Scott." The Vancouver Sun (13 March),
    p. 27.
        The first of four columns on Lowry, recounting Lowry's
    publishing and the growth of his international reputation.

50 _____. "Jack Scott." The Vancouver Sun (14 March), p. 21.
        The second of four columns, recounting the ironies and
    contradictions of Lowry's life.

51 _____. "Jack Scott." The Vancouver Sun (15 March), p. 27.
        The third of four columns, recounting Lowry's life in
    Dollarton. A fourth column (16 March, p. 31) prints the
    (at that time previously unpublished) conclusion to "The
    Forest Path to the Spring."

52 _____. "Lowry Tops at Capturing Flavor of Life by the Sea."
    The Vancouver Sun (7 June), p. 5.
        A favourable review of Hear Us O Lord.

53 STAINSBY, DONALD. "Plaque Mounted on Big Boulder Sought to
    Mark Lowry's Beach." The Vancouver Sun (14 June), p. 5.
        A request for public support to help erect a plaque.

54 STEINER, GEORGE. "Cold Ash." The Nation, 192 (27 May),
    465–66.
        Review of Hear Us O Lord from Heaven Thy Resting Place
    [sic]. "Through the Panama" is claimed as the finest work

Lowry produced after <u>Under the Volcano</u>, but the others--an incoherent whole--are dismissed as mediocre.

55 THOMPSON, JOHN. "Plot, character, etc." <u>Partisan Review</u>, 28, nos. 5-6, 707-16.
    A review article, referring (pp. 712-15) to the effortfulness of Lowry's writing in <u>Hear Us O Lord</u>.

56 TUOHY, FRANK. "Day of a Dead Man." <u>Spectator</u>, 207 (25 August), 262.
    Disputes Canadian claims to Lowry and French claims for him. Finds his poetry "heavy-footed," his symbolism pretentious rather than "experienced," and his characters 1930s stereotypes. "He is not a creator of character but an inhabitant of masks." Yet his adaptation of Joyce to alcoholic experiences is good, and the terror is true.

57 VAN O'CONNOR, WILLIAM. "The Echoing Ego." <u>Saturday Review</u>, 44 (27 May), 19.
    A review of <u>Hear Us O Lord</u> which finds no point in any of the stories, and condemns their concern about "being a writer," which stories "ought" not to have.

58 VIGORELLI, GIANCARLO. "Il romanzo dell'inferno." <u>Tempo</u> (Milan) (22 April).
    A complimentary review of the Italian translation of <u>Under the Volcano</u>, suggesting a number of parallels between Lowry and various modern European writers.

59 VILLELAUR, ANNE. "Au-dessous du volcan, dix ans après." <u>Les lettres françaises</u>, no. 858 (12-18 January), p. 2.
    A review of French criticism, examining its perspective toward the novel. Finds the symphonic images of nature and the Good Samaritan more central to appreciating the book than those explicitly Cabbalistic.

60 WOODCOCK, GEORGE. "Malcolm Lowry as Novelist." <u>B.C. Library Quarterly</u>, 24, no. 4 (April), 25-30.
    Contrasts the accomplishments of <u>Ultramarine</u> and <u>Under the Volcano</u>, the one as derivative interior monologue, in which life is incompletely fused into fiction, the other as terrifyingly real as the paintings of Bosch. Lowry was an imaginative rather than inventive writer, however. Verging on allegory, <u>Under the Volcano</u> is marred by the "heavy presence" of destiny, and the overly baroque ornamentation. Reprinted: 1970.B36.

61 _____. "Under Seymour Mountain." <u>Canadian Literature</u>, no. 8 (Spring), pp. 3-6.

1961

A review of the stories in Hear Us O Lord, appreciating
the sense of place that indicates Lowry's "mental natural-
isation" in Canada.
Reprinted: 1970.B36; 1971.A5.

1962 A BOOKS - NONE

1962 B SHORTER WRITINGS

1 ALBÉRÈS, R. M. See MARILL, RENÉ (1962.B26).

2 ANON. "Author Dead 5 Years, Book Wins Literary Prize."
Toronto Daily Star (24 February), p. 29.
A report of Hear Us O Lord winning the Governor-General's
Award for 1961.

3 ANON. "Widow Gets Lowry Award." The Vancouver Sun
(26 February), p. 8.
Announcement of Governor-General's Award for 1961.

4 ANON. Review of Ultramarine. The New Yorker, 38 (20 October),
230.
The book is an "expanded short story," of little substance but an "interesting prelude" to later work.

5 ANON. "Publisher's Note" in Malcolm Lowry, Hear Us O Lord
from Heaven Thy Dwelling Place. Philadelphia and New York:
J. B. Lippincott, Keystone edition, pp. 7-8.
Reprint of 1961.B14.

6 BEATTIE, MUNRO. "Tragic Novel Praised As a Modern Classic."
Ottawa Citizen (8 September), p. 28.
Considers Under the Volcano very good and not Canadian.

7 BIRNEY, EARLE. "Five Signallings in Darkness." Evidence,
no. 4 (Winter), pp. 76-78.
Commentary on five poems: "Prayer," "Doctor Usquebaugh,"
"Rilke and Yeats," "Self Pity," and "For Under the Volcano."

8 _____. "Foreword" to "Twelve Poems by Malcolm Lowry." North-
west Review, 5, no. 1 (Winter), 57-59.
Notes that the early poems relate closely to Ultramarine,
and that the humour and love of "quirky parallels" are
functional. Feels that "Sunrise" is a "fable of his life."

9 _____. "Introduction" to Selected Poems of Malcolm Lowry.
Edited by Earle Birney with the assistance of Margerie
Lowry. San Francisco: City Lights, pp. 7-10.

28

1962

Biographical notes on a man "innocent of defenses," with comments on the editing of the poems.

10 _____. "Malcolm Lowry, Poète Méconnu." Translated by Bernard Lafourcade. *Les lettres nouvelles*, no. 29 (October), pp. 71–81.
Translation of 1961.B21.

11 _____. "First Supplement to Malcolm Lowry Bibliography." *Canadian Literature*, no. 11 (Winter), pp. 90–95.
Primary works are divided into six categories (Short Stories and Novellas, Novels, Poetry, Articles, Letters, and Unpublished Material) and secondary works into three (Critical, Biographical, and Bibliographical).

12 BOATWRIGHT, JAMES. "The Sequel to Lowry's *Under the Volcano*." *Shenandoah*, 13, no. 2 (Winter), 65–70.
Reflects on the reputation of *Under the Volcano*, the wheel symbolism, and "The Voyage that Never Ends," then turns to comment on the stylistic brilliance and tonal variations of *Hear Us O Lord*.

13 BRADBURY, MALCOLM. Review. *Critical Quarterly*, 4, no. 4 (Winter), 377–79.
Comments on *Hear Us O Lord* and *Under the Volcano*, mentioning the wryness of Lowry's later work, the author's "curious internationalism," the themes of equilibrium and anguished artistry. Despite the faults, Lowry's imagination is large and interesting.

14 BUCKLER, ERNEST. "Down to the Sea to Prove Himself a Man Among Men." *The New York Times Book Review* (14 October), p. 5.
The strength of *Ultramarine* derives from its comedy and its exact sensory impressions, but the abrupt stylistic shifts are found "always disconcerting."

15 CABAU, JACQUES. "Au-delà de l'enfer." *L'Express* (20 September), pp. 29–30.
Finds *Hear Us O Lord* less esoteric and more human than *Under the Volcano*.

16 CHANDLER, GEORGE "The Seamy Side." *Liverpool Echo* (5 October).
A summary of Lowry's publications in a survey of Liverpool writers and literary representations of Liverpool.

1962

17   CHAVARDÈS, MAURICE. "L'univers obsessionel de Malcolm Lowry:
     du roman aux nouvelles." Le Monde (28 July), p. 9.
         A review of the French translation of Hear Us O Lord,
     stressing the serenity of the stories in contrast to Under
     the Volcano. Thematic and stylistic recurrence was to
     unify Lowry's intended cycle. Singles out specific stories
     for comment.

18   DEMPSEY, DAVID. "Sophisticated Innocence Abroad." Saturday
     Review, 45 (17 November), 30-31.
         A review, observing that Ultramarine must be read as
     Lowry's discovery that experience could not be separated
     from its "ultimate necessity for expression." The novel
     shifts intentionally between documentary realism and a
     poetic subjective monologue.

19   EDELSTEIN, J. M. "The Voyage that Never Ends." The New
     Republic, 147 (17 November), 22-23.
         A review, finding the revisions made to Ultramarine to
     be "insignificant." A "richer fulfillment" of his genius
     is to be found in the Selected Poems, which show the "dis-
     tilled bitterness" and the "agonized experiences" of his
     life.

20   HOFFMAN, FREDERICK J. Conrad Aiken. New York: Twayne, p. 31.
         Mention of Lowry's tribute to Aiken.

21   KANTERS, ROBERT. "Le dernier voyage de Malcolm Lowry." Le
     Figàro littéraire (11 August).
         Reflections on Under the Volcano and drunkenness.

22   KNICKERBOCKER, CONRAD. "Epitaph for Romantic Imagination."
     The Kansas City Star (28 October), p. 4E.
         A review, observing that Ultramarine, though uncon-
     trolled, shows the patterns of torment which afflicted the
     writer, and that his poems show intense feeling as well as
     Lowry's lack of defences.

23   LOWRY, MARGERIE. "Introductory Note" to Malcolm Lowry,
     Ultramarine. Revised edition. Philadelphia and New York,
     pp. 5-8.
         Biographical comments on Lowry at the time of writing
     Ultramarine, and notes on the revisions he made to the
     novel.
         Reprinted: 1964.B28; 1974.B57. Translated: 1965.B18;
     1969.B30.

24   MAGRINI, CÉSAR. "La ciudad métrica de Lowry." <u>Sur</u> (Buenos
     Aires), no. 277 (July-August), p. 23.
         A brief biographical summary, followed by a note on the
     difficulty of translating Lowry's lyric poems, particularly
     because of his metrical control, his balance of long and
     short syllables for particular effects. Lowry's sensibil-
     ities are seen as related to those of the 1914-18 War Poets
     generation.

25   MARCOTTE, GILLES. "Connaissez-vous Malcolm Lowry?" <u>La Presse</u>
     (Montreal) (11 August), p. 8.
         An examination of themes of menacing love, voyage, and
     native land in <u>Hear Us O Lord</u>.

26   MARILL, RENÉ [pseud., R. M. ALBÉRÈS]. <u>Histoire du roman
     moderne</u>. Paris: Editions Albin Michel, pp. 229-33, 417-18.
         Briefly describes features of <u>Under the Volcano</u>, seeing
     it as a continuation of the Kafkaesque novel of anguish.
     Translated: 1964.B30.

27   MARTIN, JAY. <u>Conrad Aiken: A Life of His Art</u>. Princeton:
     Princeton University Press, pp. 4-5, 71, 85, 195-96.
         Passing mention of Lowry.

28   MAYNE, RICHARD. "Further Arias." <u>New Statesman</u>, 63 (4 May),
     648-49.
         A review, praising the artistry of <u>Under the Volcano</u> and
     contrasting it with the "dazzling display" and volubility
     of <u>Hear Us O Lord</u> which lacks the "strictness" of art.

29   MOORE, BRIAN. "The Albatross of Self." <u>Spectator</u>, 208
     (4 May), 589.
         Review of <u>Hear Us O Lord</u>; says that it is an auto-
     biographical work, "Through the Panama" being the most
     brilliant narrative, showing Lowry emerging from his
     aliases.

30   NYE, ROBERT. "Horrors at Sunset." <u>The Tribune</u> (London)
     (2 November).
         "Being a major novelist, Lowry was a minor poet...." (A
     review of <u>Selected Poems</u>.)

31   PETER, JOHN. "Selected Poems of Malcolm Lowry." Broadcast on
     "Critics at Large," Canadian Broadcasting Corporation
     (11 September), 4 pp. typescript at The Bancroft Library,
     Berkeley, California.
         The poems offer brief glimpses of Lowry himself, but do
     not show the linguistic control of <u>Under the Volcano</u>, where

1962

the "link of memory" allows meaning to occur "between the
words."

32   POST MAN. "Merseyside Author." <u>Liverpool Daily Post</u>
     (13 April).
          Brief inexact biographical account, quoting two passages
     from <u>Under the Volcano</u> describing Leasowe.

33   PURDY, A. W. "Dormez-vous? A Memoir of Malcolm Lowry."
     <u>Canada Month</u>, 2, no. 9 (September), 24–26.
          An anecdotal account of meetings between Lowry and other
     Canadian poets--Purdy himself, A. J. M. Smith--and of poems
     Lowry was writing and revising at the time.

34   SCANNELL, VERNON. "New Fiction." <u>The Listener</u>, 67 (17 May),
     877.
          <u>Hear Us O Lord</u> is enjoyable despite the fact that it is
     overly literary and Lowry has no sense of character.

35   SCOTT, PETER DALE. "Turning New Leaves (1)." <u>The Canadian
     Forum</u>, 41 (January), 235–36.
          An account of the natural sequence of the stories in
     <u>Hear Us O Lord</u>, probing Lowry's use of an "ungainly" style
     as a "device of ignorance, to retrieve salvation from the
     world which destroyed that brilliantly dissociated person-
     ality, the Consul."

36   SHEDD, MARGARET. "Birney Discusses Malcolm Lowry." <u>The News</u>
     (Mexico City) (9 September), p. 8A.
          A salute to Earle Birney's Lowry endeavours, on the
     occasion of his visit to Mexico City.

37   _____. "Lowry's Translator, Raúl Ortiz Interviewed by Centro
     Director." <u>The News</u> (Mexico City) (9 September), p. 8A.
          Ortiz y Ortiz observes the difficulties of translating
     the density of language, feels that Lowry intentionally
     chose Mexico and the date for his setting, and stresses
     the "musical structure" of <u>Under the Volcano</u>.

38   SIGAUX, GILBERT. "'Ecoute notre voix ô Seigneur'!" <u>Democratie</u>
     (23 August).
          Considers briefly the theme of the writer in <u>Hear Us O
     Lord</u>.

39   SKELTON, ROBIN. "Let's Ban the Myth of the Poet Drowning in
     Alcohol and Guilt." <u>The Vancouver Sun</u> (10 October), p. 5.
          A review of the poems, finding an "ironic clarity and
     wit" in the best of them and a "lonely dignity" at the
     heart of the "self-destructive gestures."

40   STALLMAN, R. W. and R. E. WATTERS. "Strange Comfort Afforded
     By the Profession" in The Creative Reader. Second edition.
     New York: Ronald Press, pp. 358-62.
         Detailed notes identifying the allusions in "Strange
     Comfort Afforded By the Profession" and raising questions
     about the function of the story's techniques.

41   TROTZIG, BIRGITTA. "Dödens triumf" [Triumph of Death].
     Bonniers Litterära Magasin, 31, pp. 272-84.
         After an account of the reception of Under the Volcano
     in America and France, and a biography, compares Lowry with
     Joyce (myth and psychology), Wolfe (personal torments), and
     Flaubert (meticulous style). Explores the novel's imagery,
     particularly the volcano ("death and consummate achievement")
     and All Souls' Day. The novel's polar perceptions produce
     tension. The defeat of love becoming the triumph of death
     is a theme on which Lowry "built a monument to the despair
     of an era." Followed (pp. 285-95) by "Genom Panama," the
     Swedish translation of "Through the Panama."

42   WATT, F. W. Review of Hear Us O Lord from Heaven Thy Dwelling
     Place. University of Toronto Quarterly, 31, no. 4 (July),
     467-71.
         An extended review in the context of a survey of the
     year's work ("Letters in Canada: 1961"), acknowledging the
     "unusual" nature of the form of the stories, describing
     each, but praising its poignancy and the author's handling
     of both "complicated fatefulness" and "human happiness."

43   XTRAU, RAMÓN. "Malcolm Lowry, Poet of Cycles." The News
     (Mexico City) (9 September), p. 8A.
         A review of the "living document" that the poems com-
     prise, finding dream and death at the centre of Lowry's
     cycles, though it is not a nihilistic world. The poems
     constitute a guide to Under the Volcano.

1963 A BOOKS

1   AIKEN, CONRAD. Ushant, An Essay. London: W. H. Allen,
     365 pp.
         Reprint of 1952.A1, with the addition of a prefatory key
     to personae and place names.

1963 B SHORTER WRITINGS

1   ANDRIANNE, RENÉ. "Ecoute notre voix, ô Seigneur, par Malcolm
     Lowry." Revue nouvelle, 37, no. 2 (February), 206-10.

1963

Summarizes some of the central concerns of <u>Under the
Volcano</u>, then recounts the parallels between Lowry's life
and various details in <u>Hear Us O Lord</u> in order to demonstrate that in Lowry "the object is everything." Consciousness controls all symbols and details, which acquire
aesthetic significance. Recurrence and repetition are
features of an exact style. In the final pages of the
work, the author abandons masks and becomes himself.

2   ANON. "Rake in a Suit of Armour." <u>The Times Weekly Review</u>
    (London) (21 February), p. 13.
        Approves the realism of the crew's talk in <u>Ultramarine</u>.

3   ANON. "Lost, Lost, Lost." <u>The Times Literary Supplement</u>
    (22 March), p. 197.
        Review of <u>Ultramarine</u>, recounting some of the experiences
    that led to the writing of the book. Lowry "was closer to
    the Puritan tradition of America than to anything, or any-
    one, in England."

4   ANON. "Malcolm Lowry i jego 'Ultramaryna'" [Malcolm Lowry
    and his <u>Ultramarine</u>]. <u>Życie Literackie</u>, no. 15.
        Notes the forthcoming Polish translation of <u>Under the
    Volcano</u>, and cites the <u>Times Literary Supplement</u>'s current
    assertion that <u>Ultramarine</u> shows the major ingredients of
    Lowry's greatest work.

5   ANON. "Notes on Current Books." <u>Virginia Quarterly Review</u>,
    39, no. 1 (Winter), xiv.
        The revisions of <u>Ultramarine</u> demonstrate Lowry's
    "peculiar artistry."

6   ANON. "Publisher's Note" in Malcolm Lowry, <u>Hear Us O Lord
    from Heaven Thy Dwelling Place</u>. London: Jonathan Cape,
    pp. 7-8.
        Reprint of 1961.B14.

7   ASCHERSON, NEAL. "Lake Lowry." <u>New Statesman</u>, 65
    (15 February), 242.
        <u>Ultramarine</u> is a "noble but crippled" work, awash in
    self-pity.

8   BERL, EMMANUEL. "Homage à Malcolm Lowry." <u>Preuves</u>, no. 143
    (January), pp. 64-66.
        The true subject of <u>Under the Volcano</u>, a contrapuntal and
    polyphonic novel, is God and the condition God has made for
    Man. What matters in the book is the stance human beings
    take, the issue of whether or not they believe themselves
    to be free.

9   BROMIGE, DAVID. "Reviews." <u>Northwest Review</u>, 6, no. 1
    (Winter), 113-15.
        Observes that an awareness of Lowry--reduced to self by
    his inability to accept the compromises of love--is essen-
    tial to a reader of <u>Selected Poems</u>. If sometimes he fails
    to make art out of agony, he never succeeds in depicting
    happiness. "Sestina in a Cantina" is singled out for
    praise.

10 CABAU, JACQUES. "La saison des enfers." <u>L'Express</u> (22 August),
    p. 23.
        Finds in <u>Lunar Caustic</u>'s alcoholic isolation a symbolic
    revelation of the human drama.

11 CHAVARDÈS, MAURICE. "'Lunar Caustic,' Le purgatoire de
    Malcolm Lowry." <u>Le Monde</u> (22 June).
        Sees the novel as a minor but important part of Lowry's
    "drunken Divine Comedy."

12 COGSWELL, FRED. "Lord Jim as Byron." <u>The Canadian Forum</u>, 42
    (January), 230.
        Lowry's poems show a mingling (but not balancing) of a
    noble literary world and a depraved one of "self-experienced
    reality." His strengths as a writer are in conflict with
    his lapses into "masochistic narcissism."

13 COLOMBO, J. R. "Poetry and Legend." <u>Canadian Literature</u>,
    no. 16 (Spring), pp. 61-63.
        A review of <u>Selected Poems</u>, observing that it will
    "enhance the Lowry legend without advancing the cause of
    his poetry." The poems are romantic but not sharp, and the
    pleasure in reading them "comes from one's willingness to
    appreciate fragments."

14 [FRANCILLON, CLARISSE]. Headnote to her translation of <u>Lunar
    Caustic</u>. <u>Les lettres nouvelles</u>, 35, pp. 7-9.
        Explains the difficulties in translating the title, pro-
    vides a brief publishing history, and suggests that the
    work, because of its obsessions, is close to the spirit of
    <u>Under the Volcano</u>.

15 FRYE, NORTHROP. "To the Editor." <u>Canadian Literature</u>, no. 17
    (Summer), p. 84.
        Letter to the editor in regard to item 1963.B13, pointing
    out that Mrs. Lowry received the 1961 Governor-General's
    Award prize money.

1963

16   HAAS, RUDOLF. "Nachwort" to Malcolm Lowry, <u>Unter dem Vulkan</u>.
     Reinbek bei Hamburg: Rowohlt, pp. 395–404.
          Suggests, after a brief account of Lowry's career,
     several ways of seeing Lowry's contemporaneity. A number
     of parallels--dramatic and thematic--are drawn between
     Lowry and, for example, Williams, O'Neill, Eliot, Lawrence,
     Greene, and Faulkner. Some reference is also made to Ger-
     man influences on Lowry.

17   HORST, KARL AUGUST. "Höllenparadies der Kunst." <u>Sonntags-</u>
     <u>blatt</u> (Hamburg) (1 December).
          A review, commenting on character in <u>Under the Volcano</u>.

18   KNICKERBOCKER, CONRAD. "Malcolm Lowry and the Outer Circle
     of Hell." <u>Paris Review</u>, no. 29 (Winter-Spring), pp. 12–13.
          Notes on themes in <u>Lunar Caustic</u> and on Lowry's associa-
     tions with New York.
          Reprinted: 1968.B31; 1975.A3. Translated: 1973.B18–B19.

19   LISOWSKI, JERZY. "Pod Wulkanem" [Under the Volcano].
     <u>Twórczość</u>, 19, no. 11 (November), 67–73.
          Reprint of 1963.B20.

20   _____. "Posłowie" to Malcolm Lowry, <u>Pod Wulkanem</u> [Postscript
     to <u>Under the Volcano</u>]. Warsaw: Państwowy Instytut
     Wydáwniczy, pp. 459–67.
          Mistakenly identifies Scotland as Lowry's native country
     and asserts that Lowry fought for the Republicans in Spain.
     Acknowledges the novel's love theme and its metaphysical
     elements (the internal struggle between Good and Evil), but
     finds the political leitmotif to be most important. It
     establishes the moral atmosphere, the pervading sense of
     guilt.
          Reprinted: 1963.B19.

21   MATHEWS, ROBIN. "Canadian Poetry and Fiction." <u>Queen's</u>
     <u>Quarterly</u>, 70 (Summer), 282–83.
          Lowry's poems "possess intensity without particulariza-
     tion," their movement into generality preventing them from
     stirring readers.

22   MATTHEWS, MICHAEL. "Malcolm Lowry--Writer." <u>The Ubyssey</u>, 45,
     no. 67 (14 March), 4.
          Praises the "moral realism" of Lowry's work.

23   _____. Review of Stories and Poems. <u>British Columbia Library</u>
     <u>Quarterly</u>, 26, no. 4 (April), 31–33.
          All of Lowry's writing is one vast "monologue" by a man
     who was "omniverous for metaphor" and capable of intense,

agile, and ironic seriousness. The earnestness of the
poems does not match the substance of the stories, though
both display his "moral realism."

24 MEIJER, HENK ROMIJN. "Malcolm Lowry." Tirade (Amsterdam), 7,
     918–22.
        Observes the humour in Under the Volcano, and Lowry's
     objectivity towards the Consul. These two elements prevent
     the Consul from being tragic, but they also prevent the in-
     trusion of pathos. The theme is not love or politics, but
     drink, and the value of the novel lies in its portrayal of
     alcoholism.

25 MORAES, DOM. "Novels Back From Limbo." The Daily Telegraph
     (London) (24 May).
        A tribute to Lowry's style in Ultramarine.

26 POST MAN. "Fame Comes Too Late to a New Brighton Writer."
     Liverpool Daily Post (13 February), p. 6.
        A note on the republication of Ultramarine, quoting "a
     Mostyn correspondent" who sailed with Lowry in 1927. Com-
     ments on Liverpool sites mentioned in Ultramarine.

27 PREE, BARRY. "Special Notices." The London Magazine, 3 n.s.
     (April), 85–86.
        A review of Ultramarine, finding it a "classic" sea
     novel and an exciting story; in it Lowry's later themes
     germinate.

28 ROSE, ALEXANDER. "Pauline Johnson Honored – But What About
     Lowry?" The Vancouver Sun (14 December), p. 6.
        An account of Lowry's growing reputation around the
     world, an interview with Earle Birney, and a reflection on
     the fact that money was never raised in 1961 to erect a
     commemorative plaque [See 1961.B10–B12].

29 RUTHERFORD, MALCOLM. "Shadows of the Con-Men." Spectator,
     210 (5 April), 440.
        Ultramarine seems repetitive, but is occasionally
     powerful.

30 SCHONAUER, FRANZ. "Tod in Mexico." Deutsche Zeitung und
     Wirtschaftszeitung (Cologne) (21 December).
        A review of Under the Volcano.

31 SIMPSON, W. G. "Lowry and Grieg." The Times Literary
     Supplement (12 April), p. 249.
        A letter pointing out some of the influences of
     Nordahl Grieg upon Lowry.

1963

32 SPETTIGUE, D. Review of Ultramarine. Queen's Quarterly,
    70 (Autumn), 453.
        The book is not totally satisfying but is invaluable
    for an understanding of Lowry.

33 VUILLEUMIER, JEAN. "Lunar Caustic de Malcolm Lowry."
    Tribune de Genève (19 August).
        A summary review.

34 WEST, PAUL. The Modern Novel. London: Hutchinson,
    pp. 148–49.
        Passing mention of Lowry's "febrile" but convincing
    works.

35 WILSON, MILTON. Review of Selected Poems. University of
    Toronto Quarterly, 32, no. 4 (July), 391.
        Passing mention of Lowry in a survey of the year's work
    ("Letters in Canada: 1962"), finding him to be a good poet
    but not so good as a poem writer.

36 W[OODCOCK], G[EORGE]. "Before the Volcano." Canadian Liter-
    ature, no. 17 (Summer), pp. 83–84.
        A review of Ultramarine, finding it "derivative" but an
    apprenticeship for greater work to come.

37 ZIMMER, DIETER E. "Die Verwüstung des Gartens." Die Zeit
    (Hamburg), 41 (11 October), 20.
        Admiring review of Under the Volcano, with some account
    of Lowry's life and use of literary allusion.

1964 A BOOKS – NONE

1964 B SHORTER WRITINGS

1 AGUILERA-MALTA, DEMETRIO. "La rosa de los vientos." El Dio
    (Mexico City), "El Gallo Illustrado" supplement (14 June).
        Summary review of the Spanish translation of Under the
    Volcano.

2 ALBÉRÈS, R. M. See MARILL, RENÉ (1964.B30).

3 ALLEN, WALTER. "The Masterpiece of the Forties" in On Con-
    temporary Literature. Edited by Richard Kostelanetz.
    New York: Avon, pp. 419–21.
        A brief commentary praising Under the Volcano as the
    decade's major work. A novel about hell, it carries
    glimpses of heaven; a great tragic work, it is masterfully

organized and achieves a complete harmony between characters and external landscape.

4   . The Modern Novel in Britain and the United States.
New York: E. P. Dutton & Co., pp. 263–65, 307.
   Reprint of 1964.B5.

5   . Tradition and Dream: The English and American Novel
from the Twenties to Our Time. London: Phoenix House,
pp. 263–65, 307.
   Noting Under the Volcano's general indebtedness to
Ulysses and The Waste Land, asserts its independence from
both. It is a great tragic novel about alienation and hell,
a masterpiece of organization and organic symbolism.
   Reprinted: 1964.B4.

6   ANON. "Octubre–noviembre, 1938." Revista de la Universidad
de México, 19, no. 3 (November), p. 12.
   A summary of Mexican and international events of the two
months, as background to Under the Volcano.

7   BIEŃKOWSKI, ZBIGNIEW. "Pod Wulkanem" [Under the Volcano].
Twórczość, 20, no. 5 (May), 58–62.
   Finds the strength of the novel to come not from the
wealth of allusion but from the fact that the syncretic
structure constitutes an integrated whole. Though the
Consul's actions are simple, their symbolic reverberations
are complex, and the novel is the testimony of an "uncom-
promising moralist," a "moral maximalist like Céline."
The Consul "condemns himself in the name of values which
he continues to affirm."
   Reprinted: 1966.B3.

8   BIRNEY, EARLE. "Against the Spell of Death." Prairie
Schooner, 37, no. 4 (Winter), 328–33.
   An introduction to four of Lowry's poems, describing
the seven-part structure of the proposed collection to be
called "The Lighthouse Invites the Storm." The poems--
"exorcisms" that create a "psychic autobiography" of his
last twenty years--do not have the "wing-spread" of his
prose, but "cry more openly." The effects of his prose,
however, were achieved through "rhythm, verbal shock...,
and the intricate repetition and passionate development
of very personal symbols."

9   , comp. "Second Supplement to Malcolm Lowry Bibliography."
Canadian Literature, no. 19 (Winter), pp. 83–89.
   Primary works are divided into five categories (Short
Stories and Novellas, Novels, Poetry, Letters, Unpublished

1964

Material) and secondary works into three (Critical,
Biographical, Bibliographical).

10   BREZA, HENRYK. "Świadomość zabójcza" [Lethal Consciousness].
      Nowe Książki, no. 3, pp. 102-03.
          Although finding Under the Volcano artistically dazzling
      and intellectually subtle, concludes that the novel does
      not (as a work of genius does) transcend expectations.
      Actions are predictable; the elaborate superstructure is
      built on a conventional base; and the hero--though it is
      unusual for him to be a dipsomaniac--tours the typical hells
      of modern literature.
          Reprinted: 1967.B8.

11   BUDRECKI, LECH. "Ucieczka Malcolma Lowry" [Malcolm Lowry's
      Flight]. Odgtosy (Lodz), no. 1, p. 9.
          Lowry left behind a legend composed of stereotypes
      (unrecognized writer, rebel, hounded by failure) and a
      great novel, one in the tradition of Brontë enriched by
      the technical discoveries of Faulkner and Joyce.

12   BUREK, TOMASZ. "Jeszcze jedna podróż do piekieł" [One more
      voyage to hell]. Tygodnik Kulturalny, no. 9, p. 5.
          Under the Volcano demonstrates the modern novel's
      capaciousness: at once love story, fable, parable about
      guilt, and eschatological myth. The Consul's journey to a
      polymorphous hell derives from his sense of guilt, which in
      turn derives from the "myth of original sin and its secular
      and historical analogues: private property, imperialist
      conquest, intolerance, and war." To reject the past is to
      commit a crime against conscience; to acknowledge the con-
      science; to acknowledge the conscience is to prepare to
      change the future.

13   CHITTICK, V. L. O. "Ushant's Malcolm Lowry." Queen's
      Quarterly, 71 (Spring), 67-75.
          A summary of Conrad Aiken's portrait of Lowry as "Hambo"
      in Ushant, recounting biographical details, commenting on
      Joyce's influence on them both, and suggesting that Lowry
      also influenced Aiken, particularly through his "gift of
      'mythopoeic' creation."

14   CHOCIŁOWSKI, JERZY. "Western i symfonia" [A Western and a
      Symphony]. Trybuna Mazowiecka (Warsaw), no. 75 (30 March),
      p. 6.
          Under the Volcano is "the authentic history of a drunk-
      ard," a love story, a prophecy, and a political warning.
      Compares the novel with Antonioni's films.

40

15 CHURCHILL, VICTOR ALEXANDER SPENCER, VISCOUNT. "The Ending
   is the Beginning" in <u>All My Sins Remembered</u>. London:
   Heinemann, pp. 187–202.
       Chapter 15 of an autobiography. Mentions his friendship
   with Lowry, and recounts a few anecdotes about him.
   Reprinted: 1965.B6.

16 DAY, DOUGLAS. "Malcolm Lowry: Letters to an Editor."
   <u>Shenandoah</u>, 15, no. 3 (Spring), 3–15.
       A survey and summary of Lowry's life through his letters,
   particularly those to Albert Erskine.

17 _____. "Of Tragic Joy." <u>Prairie Schooner</u>, 37, no. 4 (Winter),
   354–62.
       Unsympathetic to Jan Gabrial, a portrait emerges of
   Lowry as an engaging "naïf," with an ability to laugh.
   An account of <u>Under the Volcano</u> refers to its patterning,
   its allusions, and the survival of Geoffrey's soul.

18 EDELSTEIN, J. M. "On Re-Reading <u>Under the Volcano</u>." <u>Prairie
   Schooner</u>, 37, no. 4 (Winter), 336–39.
       Finds the book, with its voice of guilt, a major aes-
   thetic experience.

19 ELEKTOROWICZ, LESZEK. "Pod wulkanem" [Under the Volcano].
   <u>Życie Literackie</u>, no. 31, p. 4.
       Summarizes the novel's themes and emphasizes the extent
   to which the Consul is a moralist. Finds the title superbly
   appropriate, suggesting literally the towering landscape
   and figuratively the menace of war, the evil in the heart
   of man, and the horror of universal hate which constitute
   the moral setting.
   Reprinted: 1966.B11.

20 GANZ, RAFFAEL. "Am einbrechenden Kraterrand." <u>Der Landbote</u>,
   "Sonntagspost" (Sunday Supplement) (3 January).
       A commentary on the density of <u>Under the Volcano</u>, com-
   paring Lowry with Fitzgerald.

21 HIRSCHMAN, JACK. "Kabbala/Lowry, etc." <u>Prairie Schooner</u>, 37,
   no. 4 (Winter), 347–53.
       A lyric response to Lowry's writing finding it com-
   parable in its poetic intensity to the work of Artaud and
   Djuna Barnes, among others. Lowry's obsession with language is part of an attachment to cabbalistic teaching.
   Charles Stansfeld Jones was giving Lowry lessons.

1964

22   KNICKERBOCKER, CONRAD. "Paperbacks in Review: Malcolm
       Lowry." New York Times Book Review (8 November), pp. 64-65.
          A general review of four of Lowry's books, recounting
       his life, referring to the poems as the most private reve-
       lations of his morality, tracing the theme of exile, and
       praising the originality of his talent.

23   _____. "The Voyages of Malcolm Lowry." Prairie Schooner,
       37, no. 4 (Winter), 301-14.
          Lowry was a clown when sober, a hierophant when drunk.
       Mexico was his Dark Night of the Soul. A biographical
       account, drawing attention to some of the autobiographical
       allusions in Lowry's narratives.

24   KOYAMA, OLIVE. "Ultramarine." The Canadian Reader (May),
       pp. 8-9.
          A brief account of the novel, praising Lowry's perspec-
       tive toward Dana.

25   ŁAPINSKI, ZDZISŁAW. "Malcolm Lowry: 'Pod Wulkanem'" [Under
       the Volcano]. Tygodnik Powszechny (Cracow), no. 12, p. 6.
          A review, finding the novel to be one which forces
       readers to revise their view of reality and the human
       condition.

26   LOWRY, MALCOLM. "El Jardin de Etla." Translated by Mario
       Beauregard. Mexico en la Cultura (8 March), p. 2.
          Translation of 1950.B6.

27   _____. "Le jardin d'Etla." Translated by Geneviève Serreau
       and Robert Pépin. Les lettres nouvelles (February-March)
       pp. 45-47.
          Translation of 1950.B6.

28   LOWRY, MARGERIE. "Introductory Note" to Malcolm Lowry,
       Ultramarine. Revised edition. New York: McGraw-Hill,
       pp. 5-8.
          Reprint of 1962.B23.

29   MAHON, DEREK. "Malcolm Lowry-- the Road to Parián." Icarus
       (Trinity College, Dublin), 43 (May), 20-24.
          Summaries of Lowry's life and the plot of Under the
       Volcano lead to an interpretation of the Consul as Faust,
       Prometheus, and civilization, and of History as "the long-
       drawn-out Fall of Man."

1964

30 MARILL, RENÉ [pseud., R. M. ALBÉRÈS]. Geschicte des modernen
    Romans. Translated by Karl August Horst. Düsseldorf –
    Köln: Eugen Diederichs Verlag, pp. 232-34, 238, 409, 410.
    Translation of 1962.B26.

31 MARKSON, DAVID. "Myth in Under the Volcano." Prairie
    Schooner, 37, no. 4 (Winter), 339-46.
        Points to various Joycean, Dantean, and Homeric paral-
    lels, specifying the Homeric references in Under the
    Volcano's Chapter 10. Mention is also made of Hindu epics,
    Cabbala, Bunyan, Eliot, and Jessie Weston. Berkeleyan
    philosophy is called upon to show the way in which "the
    entire narrative is meant to be seen as unreal."

32 NORDELL, RODERICK. "Malcolm Lowry in Retrospect." The
    Christian Science Monitor (4 June), p. 11 (eastern and
    midwest edition, or p. 5 of the western edition).
        A reflective glance at all of Lowry's published work,
    stressing the importance of perception, Lowry's happy as
    well as hellish visions, and Aiken's comments on Lowry's
    character.

33 NOXON, GERALD. "Malcolm Lowry: 1930." Prairie Schooner, 37,
    no. 4 (Winter), 315-20.
        Personal memoir of Lowry at Cambridge, submitting "Port
    Swettenham" to Experiment, consulting Noxon's film books,
    enjoying student life. Incorrectly remembers Lowry earning
    a class I degree.
        Reprinted: 1975.A3. Translated: 1974.B69.

34 PETIT, MARQUEL. "Good Sailors Rarely Go Home." Book Week
    (15 November), p. 26.
        A review of Ultramarine, putting it in the context of
    Lowry's other work, and praising its complex substructure,
    condensation, imaginative power, authenticity, and irony.
    Ship and self are identified; the voyage signifies rebirth;
    and the furies are transformed into mercies.

35 PONCE, JUAN GARCÍA. "Malcolm Lowry en su obra." Revista de
    la Universidad de México, 19, no. 3 (November), 10-11.
        Under the Volcano, Lowry's major, tragic work, is auto-
    biographical, yet one cannot completely identify the author
    with the Consul. The article is followed (pp. 13-22) by a
    Spanish translation of Lowry's letter to his lawyer,
    A. Ronald Button, in connection with his imprisonment in
    Mexico.

1964

36 SADKOWSKI, WACŁAW. "Śmierć w Meksyku" [Death in Mexico].
    Trybuna Ludu (Warsaw), no. 101 (12 April), p. 4.
        Though antagonistic to works which deal with man's
    dark heart—works which make man terrified of himself—
    admires the perfection of the formal structure of Under
    the Volcano, and praises the novel's refusal "to come to
    terms with evil."
        Reprinted: 1968.B42.

37 SCHALJKWIJK, BOB. "El volcán de Quauhnáhuac." Revista de
    la Universidad de México, 19, no. 3 (November), 23–27.
        Photographs of the town, with quotations from Lowry as
    captions.

38 SKWARNICKI, MAREK. "Wulkany" [Volcanoes]. Znak, no. 119,
    pp. 614–17.
        Reflects that novels like Under the Volcano, which
    separate the perceiving subject from external reality and
    lead to alienation and despair, were once popular in Poland,
    but now being sought are works which show faith in order.
    Lowry's novel brings no artistic catharsis. The descrip-
    tions of nature still impress, whereas the symbolic and
    thematic superstructure shows signs of wear.

39 TERRÉS, JAIME GARCÍA. "La feria de los días." Revista de
    la Universidad de México, 19, no. 3 (November), 3.
        Brief comments on Lowry's connection with Mexico.

40 XIRAU, RAMÓN. "Malcolm Lowry: Intención de una obra
    incompleta." Revista de la Universidad de México, 19,
    no. 3 (November), 34–35.
        An account of Lowry's response to Nietzche and
    Swedenborg, and of the note of reconciliation which "The
    Forest Path to the Spring" brings to his work.

1965 A BOOKS

1 BREIT, HARVEY and MARGERIE BONNER LOWRY, eds. Selected Letters
   of Malcolm Lowry. Philadelphia and New York: J. B.
   Lippincott, xix + 459 pp.
       Assembles a selection of the letters held by The Univer-
   sity of British Columbia Special Collections Division. Included are letters to friends, relatives, editors, reviewers,
   etc., from 1928 to 1957. Appended are several letters to
   him or about him, bearing upon or answering some of the
   points in his own letters, by editors and agents such as
   Harold Matson, Jonathan Cape, Maxwell Perkins, Charles

Scribner, and Robert Giroux, together with letters from
other writers--James Agee, Christopher Isherwood, Ralph
Gustafson, Alfred Kazin, and Jacques Barzun--and letters by
Margerie Lowry. A biographical chronology is also included.
The book is indexed.

Lowry's letters range from witty, friendly gestures to
angry declarations about the critical reception of his work,
and from plaintive accounts of his personal circumstances
to reflections upon the intent, structure, and direction of
his writing. A subjective sourcebook for biographical attitudes, the book also contains a number of key statements
about Lowry's work. Notable among these is the letter to
Jonathan Cape (1946, pp. 57-88) defending Under the Volcano's setting, flashbacks, references to alcoholism, and
providing a chapter-by-chapter exegesis, alluding to the
Dantesque parallels, Cabbalistic and political overtones,
and general symbolic design. Other letters include those
to James Stern (1940, pp. 27-31) about the potential of
the short story form; to A. Ronald Button (pp. 91-112)
about his 1946 imprisonment in Mexico; to Jacques Barzun
(1947, pp. 143-48) attacking his review; to Derek Pethick
(1950, pp. 197-201) on patterns in Under the Volcano; to
David Markson (1951, pp. 247-66) explaining the trilogical
pattern in which he initially planned to fit Under the Volcano; to Albert Erskine (1953, pp. 333-40, 344-46) concerning Gabriola and Hear Us O Lord.
Reprinted: 1967.A1; 1969.A2. Translated: 1968.A1.

2   EDMONDS, DALE H. "Malcolm Lowry: A Study of His Life and
    Work." Ph.D. dissertation, University of Texas (Austin),
    488 pp.
       Drawing much information from Margerie Lowry, writes a
    biographical commentary, followed by an examination of sym-
    bol and story in the major works, concentrating (four chap-
    ters))on Under the Volcano. Influences on Ultramarine are
    explored, and there is some discussion of the short stories
    and poems.

3   KILGALLIN, ANTHONY R. "The Use of Literary Sources for Theme
    and Style in Lowry's Under the Volcano." Master's thesis,
    University of Toronto, 125 pp.
       Traces a number of allusions. Much of the material, in
    revised form, appeared in 1973.A5.

4   THOMAS, HILDA L. "Malcolm Lowry's Under the Volcano: An
    Interpretation." Master's thesis, The University of British
    Columbia, 71 pp.
       Argues that the doctrine of "universal analogy," as it
    influenced the Romantic and Symbolist movements, is an

essential part of the theme and design of Lowry's novel.
The wheel and abyss symbols, and the Consul's tragic stat-
ure, are illuminated by this understanding.

1965 B SHORTER WRITINGS

1   ANON. "Dipso to Dachau." The Times Literary Supplement
        (18 November), p. 1017.
          Review of A. D. Maclean's Winter's Tales 11, in which
        "The Element Follows You Around, Sir!" appears. It is
        singled out for praise, for Lowry's "feverish, incautious"
        writing "is yet controlled as if by an inner music."

2   ANON. "Harrowing Hell." Newsweek, 66 (20 December), 105-07.
          Compares Lowry's letters with Fitzgerald's, insofar as
        both reveal openly the personality of the writer.

3   BREIT, HARVEY. "Introduction" to Selected Letters of Malcolm
        Lowry. Philadelphia and New York: J. B. Lippincott,
        pp. xi-xv.
          Refers to the importance of the supernatural in Lowry's
        life and work, and to his intimate knowledge of despair,
        asserting that the letters, despite their frequent wit,
        cumulatively reveal a moving portrait of the tragic human
        condition.
          Reprinted: 1967.B7; 1969.B8.

4   CARROY, JEAN-ROGER. "Postface: Malcolm et les ambiguïtés"
        in Malcolm Lowry, Ultramarine. Paris: Editions Denoel,
        pp. 235-265.
          Examines the principle of "doubling" in the novel, the
        antagonism and identification between Dana and Andy, then
        examines Lowry's relation to Melville and his relationship
        with Conrad Aiken. Dana's symbolic progress is traced,
        though some doubt is cast on Lowry's total acceptance of
        hermetic systems. The novel is linked with Lowry's other
        works, with the myth he created and his exploration of the
        ambivalence of human potential.

5   CHRISTELLA MARIE, SISTER. "Under the Volcano: A Considera-
        tion of the Novel by Malcolm Lowry." Xavier University
        Studies, 4, 13-27.
          A summary of the novel, identifying Lowry as modern
        Promethean Man and the Consul as a doomed Faust figure.
        The novel pits man against both himself and God.

6   CHURCHILL, VICTOR ALEXANDER SPENCER, VISCOUNT.   Be All My Sins
    Remembered.   New York: Coward-McCann.
        Title revised.
        Reprint of 1964.B15.

7   DAVENPORT, JOHN.   "A Tortured Life Is Key to a Masterwork."
    Life, 59, no. 24 (10 December), 12, 20.
        A brief account of Lowry's life, by way of reviewing the
    personal force of Under the Volcano.

8   EDMONDS, DALE.   "Lowry=Volcano=Mexico=."   Riata (University
    of Texas) (Spring), pp. 11-20.
        Asserts that Lowry's work must be "lived" rather than
    talked about.   The writer's humour colours the biographical
    commentary and the judgments of Under the Volcano, the
    poems, and the "interesting" short pieces.

9   FREMONT-SMITH, ELIOT.   "In the Jaws of the Abyss."   The New
    York Times (15 December), p. 45.
        Praises Lowry's letters as a guide to the "responsibility
    of consciousness" in his novels.

10 HICKS, GRANVILLE.   "One Great Statement."   Saturday Review,
    48 (4 December), 39-40.
        A survey of Lowry's publications, picking out his let-
    ters to Cape and Ronald Button for special notice and
    claiming Under the Volcano as "one of the major novels of
    our time."

11 JACKSON, CHARLES.   "We Were Led to Hope for More."   New York
    Times Book Review (12 December), pp. 4, 20.
        A review of Lowry's letters, finding Lowry too self-
    preoccupied, therefore "fortunate in his death."   Reflects
    also on Lowry's concerns about The Lost Weekend and Under
    the Volcano.

12 KILGALLIN, ANTHONY R.   "Eliot, Joyce & Lowry."   Canadian
    Author and Bookman, 41, no. 2 (Winter), 3-4, 6.
        An account of some of Lowry's allusions to and borrow-
    ings from Eliot and Joyce.

13 _____.   "Faust and Under the Volcano."   Canadian Literature,
    no. 26 (Autumn), pp. 43-54.
        Traces through the novel various references to Faust,
    Dr. Faustus, and Faustian patterns, in order to demonstrate
    how the use of the archetype allows Lowry to achieve a sense
    of ironic difference and human continuity between Geoffrey
    and his "exemplars."
        Reprinted: 1971.A5.

1965

14 KIM, SUZANNE. "Les oeuvres de jeunesse de Malcolm Lowry."
    Etudes anglaises, 18, no. 4 (October–December), 383–94.
        Surveys Lowry's writings for The Fortnightly and his
    other juvenilia. Uneven in quality, his hockey reporting
    shows him developing his style and searching for the right
    word. His tartness was typical. In "A Repulsive Tragedy"
    he approaches his adult themes; in a poem called "Number 8
    Fireman" (June 1, 1928), he had found his voice.
        Revised: 1974.B53.

15 _____. "Par l'eau et le feu: deux oeuvres de Malcolm Lowry."
    Etudes anglaises, 18, no. 4 (October–December), 395–97.
        Ultramarine and Hear Us O Lord are dominated by the
    water element, as Under the Volcano is by fire; they give
    some indication of the polar opposites Lowry's work
    attempted to reconcile.

16 KNICKERBOCKER, CONRAD. "Hooking His Own White Whale." Book
    Week (26 December), pp. 5, 11.
        Anecdotes about Lowry in New York in 1947 preface a
    biographical account of Lowry's letters and a tribute to
    Under the Volcano.

17 KOSTELANETZ, RICHARD. "From Nightmare to Seredipity [sic]:
    A Retrospective Look at William Burroughs." Twentieth
    Century Literature, 11, no. 3 (October), 123–30.
        A passing comparison between Naked Lunch and Under the
    Volcano, suggesting that in both works the fusion between
    a "neglected experience" and "a resonant literary tech-
    nique" takes narrative out of reportage.

18 LOWRY, MARGERIE. "Avant-propos à l'édition américain" in
    Malcolm Lowry, Ultramarine. Translated by Clarisse
    Francillon and Jean-Roger Carroy. Paris: Editions Denoel,
    pp. 11–12.
        Translation of 1962.B23.

19 McPHERSON, HUGO. "Canadian Writing: Present Declarative."
    English, 15, no. 90 (Autumn), 212–16.
        Passing mention of Lowry's contribution to the Canadian
    literary imagination.

20 _____. "Fiction 1940–1960" in Literary History of Canada.
    Edited by Carl F. Klinck. Toronto: University of Toronto
    Press, pp. 716–17.
        Lowry's prose poems show a "possessed" imagination,
    but the uncontrolled technique of Under the Volcano ob-
    scures its structure.
        Revised: 1976.B11.

21   MAGEE, A. PETER R. "The Quest for Love." Emeritus (London,
     Ontario), 1 (Spring), 24–29.
          Tracing the motifs of river and volcano, compares Under
     the Volcano with Wolfe's Of Time and the River, finding
     both to be concerned with themes of love.

22   M.[IHELIČEVA], M.[IRA]. "Malcolm Lowry (1909–1957)" in
     Malcolm Lowry, Pod ognjenikom [Under the Volcano].
     Ljubljana: Cankarjeva založba, pp. 437–41.
          A biographical note to accompany the Slovenian transla-
     tion of the novel. Asserts that Chapter I of the novel is
     effectively its conclusion, and that for the Consul, like
     Faust, man's best view of life is from hell.

23   MOORE, HARRY T. "Malcolm Lowry in Retrospect." The Tribune
     (Chicago) (26 December), p. 3.
          A tribute to the dignity, humour, and lack of self-pity
     in Lowry's letters.

24   SIMONSON, HAROLD P. "Malcolm Lowry: 'The Bravest Boat'" in
     Instructor's Manual to accompany Trio: A Book of Stories,
     Plays, and Poems. Second edition. New York: Harper &
     Row, pp. 6–8.
          A brief exposition of the story (followed by discussion
     questions and suggestions for further readings), concen-
     trating on the imagery, the lyricism, and the reminders
     of melancholy.

25   SNOJ, JOŽE. "Med knjigami: Malcolm Lowry: Pod ognjenikom"
     [Among Books: Malcolm Lowry: Under the Volcano]. Delo,
     no. 342 (19 December), p. 7.
          A review of the Slovenian translation, providing sum-
     maries of the plot of the novel and of Lowry's "bohemian
     life, and stressing the book's psychological elements.
     Observes that "action is in the hands of an alcoholic" and
     that "the whole book is the aimless search of a man falling
     from vision to vision." The novel attempts the impossible:
     to succeed both as symbolic artifice and as reality. The
     best way to read it is to see it as "the inner quest of a
     consular official and the pathology of a private person."

26   SPENDER, STEPHEN. "Introduction" to Malcolm Lowry, Under the
     Volcano. Philadelphia and New York: J. B. Lippincott,
     pp. vii–xxvi.
          An account of the differences between the novel and the
     short story of the same name, followed by a summary of the
     novel's themes. Certain features are noted: the Consul
     as "anti-hero," the use of symbolic myth as metaphoric

1965

analogy, the differences between Lowry and Joyce, Lowry's "kinetic" cinematic form, the relation between consciousness and individuality, the force of Lowry's sense of himself. Brief biographical details are followed by further consideration of Under the Volcano, finding its "central paradox" to be that it is a novel about "action negated." The Consul's despair is religious "acedia" and the novel traces the progress of a soul.
Reprinted: 1966.B28; 1967.B36.

27 THORPE, DAY. "Lowry's 'Volcano' Novel Called a Modern Classic." The Washington Star (12 December).
A review, placing Under the Volcano in the context of the letters, praising Lowry's handling of character and allegory.

1966 A BOOKS

1 BLACK, PAUL J. "Malcolm Lowry's Under the Volcano: A Critical Reception Study." Master's thesis, University of Windsor, 68 pp.
Traces the novel's critical support—from the "underground" enthusiasm to general critical acclaim.

2 JEWISON, DONALD BRUCE. "Great Circle Sailing: A Study of the Imagery of Malcolm Lowry." Master's thesis, University of Manitoba, 104 pp.
A consideration of the development of theme and symbol in Lowry's work, focussing on the "principle of circularity."

3 ROBERTSON, ANTHONY. "Aspects of the Quest in the Minor Fiction of Malcolm Lowry." Master's thesis, The University of British Columbia, 95 pp.
Considers the "quest for self" in Lunar Caustic, "Through the Panama," and "The Forest Path to the Spring," arguing that the design of the quest is redemptive although Lowry's literary reconstruction of it was "destructive."

1966 B SHORTER WRITINGS

1 ALBÉRÈS, R. M. See MARILL, RENÉ (1966.B21).

2 BANNERMAN, JAMES. "See Hell on 65 Double Rums a Day." Maclean's, 79, no. 3 (February), 42.
Praise for Under the Volcano, declaring that what happens in it is less important than "how what happens is presented."

3 BIEŃKOWSKI, ZBIGNIEW. "Pod Wulkanem" in his <u>Modelunki</u>
   [Formations]. Warsaw: Czytelnik, pp. 51–60.
   Reprint of 1964.B7.

4 CLARK, CECIL. "Legend grows around Vancouver Author." <u>The</u>
   <u>Daily Colonist</u> (Victoria) (16 January), p. 12.
   An interview with Lowry's Victoria friends, George and
   Greta Stevenson.

5 CLUNY, CLAUDE MICHEL. "Malcolm Lowry." <u>La nouvelle revue</u>
   <u>française</u>, 27 (1 June), 1108–10.
   A review of <u>Ultramarine</u>, praising the style, the odyssey
   theme, the passion of the book.

6 COLOMBO, JOHN ROBERT. "Malcolm Lowry: A Flat-Broke Success."
   <u>The Canadian</u> (26 February), pp. 29–30.
   Comments on the humour in Lowry's letters.

7 CORRIGAN, MATTHEW. Review of <u>Selected Letters</u>. <u>The</u>
   <u>Dalhousie Review</u>, 46 (Spring), 118–19, 121.
   The letters reveal insights into writing and the human
   soul, and it was primarily the "infernal regions of the
   soul that he wanted to write about."

8 COSTA, RICHARD H[AUER]. "Volcano." <u>The New York Times Book</u>
   <u>Review</u> (9 January), p. 42. Reply by Charles Jackson.
   Letter to the editor complaining about Charles Jackson's
   review of <u>Under the Volcano</u> (<u>See</u> 1965.B11) and his concern
   for his own book, <u>The Lost Weekend</u>; with Jackson's rebuttal.

9 _____. "The Volcano Revisited." <u>Utica College News</u>, 3,
   no. 3 (November), 1, 16.
   Reflections on his preparation of his own book <u>Malcolm</u>
   <u>Lowry</u> (1972.A2).

10 DONOGHUE, DENIS. "Ultra Writer." <u>The New York Review of</u>
   <u>Books</u>, 6 (3 March), 16–18.
   Finds that Lowry's "self-embattled" and carelessly
   edited letters are best read as footnotes to the novels;
   <u>Ultramarine</u> is "absurd" and a "mess," the middle letters
   are "repetitive and tedious," throwing light on <u>Under the</u>
   <u>Volcano</u>, which has "a plenitude" of sensations even though
   it is weak on character; Lowry turned realities into symbols because he didn't see realities outside himself.

11 ELEKTOROWICZ, LESZEK. "Pod Wulkanem" in his <u>Zwierciadło w</u>
   <u>okruchach</u> [A mirror in fragments]. Warsaw: Panstwowy
   Instytut Wydåwniczy, pp. 107–15.
   Reprint of 1964.B19.

1966

12 GREENE, GEORGE. Review of <u>Selected Letters</u>. <u>Commonweal</u>, 84,
    no. 4 (15 April), 124-27.
        The letters reveal a Lowry "more persuasive as a witness
    to a psychological problem than as a technician." A sum-
    mary of his life follows.

13 HRISTIĆ, JOVAN. "Predgovor" to Malcolm Lowry, <u>Ispod Vulkana</u>
    [Preface to <u>Under the Volcano</u>]. Belgrade: Nolit, pp. 9-14.
        Finds the novel to be increasingly important because of
    the way it combines several modern fictional strains.
    Lowry is one of the rare writers who is as American as he
    is English. Biographical and plot summaries are followed
    by quotations from the French critics Nadeau and Myrer.
    Stresses the humanity of <u>Under the Volcano</u>, which makes
    its vision of hell atypical of modern literature.

14 KANŌ, HIDEO. "Kaisetsu" [Commentary] in his translation of
    Malcolm Lowry, <u>Kakkazan no shita</u> [<u>Under the Volcano</u>].
    Tokyo: Hakusuisha, pp. 389-95.
        A brief biographical account followed by a short critique
    of the novel, contending that its value can be measured by
    appreciating how tightly the influences of Joyce (the tech-
    nique of handling time) and Aiken (the creation of setting)
    are woven into it. The theme—man's powerlessness against
    death—is both comic and tragic, expressing some hope of
    reconciliation. Mexico is represented as a boat in the sea
    of the world in which two national ideologies (totalitar-
    ianism and freedom) are competing with each other.

15 KILGALLIN, TONY. "Malcolm." <u>Canadian Author and Bookman</u>, 41,
    no. 4 (Summer), 11.
        A brief review of Lowry's letters, stressing their use-
    fulness as a guide to Lowry's character.

16 KLINCK, CARL F. and R. E. WATTERS. "Malcolm Lowry" in their
    <u>Canadian Anthology</u>. Second edition. Toronto: Gage,
    pp. 359-60.
        Revised and expanded version of 1955.B2.

17 KNICKERBOCKER, CONRAD. "Swinging the Paradise Street Blues:
    Malcolm Lowry in England." <u>Paris Review</u>, 38 (Summer),
    pp. 13-38.
        An attempt to trace Lowry's early life, and to interview
    people who knew him, including John Davenport and Martin
    Case. Some of the stories about Lowry are unsubstantiated.
    Lowry is called a syphilophobe and a "possessed" person-
    ality; he is declared fearful of authority and (because he
    was trustful) the "perfect butt" for practical jokes.

Destiny appeared always to strike him, yet he had many
friends. The Taskersons of <u>Under the Volcano</u> are identified
with the Hepburn family. On p. 21 is a photograph of the
title page of Lowry's 1927 musical composition, <u>Three Little
Dog-Gone Mice</u>. The whole is prefaced by an editor's note
on Knickerbocker's 2 April 1966 suicide.
Reprinted: 1967.B23.

18 LEVINE, NORMAN. "A Lonely Hunter." <u>The Atlantic Advocate</u>,
56, no. 7 (March), 72.
A review of Lowry's letters, summarizing his life and
paying tribute to Lowry's energy, articulateness, intelligence, and humour.

19 LYTLE, ANDREW. <u>The Hero with the Private Parts: Essays</u>.
Baton Rouge: Louisiana State University Press, pp. 54–59.
An account of the Consul being in exile and solitary
because of the murder he committed. The offer of love
brings death because the only communion can be with damna-
tion. His flight from self is well created, and his own
death parodies the earlier murder. But the literary per-
formance is damaged because the first person point of view
is controlled by a "cultural disorder" which represented
"the Ego."

20 MACHLEIDT, DOROTHEA. "Bewährungfrist vor dem Tode."
<u>Zeitwende die neue Furche</u>, 37, no. 9 (September), 638–39.
Summary review of <u>Hear Us O Lord</u>.

21 MARILL, RENÉ [pseud., R. M. ALBÉRÈS]. "Le lyrisme et le
mythe: de Joyce à Malcolm Lowry" in his <u>Métamorphoses du
Roman</u>. Paris: Editions Albin Michel, pp. 119–31.
Sees Lowry in connection with Joyce and Butor. In <u>Under
the Volcano</u> everything is both real and symbolic, the whole
rendered novelistically, without Joyce's stylistic games,
thus answering the kind of paradox Joyce's work proposed.

22 MARKSON, DAVID. "The Dollarton Squatter: Reminiscences of
Lowry." <u>The Sun</u> (Vancouver) (15 February), p. 5.
Excerpts from 1966.B23.

23 _____. "Malcolm Lowry: A Reminiscence." <u>Nation</u>, 202,
no. 16 (7 February), 164–67.
An account of meeting Lowry, largely concerned with
Lowry's visit in New York on the way to Europe.
Reprinted: 1966.B22, B24; 1975.A3.

1966

24 _____. "The Ones that Burn: A Memoir of Malcolm Lowry."
   Books and Bookmen, 11 (November), 22-23, 102.
   Reprint of 1966.B23.

25 MONSARRAT, NICHOLAS. Life Is a Four-Letter Word. Vol. I:
   Breaking In. London: Cassell, pp. 311-12, 438.
   Passing reference to Lowry at Cambridge.

26 RAPIN, RENÉ. "Sur l'art de Malcolm Lowry dans Under the Volcano" in Mélanges Offert à Monsieur Georges Bonnard à
   l'occasion de son quatre-vingtième anniversaire. Geneva:
   Librairie Droz, pp. 99-104.
   An examination of two stylistic devices--quotations from
   Spanish and departures from standard English vocabularly
   and syntax--to demonstrate that they do not merely add
   local colour but also contribute to the book's moral
   atmosphere.

27 SCHIEDER, RUPERT. "What Is Really Under the Volcano?" The
   Telegram (Toronto) (5 March), p. 25.
   A brief tribute to the importance of Lowry's letters.

28 SPENDER, STEPHEN. "Introduction" to Malcolm Lowry, Under the
   Volcano. New York: Signet, New American Library; Toronto:
   New American Library of Canada, pp. vii-xxvi.
   Reprint of 1965.B26. [This edition omits the final page
   of the novel.]

29 STANSKY, PETER and WILLIAM ABRAHAMS. Journey to the Frontier:
   Julian Bell and John Cornford, their lives and the 1930s.
   London: Constable, pp. 50-52.
   Comments on the Cambridge rivalry between two literary
   magazines, Experiment and The Venture, to which Lowry and
   Bell, among others, contributed.

30 THOMAS, HILDA. "Lowry's Letters." Canadian Literature,
   no. 29 (Summer), pp. 56-58.
   A brief commentary on ways in which the experiences in
   Lowry's life, as revealed in the letters, provided him with
   material for his fiction. Item 1971.B32, using the same
   title, is a different essay.

31 VANDENBERGH, JOHN. "Inleiding" to Malcolm Lowry, Onder de
   Vulkaan. Amsterdam: Uitgeverij de Bezige Bij, pp. 7-17.
   A romantic biographical account is followed by a summary
   of the four levels--autobiographical, alcoholic, political,
   and inter-personal--of Under the Volcano. Influenced by
   Joyce (word-play), Lawrence (symbolism and relation to the

natural world), and Faulkner (atmosphere and sense of the past), Lowry in turn influenced the Dutch author Bert Schierbeek.

32 WAIN, JOHN. "Lowry's Subjective Equipment." New Republic, 154 (15 January), 23-24.
  A review of Selected Letters which concentrates on Lowry's letter to Cape, praising the kind of illumination it brings to his fiction, which in turn balances introspective impulses with the universalizing impersonality of myth.

1967 A BOOKS

1 BREIT, HARVEY and MARGERIE BONNER LOWRY, ed. Selected Letters of Malcolm Lowry. London: Jonathan Cape, xix + 459 pp.
  Reprint of 1965.A1.

2 BUTSON, BARRY. "Structural Organization in Under the Volcano." Master's thesis, University of Western Ontario, 99 pp.
  Suggests that the structural unity of the novel benefits from the traditions of the classical unities and the American transcendentalists. The refined humour and tonal rhythms strengthen the novel's suspense.

3 CASARI, LAURA ELIZABETH RHODES. "Malcolm Lowry's Drunken Divine Comedy in Under the Volcano and Shorter Fiction." Ph.D. dissertation, University of Nebraska, 343 pp.
  Attempts to trace "The Voyage that Never Ends," from Ultramarine and Under the Volcano to Lunar Caustic and "The Forest Path to the Spring," showing how the pilgrimage relates to Dante.

4 EPSTEIN, PERLE SHERRY. "Cabbalistic Elements in Malcolm Lowry's Under the Volcano." Ph.D. dissertation, Columbia University, 381 pp.
  A brief biographical sketch, followed by a history of Jewish cabbala (with glossaries) and an examination of Lowry's hermetic symbolism. An appendix (pp. 369-73) prints some selected, previously unpublished notes from Lowry's journal.
  Revised and published: 1969.A5.

5 LLOYD, RODNEY OSTEN. "Mexico and Under the Volcano." Master's thesis, University of Western Ontario, 130 pp.
  Examines Lowry's symbolic representation of Mexican landscape and history, and the "psychological polarity

1967

of the Mexican character," both for their "unique attitude
to life and death" and as "properties of the human soul."

6   MARY ROSALINDA, SISTER. See NYLAND, AGNES CECILIA (1967.B8).

7   MAUREY, PIERRE. "Malcolm Lowry, The Man and His Work: The
     Road to Damascus." Diplôme d'études supérieures thesis,
     Université de Caen, 131 pp.
          A biographical chapter is followed by two sections: an
     explanation of themes of social and individual degradation
     and salvation throughout Lowry's book-length published
     prose, and a consideration of Lowry's search for an
     adequate mode of expression (dualism, archetypes, tone,
     breaks from realism). An appendix contains synopses of
     Lowry's works.

8   NYLAND, AGNES CECILIA [SISTER MARY ROSALINDA]. "The Luminous
     Wheel: A Study of Malcolm Lowry." Ph.D. dissertation,
     University of Ottawa, 222 pp.
          Considers, from his adolescent to his later writings,
     Lowry's developing ability to fuse "matter, manner, and
     personality." The study of style has a biographical con-
     cern behind it.
          Chapter II reprinted: 1975.B25.

9   WILD, SISTER BERNADETTE. "Malcolm Lowry: A Study of the Sea
     Metaphor in Ultramarine and Under the Volcano." Master's
     thesis, University of Windsor, 76 pp.
          Suggests that the complexity of the metaphor in the
     later novel shows Lowry's developing artistic skill.

1967 B SHORTER WRITINGS

1   AIKEN, CONRAD. "Malcolm Lowry." The Times Literary Supple-
     ment (16 February), p. 127.
          A letter to the editor responding to item 1967.B5,
     correcting statements made concerning Lowry's relationship
     with Aiken. Comments on the composition of Ultramarine
     and its derivation from Blue Voyage, on Lowry's ability
     to record verbatim scenes from his own life, and on other
     characteristic Lowry phrases which came directly from
     Aiken. Asserts that Lowry was constantly jesting in his
     works.

2   ALLEN, TREVOR. "Malcolm Lowry's Letters." Contemporary
     Review, 210 (February), 108-09.

A review of the letters, urging that they be read as a story, which incidentally finds the symbolism of <u>Under the Volcano</u> "abstruse."

3   ANON. "Novelist Who Recorded His Own Self-Made Myth." <u>The Times</u> (London) (19 January), p. 14.
A review of Lowry's letters, seeing them as a "footnote" to his art, which in turn demands the fusion of a "prophet's vision" and "creative invention."

4   ANON. "Dead B.C. Writer Declared Genius." <u>The Vancouver Sun</u> (23 January), p. 12.
A summary of recent London reviews of Lowry's works.

5   ANON. "Malcolm Lowry." <u>The Times Literary Supplement</u> (26 January), pp. 57–59.
A review of <u>Under the Volcano</u> and <u>Selected Letters</u>, recounting his writing in the context of his life. <u>Under the Volcano</u> is praised for its attention to minutiae, its realistic perceptions which are then put to symbolic purpose; it is "as rich and humorous as <u>Ulysses</u> and far more poetic." The comic element in the novel is stressed, and Spender's introduction is contrasted with Lowry's explanatory letter to Jonathan Cape.

6   BOATWRIGHT, JAMES. "Réflexions sur Styron, ses critiques et ses sources." Translated by Paul Rozenberg. <u>Revue des Lettres Modernes</u>, nos. 157–161, pp. 123–35.
Explores thematic and rhetorical parallels between William Styron's work and <u>Under the Volcano</u>, suggesting the presence of an affinity between the two writers and not just the influence of one on the other.

7   BREIT, HARVEY. "Introduction" to <u>Selected Letters of Malcolm Lowry</u>. London: Jonathan Cape, pp. xi–xv.
Reprint of 1965.B3.

8   BREZA, HENRYK. "Świadomość zabójcza" in his <u>Doświadczenia z lektur prozy obcej</u> [Experiences from the reading of foreign prose]. Warsaw: Państwowy Instytut Wydáwniczy, pp. 190–92.
Reprint of 1964.B10.

9   BROOKE-ROSE, CHRISTINE. "Mescalusions." <u>London Magazine</u>, 7, no. 1 (April), 100–05.
Asserts that the letters clearly show that Lowry was not a genius, but an innocent man, and that they also show him to be ignorant of contemporary literature, and to be an old-fashioned Germanic Romantic. <u>Under the Volcano</u>, moreover,

1967

though brilliant about drunkenness, is tedious, structurally
wayward, and weak in character drawing. A modern novelist
"can no longer split a man into humours...or aspects."
Lowry's letters to Barzun and Cape are "hysterical"; the
Cabbalistic and other meanings in the novel are "preten-
tious"; and the humour, "delicious" in his letters, is out
of place in the novel.

10   BRUMM, URSULA. "Symbolism and the Novel" in The Theory of the
Novel. Edited by Philip Stevick. New York: The Free
Press; London: Collier-Macmillan, pp. 366-68.
     Reprint of 1958.B1.

11   BURGESS, ANTHONY. See WILSON, JOHN ANTHONY BURGESS
(1967.B43-B44).

12   CALDER-MARSHALL, ARTHUR, comp. "A Portrait of Malcolm Lowry."
The Listener, 78 (12 October), 461-63.
     An edited version of a BBC Third Programme broadcast on
16 September 1967, produced by Robert Pocock. A biography
based on comments by various people who knew him (Stern,
Parsons, John Sommerfield, and others), and by Douglas Day,
the whole composed and narrated by Calder-Marshall.
     Translated: 1974.B20.

13   COSTA, RICHARD HAUER. "The Lowry/Aiken Symbiosis." The
Nation, 204 (26 June), 823-25.
     Catalogues a series of puns involving William Blackstone.
Asserts that Firmin is largely built on the conflict be-
tween Aiken and Lowry.

14   _____. "Ulysses, Lowry's Volcano, and The Voyage Between: A
Study of an Unacknowledged Literary Kinship." University
of Toronto Quarterly, 36, no. 4 (July), 335-52.
     Lowry always seemed to be exorcising Joyce, sharing his
impatience with usual means of narrative expression. "Hotel Room in Chartres" shows the method being learned, but
as he approaches Aiken's method in Blue Voyage, he
approaches Joyce. "La mordida" is identified with
"agenbite = the remorse of conscience," as Joyce uses
the word in Ulysses. Spender's series of contrasts between Joyce and Lowry does not trace the parallels as they
appear transfused through Aiken.
     Adapted in: 1972.A2.

15   EDMONDS, DALE. "The Short Fiction of Malcolm Lowry." Tulane
Studies in English, 15, pp. 59-80.

Surveys Lowry's published adult stories, as of 1967.
Early works were ephemeral, mawkish, though sometimes show-
ing a sense of comedy. "The Element Follows You Around,
Sir!" is full of "over-wrought, digressive" prose. Shows
parallels between Plantagenet, Cosnahan, and Hugh Firmin,
but finds Lunar Caustic to be without the style of "The
Bravest Boat" and to have an unsatisfactory conclusion.
Surveys the mixed criticism of Hear Us O Lord from Heaven
Thy Dwelling Place, and finds only "Through the Panama" and
"The Forest Path to the Spring" to be "minor triumphs."
There is insufficient vitality in the whole; the motifs are
boring; the women are unconvincingly drawn; the three Wil-
dernesses, being inconsistent, are indefensible; the style
is excessively mannered; yet there are rich ironies. Lowry
tells his basically simple pattern (paradise, expulsion,
the illusion of safety) in a tone of high seriousness.

16   ENRIGHT, D. J. "Malcolm Lowry." New Statesman, 73
     (27 January), 117–18.
         Impressed by Lowry's letter to Cape, but appreciative
     also of the publisher's reader's report. Asserts that
     Lowry's symbols work because of their rootedness in reality,
     but complains that too much is left unexplained (e.g. what
     motivates the Consul and whether or not Yvonne dies).
         Reprinted: 1972.B11.

17   FOUCHET, MAX-POL. "Le feu central" in Les appels. Paris:
     Mercure de France, pp. 95–105.
         After a summary of the plot and an account of the impor-
     tance of Chapter I of Under the Volcano as the beginning of
     a mythological tragedy, this chapter explains the relation
     between the sexual laws of the Zohar and the novel's themes
     of love and chaos. The concern for time places Lowry be-
     side Eliot and Joyce; the Faustian recurrence theme has
     ultimately a liberating function. Incorporates material
     published in 1960.B6.

18   GLASS, NORMAN. "On a Tough Idyll." Books and Bookmen, 12
     (May), 46.
         A letter to Lowry, by way of reviewing Lowry's letters
     appreciatively, finding the author lucid, vigorous, and
     charitable.

19   GREENE, T. E. "Malcolm Lowry." The Times Literary Supplement
     (23 March), p. 259.
         A letter to the editor from a medical friend of Lowry's
     doctor (C. McNeill) concerning Lowry's varicose veins and
     simian stance.

1967

20   HANNAH, PIERCE. "Non-Novels." The Times (London)
     (26 January), p. 14.
          A reflection on the fact that Lowry's works will not
     reach mass markets.

21   HARRIS, WILSON. "Tradition and the West Indian Novel" in
     Tradition The Writer and Society: Critical Essays. London
     and Port of Spain: New Beacon, p. 35.
          Mention of Under the Volcano in a commentary on experi-
     mental renderings of time. The essay was first delivered
     as a London West Indian Students' Union lecture, 15 May 1964,
     and first published as a Students' Union pamphlet.
     [The pamphlet was not located.]

22   KNICKERBOCKER, CONRAD. "Lowry à vingt ans." Translated from
     English by Serge Fauchereau. Les lettres nouvelles
     (March-April), 68-94.
          A biographical account of Lowry's early years, particu-
     larly 1927-1933, based in part upon interviews with Martin
     Case, John Davenport, Arthur Calder-Marshall, Ralph Case,
     James Hepburn, and others.

23   _____. "Swinging the Paradise Street Blues: Malcolm Lowry in
     England" in Best Magazine Articles: 1967. Edited by
     Gerald Walker. New York: Crown Publishers, Inc.,
     pp. 128-45.
          Reprint of 1966.B17.

24   KUNDA, BOGUSŁAW SŁAWOMIR. "Rozmowy z Konsulem" [Conversations
     with the Consul]. Agora, no. 18, pp. 58-60.
          Argues that the Consul's predicament derives from the
     paradoxes he wills himself to point out. A "maximalist"
     (ruled by a principle of "all or nothing"), he can neither
     accept the world (with its evils) nor reject it (because
     of its many virtues).

25   LYKIARD, ALEXIS. "Malcolm Lowry." The Times Literary Supple-
     ment (2 February), p. 87.
          A letter to the editor urging more English publications
     of his works now that "Lowry's status as a major writer
     rests assured."

26   McCONNELL, FRANK D. "William Burroughs and the Literature of
     Addiction." Massachusetts Review, 8 (Autumn), 665-80.
          Passing mention of Lowry as part of a tradition
     (Coleridge, de Quincey) in which Burroughs' work should be
     read.

27   MONTAGUE, JOHN. "Psychological Melodrama." <u>Manchester Guardian Weekly</u>, 96, no. 7 (16 February), 10.
    A general review of Lowry's published work, comparing <u>Under the Volcano</u> tangentially with <u>Tender Is the Night</u> and finding that it lacks a social context. Suggests that the Cabbalistic elements may have been intended comically.

28   PARSONS, IAN. "Malcolm Lowry." <u>The Times Literary Supplement</u> (13 April), p. 317.
    A letter to the editor, recalling Parsons' experience (as a partner in Chatto & Windus) when he lost the manuscript of <u>Ultramarine</u> in 1932; the letter corrects Lowry's own letter of 22 June 1946 to Albert Erskine. Quotes from Oliver Warner's report on the novel for Chatto and Windus, and explains Lowry's move from Chatto to Cape.

29   PAZ, OCTAVIO. "Paisaje y novela en México" in his <u>Corriente alterna</u>. Mexico City: Siglo veintiuno editores, pp. 16-18.
    Contrasts <u>Under the Volcano</u> with Lawrence's <u>The Plumed Serpent</u> and Juan Rulfo's <u>Pedro Páramo</u>, finding Lowry's theme to be the expulsion from Paradise, and declaring that the rendering of landscape makes it more than setting or symbol: makes it a voice and a character, pointing beyond itself, like a metaphysic.
    Translated: 1973.B25.

30   PEMBERTON, NICHOLAS. "Malcolm Lowry." <u>The Times Literary Supplement</u> (9 February), p. 107.
    A letter pointing out that <u>Under the Volcano</u>, nearly ten years earlier, was required reading at the University of Brussels.

31   PRYCE-JONES, DAVID. "Genius Self-destroyed." <u>The Financial Times</u> (19 January), p. 26.
    Praises Lowry's delight in language and capacity for lyricism, as revealed in the letters and <u>Under the Volcano</u>.

32   RABINOWICZ, WŁODZIMIERZ. "Pod wulkanem" [Under the Volcano]. Współczesność (Warsaw), no. 9, p. 10.
    The novel acquires its visionary quality from the symbolic topography it employs. Though in a hierarchically ordered cosmos, the sacred volcano "higher" than the infernal abyss, the volcano is also destructive and the ravine the romantic chasm of Coleridge's Kubla Khan. The Consul chooses pessimistically though he could do otherwise.

33   REDGRAVE, MICHAEL. "High Wire to the Crater." <u>The Sunday Times</u> (29 January), p. 48.

1967

> A memoir of Lowry at Cambridge, finding that he disliked academicism but was no rebel. Asserts the influence of Henry James on Lowry's work.

34   RONSON, ROBERT. "Malcolm Lowry." The Times Literary Supplement (2 March), p. 176.
A letter indicating Lowry's exact birthplace (Wallasey).

35   SHUTTLEWORTH, MARTIN. "New Novels." Punch, 252 (1 February), 174.
A descriptive review of the reissue of Under the Volcano, finding it "one of the very great books of the century."

36   SPENDER, STEPHEN. "Introduction" to Malcolm Lowry, Under the Volcano. London: Jonathan Cape, pp. vii–xxvi.
Reprint of 1965.B26.

37   _____. "Malcolm Lowry." The Times Literary Supplement (2 February), p. 254.
A letter to the editor, correcting a point in item 1967.B5 concerning Spender's introduction to Under the Volcano.

38   STERN, JAMES. "Malcolm Lowry: A First Impression." Encounter, 29 (September), 58–68.
Memoir about first meeting Lowry--and the humour of that meeting--in Paris in 1933. Recounts Lowry's own stories of sailing, meeting Grieg and Aiken, and being fascinated with voodoo.
Reprinted: 1975.A3. Translated: 1968.B46.

39   STORY, NORAH. The Oxford Companion to Canadian History and Literature. Toronto, London and New York: Oxford University Press, p. 471.
A brief account of Lowry's life and work. The biographical details are inexact and the novels are read as autobiography.

40   SYLVESTRE, GUY, BRANDON CONRON and CARL F. KLINCK. Canadian Writers: écrivains canadiens. Revised edition. Toronto: Ryerson, pp. 96–97.
A brief biocritical summary, inexact in some biographical details, praising the organization and rich allusiveness of Under the Volcano.

41   TOYNBEE, PHILIP. "On the Edge of the Volcano." The Observer (22 January), p. 26.

Comments on Lowry's romanticism, on the lovableness of his character, and on the self-absorption which limits the excellence of his fiction.

42   TREVOR, WILLIAM. "Besides the Volcano." The Listener, 77 (9 February), 202.
      A sympathetic response to the "Lowry of the letters."

43   WILSON, JOHN ANTHONY BURGESS [pseud., ANTHONY BURGESS]. "Europe's Day of the Dead." Spectator, 218 (20 January), 74.
      Sees Lowry's letter to Cape as eloquent and frank, and condemns the first English reviewers for wanting provincialism instead of profundity in a novel. Lowry's superiority to Aiken lies in the success of his Promethean character, the Consul, an "exact symbol of Europe" who contains within himself all the tragic heroes and is a fresh tragic creation in his own right.

44   _____. The Novel Now: A Student's Guide to Contemporary Fiction. London: Faber & Faber, pp. 69–72.
      A brief account of the Faustian motifs of Under the Volcano, the experimentalism of Hear Us O Lord, and the Joycean origins of Lowry's style.

1968 A BOOKS

1   BREIT, HARVEY and MARGERIE BONNER LOWRY, eds. Choix de Lettres. Translated by Suzanne Kim. Paris: Denoël, 389 pp.
      Abridged translation of 1965.A1.

2   COSTA, RICHARD HAUER. "Quest for Eridanus: Malcolm Lowry's Evolving Art in Under the Volcano." Ph.D. dissertation, Purdue University, 193 pp.
      Examines the various short story and manuscript versions of Under the Volcano, and traces its development. Much of the material was published in 1972.A2.

3   DOYEN, VICTOR. "Under the Volcano by Malcolm Lowry: An Ergocentric Approach." Licentiate dissertation. Katholicke Universiteit Leuven, 226 pp.
      An extended study of the first chapter, followed by commentaries on the later chapters, concerned with Lowry's style, his use of spatial forms: signs, images, alienating image sequences, gibberish, and other devices.

1968

4   MILICI, DIRK.   "Malcolm Lowry's Mysticism in <u>Under the Volcano</u>
     and 'The Forest Path to the Spring.'"   Master's thesis,
     University of Toronto, 113 pp.
         Asserts that Lowry showed himself to be not a mystic but
     a writer concerned with the conflict between vision and
     routine.   Traces associative patterns in Lowry's work, and
     the integration of religious and personal themes.   Finds
     sources in Faustian and other myths, Cabbala, Stansfeld-
     Jones, Hesse, and Indian holy books.

5   MONBET, JOSINE.   "Malcolm Lowry's <u>Under the Volcano</u>:   or, An
     Introduction to a Modern Descent into Hell."   Diplome
     d'études supérieures thesis, Université de Bordeaux, 147 pp.
         An elucidation of historical and political, ethical and
     psychological, symbolic, and mythical "levels" of Lowry's
     novel.

6   TIESSEN, PAUL G.   "<u>Under the Volcano</u>:   Lowry and the Cinema."
     Master's thesis, University of Alberta, 97 pp.
         Suggests that Lowry's wheel and barranca imagery act as
     a controlling metaphor affecting the novel's theme and
     modes of perception, and that these--like montage--derive
     from the cinema.

7   [WOOLMER, J. HOWARD].   <u>A Malcolm Lowry Catalogue</u>.   New York:
     J. Howard Woolmer, 57 pp.
         Contains two poems by Lowry, with a note on them by
     Earle Birney, essays by Perle Epstein and Richard Hauer
     Costa (<u>See</u> 1968.B7, B16, and B21), and an extensive gen-
     erally reliable catalogue of works on and by Lowry.   Some
     of these works were not available from Woolmer at the time;
     others are priced.   The catalogue is divided into two sec-
     tions, Books and Periodicals.   Not as complete as the
     Birney bibliography on periodical and newspaper reviews.

<u>1968 B SHORTER WRITINGS</u>

1   AIKEN, CONRAD.   "The Art of Poetry IX: Conrad Aiken: an
     interview."   <u>Paris Review</u>, no. 42 (Winter-Spring), 97-124.
         In the course of an interview (pp. 108-11), recalls
     meeting Lowry and reflects on the composition of
     <u>Ultramarine</u>.

2   ANON.   "The Outer Ring of Hell."   <u>The Times Literary Supple-
     ment</u> (21 March), p. 285.
         A review of <u>Lunar Caustic</u>, finding it less interesting
     as a novella than as an example of how Lowry worked, and
     summarizing Lowry's connections with New York.

3   ANON. "Death of the Optimist." <u>Time</u> (Canada edition), 91, no. 26 (28 June), BC8, BC10, BC12.
        A review of <u>Dark as the Grave</u>, questioning whether Wilderness goes to Mexico to "reconnect with old sources of life or to seek out a familiar place to die." The novel "gives the struggle between good and evil the dignity of an even match."

4   ANON. "Piquefort's Column." <u>The Canadian Forum</u>, 48 (July), 88.
        Review of <u>Lunar Caustic</u>, finding it a "haunting little masterpiece" despite being a mélange; the book also links North American and European literatures, Mr. Battle being "half Jim and half Pip."

5   ANON. Review of <u>Dark as the Grave Wherein My Friend Is Laid</u>. <u>Virginia Quarterly Review</u>, 44 (Autumn), cxliv.
        A brief note finding the novel "profoundly engrossing."

6   BESTERMAN, THEODORE. "The Outer Ring of Hell." <u>The Times Literary Supplement</u> (28 March), p. 325.
        A reaction to item 1968.B2, pointing out that he coined the word "autobibliographer."

7   BIRNEY, EARLE. "A Note on the Poems" in <u>A Malcolm Lowry Catalogue</u>. New York: J. Howard Woolmer, p. 11.
        Comments on the significance of the title of "Conversations with Goethe" and "Reflection to Windward."

8   CHALKER, JOHN. "Under the Volcano: Geoffrey's Unposted Letter." <u>The London Review</u> (Autumn), pp. 26–33.
        Suggests that Geoffrey's letter (Chapter I) introduces major images (dead souls, abyss) and themes (self-entrapment, fear), and is particularly important because at that point Geoffrey has readers' sympathy; what follows them is tragic loss.

9   CHAPELAN, MAURICE. "Prétentieux mais emouvant." <u>Le figaro littéraire</u>, no. 1163 (19–25 August), p. 21.
        A review of Lowry's letters, noting that his age at death was a multiple of twelve.

10   CLEMENTS, ROBERT J. "European Literary Scene." <u>Saturday Review</u>, 51 (4 May), 23–24.
        A brief account of lack of "breadth" in <u>Lunar Caustic</u>.

11   COLEMAN, JOHN. "Mucking About with H.G." <u>The Observer</u> (25 February), p. 29.

1968

A brief descriptive review of Lunar Caustic, praising
its compassionate portraits and "fine intelligence."

12 COOK, BRUCE. "Malcolm Lowry Tells the Story of a Masterpiece."
National Observer, 7 (9 September), B1.
An approving review of Dark as the Grave and Lunar Caus-
tic, which praises Under the Volcano's formal control.

13 CORRIGAN, MATTHEW. "Masks and the Man: The Writer as Actor."
Shenandoah, 19, no. 4 (Summer), 89–93.
A review of Dark as the Grave, summarizing the work and
pointing to its merits as an exploration of the "angle of...
seeing" and the coincidences that identify the illusory and
the real.

14 _____. Review of Dark as the Grave Wherein My Friend is Laid.
Dalhousie Review, 48, no. 3 (Autumn), 419–21.
Finds the novel to be psycho-critical, an "advance"
upon Under the Volcano, and a demonstration of Lowry's
writing out an "architectonics of hope."

15 COSTA, RICHARD HAUER. "Mythologized Megalomania." The Nation,
207, no. 6 (2 September), 188–89.
A review of Dark as the Grave, praising it as a fine
revelation of Lowry's theory of art, inseparable from his
view of experience and "ultimately messianic."

16 _____. "Lowry's Overture as Elegy" in A Malcolm Lowry Catalogue. New York: J. Howard Woolmer, pp. 26–44.
Referring to Lowry's letter to Cape, tries to defend the
first chapter of Under the Volcano. The "weight of the
past"--a central theme of the book--is clearly introduced
in the chapter, and an elegiac tone established. The article traces the plot, surveys the textual changes affecting
the chapter in the several drafts of the novel, and further
comments on Lowry's method. Comparison is made with
Remembrance of Things Past. Lowry's book is contemporary,
its "texture reflecting maelstrom."
Adapted in 1972.A2.

17 DAY, DOUGLAS. "Preface" to Malcolm Lowry, Dark as the Grave
Wherein My Friend Is Laid. Edited by Douglas Day and
Margerie Lowry. New York: New American Library,
pp. ix–xxiii.
Observes that Lowry was not really a novelist but--a
unique genius--something more than a diarist and poet
manqué. Suggests some of the paradoxes and compulsions
in his character and comments on the internal action of

Lowry's books. Then provides biographical background to
<u>Dark as the Grave</u> and notes on the process of editing the
three texts of the novel on which Lowry had been working
consecutively. The editors spliced texts, removed repeti-
tions and unintegrated passages, changed "Malcolm" to
"Sigbjørn" in a number of places and developed a number of
the pseudonyms in this roman-à-clef. An account of the
themes of ascent and descent follows together with notes on
the novel's weaknesses of dialogue, uncontrolled style, and
yet its residual power.
Reprinted: 1968.B18; 1969.B12; 1972.B10. Translated:
1968.B19; 1971.B9.

18 _____. "Preface" to Malcolm Lowry, <u>Dark as the Grave Wherein</u>
<u>My Friend Is Laid</u>. Edited by Douglas Day and Margerie
Lowry. London: Jonathan Cape, pp. v–xviii.
Reprint of 1968.B17.

19 _____. "Prefacio" to Malcolm Lowry, "Oscuro como la tumba
donde mi amigo yace." Translated by Alicia Jurado. <u>Revista</u>
<u>Nacional de Cultura</u> (Caracas), no. 186 (October, November,
December), pp. 32–41.
Translation of 1968.B17. Reprinted: 1969.B13.

20 EDMONDS, DALE. "<u>Under the Volcano</u>: A Reading of the 'Immediate Level.'" <u>Tulane Studies in English</u>, 16, pp. 63–105.
The finest novel written since World War II, <u>Under the</u>
<u>Volcano</u> communicates most effectively at the level of per-
son, place, and event. There follows an account of the
characters' interrelationships (involving some conjecture
about motivations), the roles in relation to Geoffrey,
Geoffrey's involvement with anti-fascist elements (including an historical account of Mexican bank/land/credit
practice), the drunkard's distortion of reality, and the
failure of love.

21 EPSTEIN, PERLE. "Malcolm Lowry: In Search of Equilibrium"
in <u>A Malcolm Lowry Catalogue</u>. New York: J. Howard
Woolmer, pp. 15–25.
Observes that, the arcane symbolism notwithstanding,
Lowry's essential personal vision was of simple religious
people searching for peace and stumbling inadvertently into
evil. His revolving literary pattern is sixfold: recognition of nameless sin, attempted expurgation through drink,
guilt, mystical illumination, creative cleansing work,
catharsis through love. Wilderness, Plantaganet, and the
Consul are all shown to illustrate this pattern. After
some mention of the stories, the author focuses on <u>Under</u>

1968

the Volcano. The last manuscripts show Lowry still working
to resolve his old preoccupations.

22   FREMONT-SMITH, ELIOT. "Recapitulation of a Masterpiece."
      The New York Times, 117 (8 July), 37.
          A summary of Lowry's publications and Day's comments in
      his introduction to Dark as the Grave.

23   GILLANDERS, CAROL. "Cain Shall Not Slay Abel Today" in Guide-
      book for Theme & Image Book 2. Toronto: Copp Clark,
      pp. 484-95.
          Provides the Biblical and Melvillean background to
      Lowry's poem, traces the sea image, and suggests some ways
      of reading it. Thirteen "questions" are appended.

24   HICKS, GRANVILLE. "Fragments from Beyond." Saturday Review,
      51, no. 27 (6 July), 19-20.
          A biographical reading of Dark as the Grave, questioning
      Lowry's motivation to return to Mexico.

25   JANEWAY, ELIZABETH. "Mega-Prone to Catastrophe." The New
      York Times Book Review, 73 (4 August), 4-5.
          A review, stressing the biographical background to Dark
      as the Grave and the fascination of watching the process of
      a writer structuring chaos into "meaningful pattern."

26   JUNKOLA, AAPO. "Sammunut tulivuori" [Extinct volcano].
      Aamulehti (22 December), p. 13.
          A mixed review of Under the Volcano, finding it an able
      rendering of an alcoholic's perceptions, yet full of banal-
      ities. Finds that it reads like Lowry's autobiography, and
      has probably been admired for the wrong reasons. Depressing
      and humourless, it is authentic and therefore maybe impres-
      sive. Finds it unbelievable that someone could write about
      hell from within hell.

27   KAYE, HOWARD. "Autobiography and Novel." New Republic, 159
      (12 October), 38-41.
          A review of Dark as the Grave, stressing its autobio-
      graphical elements and observing that, for Wilderness,
      "Life cannot be perceived independently of art."

28   KIELY, ROBERT. "Mexican Pilgrimage." The Christian Science
      Monitor (Eastern edition) (1 August), p. 5.
          A summary review of Under the Volcano, locating themes
      of alcoholism, neurosis, nostalgia, and the tasks of the
      artist ("to recognize his imperfection and bear it toward
      perfection").

29   KILGALLIN, TONY. "'Why has God given this to us?' But what
     God gave, the city took. The story of Malcolm Lowry in
     Vancouver." Vancouver Life, 3, no. 4 (January), 29–31, 48.
        A portrait of Lowry, drawing on his letters, his descrip-
     tions of the Vancouver area, and on memoirs by Norman Newton
     and William McConnell.

30   _____ and JOHN WHITLEY. "Widow, Birney Present Unfinished
     Lowry." The Vancouver Sun, "Leisure" supplement (26 July),
     p. 23A.
        Modified praise for the "embryonic" and "companion"
     volumes: Dark as the Grave and Lunar Caustic. (Two
     separate reviews under the one title.)

31   K[NICKERBOCKER], C[ONRAD]. "Malcolm Lowry and the Outer Circle
     of Hell" in Malcolm Lowry, Lunar Caustic. Edited by Earle
     Birney and Margerie Lowry. London: Jonathan Cape, pp. 5–7.
     Reprint of 1963.B19.

32   LEECH, CLIFFORD. "The Shaping of Time: Nostromo and Under
     the Volcano" in Imagined Worlds: Essays on some English
     Novels and Novelists in Honour of John Butt. Edited by
     Maynard Mack and Ian Gregor. London: Methuen, pp. 323–41.
        Surveys Elizabethan dramatic conventions regarding time,
     and their influence upon early prose narratives, as a pref-
     ace to discussing twentieth century novelists' departures
     from simple progression. The novel and film are the basic
     modern media because in part of the freedom they allow in
     the representation of time, a freedom represented by
     Conrad's careful analysis of chance and Lowry's demonstra-
     tion of the "cultural complexity" of memory. Lowry, estab-
     lishing the simultaneous brevity and extensiveness of a
     single day, creates a strong sense both of the single mo-
     ment and of the moment as a point of departure into a
     world where readers' minds must share in the shaping.
     Reprinted: 1970.B19.

33   LEHTONEN, REIJO. "Armonajan oppaaski" [Penitent's guide].
     Suomen sosialdemokraatti (24 December).
        Very brief summary review of Under the Volcano.

34   LINDSAY, JACK. Meetings with Poets. London: Frederick
     Muller, pp. 128–31.
        Passing mention of his association with the journal
     Arena, of Lowry's contributions to it, and of the absence
     of any critical reception.

1968

35 LOPOS, GEORGE J. "Selected Poems of Malcolm Lowry." Poet and
    Critic, 5, pp. 41-42.
        A brief review, identifying Lowry as a "fusion of
    energies."

36 MARKSON, DAVID. "After the Volcano." Book World, 2 (30 June),
    8.
        A review, welcoming the appearance of Dark as the Grave.

37 NEW, WILLIAM H. "A Wellspring of Magma: Modern Canadian
    Writing." Twentieth Century Literature, 14, no. 3
    (October), 123-32.
        Mentions Lowry in a survey of Canadian writers.

38 O'MALLEY, MICHAEL. "Bid and Made." Critic, 27 (October-
    November), 95-99.
        A review, praising Dark as the Grave's "heart" and
    command of language.

39 PRICE, R. G. G. "New Fiction." Punch, 254 (6 March), 358.
        Brief approving notice of Lunar Caustic.

40 [PURDY] something or other, AL. "Turning New Leaves." The
    Canadian Forum, 48 (May), 40-41.
        Quotes the mention of himself in Lowry's Selected Letters
    (as "Al something or other") to comment anecdotally about
    the man, his affinities with Canada, and his concern for
    writing.

41 REYNOLDS, STANLEY. "Image Fakers." New Statesman, 75
    (23 February), 243.
        A brief notice of Lunar Caustic in the context of a
    longer review, by a critic who openly declares an antipathy
    to Lowry's "soft centred" works, a fault recorded again in
    this novella where the DTs are "too poetic to ring true."

42 SADKOWSKI, WACŁAW. "Nadmiar wrażliwości" [Excessive sensitiv-
    ity] in his Drogi i rozdroża literatury Zachodu [The Direc-
    tions and Crossroads of Western Literature]. Warsaw:
    Książka i Wiedza, pp. 242-46.
        Reprint, with slight changes, of 1964.B36.

43 SCHROEDER, ANDREAS. "Lunar Caustic." The Province
    (Vancouver), "Spotlight" supplement (31 May), p. 4.
        A summary review, commenting on the pain of over-
    sheltering, and the blend between documentary and lyric
    styles.

70

1968

44   SEYMOUR-SMITH, MARTIN. "A Missing Link." Spectator, 220
         (23 February), 234.
            A review of Lunar Caustic, observing that its simple
         events describe a "voyage through purgatory" and praising
         the "healing power and authority" that derive from its
         seriousness.

45   SPETTIGUE, D. O. Review of Dark as the Grave Wherein My
         Friend is Laid. Queen's Quarterly, 75 (Winter), 746-48.
            Acknowledges the dramatic tension in the book.

46   STERN, JAMES. "Ma première rencontre avec Malcolm Lowry."
         Translated by Françoise and Tony Cartano. Les lettres
         nouvelles (November-December), pp. 29-46.
            Translation of 1967.B38. Reprinted: 1974.B78.

47   SUMMERS, EILEEN. "Journey to Self-Discovery." The Catholic
         World, 208 (December), 140.
            Dark as the Grave is a tense novel, displaying a charac-
         teristic mixture of "whimsy, honesty, and anguish."

48   WAIN, JOHN. "Another Room in Hell." The Atlantic, 222
         (August), 84-86.
            A review of Dark as the Grave, noting Douglas Day's
         commentary and disagreeing with its premise about Lowry's
         abilities. Lowry's "tendency to cerebrate" doesn't con-
         vince in specific passages; his mind was ordinary; he lacked
         invention, and made use only of himself as subject. The
         "cult of subjectivism" in literature is attacked, and the
         "romantic cult of the individual" found inadequate as a
         theory of art. Dark as the Grave is then praised for its
         lack of "inflation," and for showing its natural outlines
         as a "gifted" writer first made them.

49   WEBB, W. L. "Novelist's Purgatory." Manchester Guardian
         Weekly, 98, no. 9 (29 February), 10.
            A review, finding Lunar Caustic to be too unmotivated
         and too obscure, although the first and final chapters are
         praised highly.

50   WEINTRAUB, STANLEY. The Last Great Cause: The Intellectuals
         and the Spanish Civil War. New York: Weybright and Talley,
         p. 308.
            Mentions Under the Volcano, focussing on Hugh's feelings
         about Spain, in an epilogue called "The Persistence of
         Rudinism."

1968

51 WILBUR, ROBERT HUNTER. "Conrad Aiken: An Interview." <u>Paris
    Review</u>, no. 42 (Winter-Spring), pp. 97–124.
        Comments in part on his association with Lowry, giving
    him writing exercises, for example.

52 WILD, BERNADETTE. "Malcolm Lowry: A Study of the Sea Meta-
    phor in <u>Under the Volcano</u>." <u>The University of Windsor
    Review</u>, 4, no. 1 (Fall), 46–60.
        Whereas the sea is used conventionally in <u>Ultramarine</u>,
    it is a complex metaphor in <u>Under the Volcano</u>, offering
    regeneration to Yvonne and Hugh, but ("the sea of alcohol")
    only destruction to Geoffrey. Hugh's association with the
    sea is traced at some length to show the importance of his
    role in the novel both in his own right and as Geoffrey's
    "other self." The sea metaphors are linked with those in-
    volving death, alcohol, and love, showing the sea not
    romantically but as the grim arena from which self-knowledge
    comes.

53 WOOLMER, J. HOWARD. "Malcolm Lowry's <u>Ultramarine</u>." <u>Anti-
    quarian Bookman's Weekly</u> (26 August).
        A comment on the scarcity of the 1933 edition of
    <u>Ultramarine</u>, describing it.

<u>1969 A BOOKS</u>

1   BENHAM, DAVID S. "A Liverpool of Self: A Study of Lowry's
    Fiction Other than <u>Under the Volcano</u>." Master's thesis,
    The University of British Columbia, 98 pp.
        The concurrent pull towards solipsism and community is
    seen as a characteristic dilemma of <u>Lunar Caustic</u> and the
    stories.

2   BREIT, HARVEY and MARGERIE BONNER LOWRY, eds. <u>Selected Let-
    ters of Malcolm Lowry</u>. New York: Capricorn Books,
    xix + 459 pp.
        Reprint of 1965.A1.

3   DAVIDSON, MARGARET NORMANTON. "Malcolm Lowry--The Cinematic
    Devices Used in <u>Under the Volcano</u>." Ph.D. dissertation,
    Washington State University, 93 unnumbered pp.
        A summary of Lowry's knowledge and application of 1920s
    and 1930s experimental film technique in "Tender is the
    Night" and <u>Under the Volcano</u>.

4   EASTON, T. R. "The Collected Poetry of Malcolm Lowry."
    Graduating Essay, The University of British Columbia,
    25 + vi pp.

A brief commentary on 169 published and 4 unpublished poems.

5   EPSTEIN, PERLE S. The Private Labyrinth of Malcolm Lowry: "Under the Volcano" and the Cabbala. New York, Chicago, and San Francisco: Holt, Rinehart and Winston, 241 pp.
    A brief account of Lowry's associations with Cabbala, and an extended history of the doctrines and symbols of Jewish and Christian Cabbala, are followed by a detailed examination of Under the Volcano. The novel's cabbalistic symbolism is specified: among them Tarot designs, numerical reiterations, alchemy, zodiacal patterns, volcanoes and lightning. A chapter-by-chapter reading of the novel follows, identifying the Consul as a black magician and tracing the occult significance of the symbols as a support of this interpretation. Preceding the bibliography and index are five appendices, containing a list of occult works Lowry read, a glossary of cabbalistic terms, a glossary of the novel's motifs, a list of Orphic and Dionysian elements in Eleusinian Mysteries relating to the novel's symbols, and excerpts from Lowry's previously unpublished journal notes on two of his stories: the "Outward Bound" chapter from October Ferry to Gabriola and "Ghostkeeper." These notes mention "diabolical possession," white magicians, alchemy, symbolism, names, demons, and the theme of rebirth.

6   JOHNSON, CARRELL. "The Making of Under the Volcano: An Examination of Lyrical Structure, with Reference to Textual Revisions." Master's thesis, The University of British Columbia, 103 pp.
    Tries to define the term "lyrical novel" and examines Lowry's use of simultaneity, leitmotif, and counterpoint.

1969 B SHORTER WRITINGS

1   ANON. "Publisher's Note" in Malcolm Lowry, Hear Us O Lord from Heaven Thy Dwelling Place. Harmondsworth: Penguin, pp. 7–8.
    Reprint of 1961.B14.

2   ANON. "Publisher's Note" in Malcolm Lowry, Hear Us O Lord from Heaven Thy Dwelling Place. New York: Capricorn, pp. 7–8.
    Reprint of 1961.B14.

1969

3   ANON. "Revisitation." <u>The Times Literary Supplement</u>
       (3 July), p. 721.
           A review of <u>Dark as the Grave</u>, pointing to its "magnif-
       icent comic scenes."

4   ATKINS, ELIZABETH. "Aspects of the Absurd in Modern Fiction,
       with Special Reference to <u>Under the Volcano</u> and <u>Catch 22</u>."
       Master's thesis, The University of British Columbia, 160 pp.
           Lowry and Heller are used as examples of writers whose
       spiritual affirmations protect the "absurd" debilitating
       existential anxiety characteristic of mid-twentieth century
       literature.

5   BARNES, JIM. "The Myth of Sisyphus in <u>Under the Volcano</u>."
       <u>Prairie Schooner</u>, 42, no. 4 (Winter), 341-48.
           Finds that the Consul looks at himself when he sees a
       madman <u>"eternally committed</u> to an absurd task." The rolling
       wheel of the novel is likened to Sisyphus' stone, and the
       hellish references are also used as evidence. Observes
       that other Greek myths--of Odysseus, Ixion, Prometheus, and
       Tantalus--are also present.

6   BATES, LEWIS. "Sunday Best." <u>Punch,</u> 256 (25 June), 951.
           Finds that <u>Dark as the Grave</u> has only biographical
       interest.

7   BRAEM, HELMUT M. "Lowry, Malcolm" in <u>Encyclopedia of World</u>
       <u>Literature in the 20th Century</u>. Volume 2. Edited by
       Wolfgang Bernard Fleischmann. New York: Frederick Ungar,
       pp. 335-36.
           Brief biocritical entry with a very selective bibliog-
       raphy. Observes that Lowry sees man as a "Janus-faced
       creature of nature and history and the androgynous Adam."

8   BREIT, HARVEY. "Introduction" to <u>Selected Letters of Malcolm</u>
       <u>Lowry</u>. New York: Capricorn Books, pp. xi-xv.
           Reprint of 1965.B3.

9   BRYDEN, RONALD. "Stations of the Cross." <u>New Statesman</u>, 78
       (25 July), 116.
           An account of Lowry's personal return to Mexico and of
       the failure of the novel that emerges from it, a failure
       at least in part because Wilderness merely looks into the
       abyss where the Consul lived.

10   CRAWFORD, JOHN. "Primitiveness in 'The Bravest Boat.'"
       <u>Research Studies</u> (Washington State University), 37, no. 4
       (December), 330-33.

Suggests that Lowry's purpose in juxtaposing images in the story is to contrast nature's values with civilization's corruption.

11   CUDDON, J. A. "Sense of Tragedy." Books and Bookmen, 14 (September), 52–53.
Modified praise for Dark as the Grave.

12   DAY, DOUGLAS. "Preface" to Malcolm Lowry, Dark as the Grave Wherein My Friend Is Laid. Edited by Douglas Day and Margerie Lowry. New York and Cleveland: World Publishing, Meridian Books, pp. ix–xxiii.
Reprint of 1968.B17.

13   _____. 'Prefacio' to Malcolm Lowry, Oscuro como la tumba donde yace mi amigo. Translated by Alicia Jurado. Caracas: Monte Avila Editores, pp. 7–24.
Reprint of 1968.B19.

14   DOYEN, VICTOR. "Elements Towards a Spatial Reading of Malcolm Lowry's Under the Volcano." English Studies, 50, no. 1, 65–74.
Observes how symbolic references—elements of spatial form—constitute and interlink the themes of love, war, and personal conflict. After tracing several strands of spatial imagery, focuses on the wounded Indian scene to demonstrate the density of the work.

15   FERNANDEZ, DIANE. "Malcolm Lowry et le feu infernal." Preuves, no. 215–216 (February–March), pp. 129–34.
A commentary on the letters and on the importance of letters (unwritten, lost, and forgotten: the important things being created but incommunicable) in Lowry's work. Several of the themes in the fiction are located in particular letters, which reveal corners of Lowry's personal hell.
Reprinted: 1974.B33.

16   FRENCH, WARREN. "February 19, 1947" in his The Forties: Fiction, poetry, drama. Deland, Fla.: Everett Edwards, p. 215.
Introduction to 1969.B43.

17   HELWE, ULLA. "Hitaasti kypsynyt—ponnistellen luettava" [Slowly ripened—strenuous reading]. Keskisuomalainen (Jyväskylä, Finland) (4 January).
Notes Lowry's French reputation. Biographical background is linked to the publishing of Under the Volcano.

1969

Lowry's "old-fashioned" rather than "classic" text is part
of his contemporary point: we all live under the shadow of
war.

18 HEMMINGS, JOHN. "Hell or Mexico?" The Listener, 82 (3 July),
24.
    Finds that Wilderness's return to Mexico, though impres-
sive, lacks the sweep of the Consul's story.

19 HOUSTON, PENELOPE. "In the Wilderness." Spectator, 223
(9 August), 177.
    In a review of the "companion volumes," Dark as the
Grave and Hear Us O Lord, observes that the technique of
"superimposition" allows Lowry to write autobiography without quite confronting the self. "Equilibrium" is shown
also to be "a precarious and romantic condition."

20 IVĂNESCU, MIRCEA. "Malcolm Lowry şi momentul contemporan"
[Malcolm Lowry and the Present Time]. România literară
(Bucharest), 47 (November), 20.
    Despite its limitations--the parable form, the unattrac-
tiveness of the love story, the ordinariness of the characters, the pathological nature of the details, the forced
symbols, the baroque abundance, the contrived coincidences--
Under the Volcano is both fascinating and important. Its
apparent weaknesses show the force of Lowry's observation
of the contemporary, Kafka-esque world. He lacks Joyce's
capacity for tragedy, but his work is at once more human,
more authentic, and more naive than that of Beckett.

21 JARVINEN, SEPPO J. "Eräs kärsimysh istoria" [A history of
suffering]. Kansan Lehti (Kampere, Finland) (8 August).
    A review, praising Juhani Jaskari's translation of
Under the Volcano, and commenting on Lowry's similarities
to Dante, Proust, Durrell.

22 KALEMAA, KALEVI. "Juoppohullu uni ihmisestä ja yhteiskunnasta"
[Crazy drunk dream of people and society]. Kansan Uitiset
(2 February).
    Finds Under the Volcano to be one of the best renderings
of an alcoholic's vision, but is critical (the journal is
a leftwing party paper) of Hugh's position, for he sees
Communism only as an ideal and not as an economic system.

23 KANGASLUOMA, TUUKKA. "Vetoinen kuolema joka tikitti ja ähki
[Drafty death which ticked and panted.] Helsingin Sanomat
(16 February), p. 22.
    A summary review, finding that Under the Volcano starts
too slowly and ends too quickly.

24   KENNER, HUGH. "The Scene Is Bellevue, the Hero a Drunk, the
     Structure Melville's." The New York Times Book Review
     (27 July), p. 8.
           A brief review of Lunar Caustic and Epstein's The Private
     Labyrinth of Malcolm Lowry, pointing to the disparities
     that exist in stories about Lowry himself and acknowledging
     that Lowry's quest for "Significance" in everything led to
     much of the "clutter" in his work.

25   KILGALLIN, TONY. "Cyclopean Author-Critic Shredded." The
     Vancouver Sun, "Leisure" supplement (3 October), p. 32A.
           A punning dismissal of Epstein's The Private Labyrinth
     of Malcolm Lowry.

26   _____. "Lowry Posthumous." Canadian Literature, no. 39
     (Winter), pp. 80-83.
           Review of the meritorious Lunar Caustic and the frag-
     mentary Dark as the Grave, describing the process of com-
     position and explaining some of the allusions in the books.

27   KIM, SUZANNE. "Les lettres de Malcolm Lowry." Etudes
     anglaises, 22, no. 1 (January-March), 58-61.
           Observes that Lowry's letters are important documents
     for tracing the genesis of his fiction, examines some of
     their stylistic variations, and suggests ways in which
     they reveal and explain Lowry's psychological need to write.

28   LEHTONEN, REIJO. "Maailma on puutarha eikä pelto" [The world
     is a garden and not a field]. Suomen Sosialidemokraatti,
     no. 96, p. 6.
           A review of the Finnish translation of Under the Volcano,
     approving its fluency--the shifts from complex and excited
     to direct and everyday language, which support different
     approaches to the work. The novel is an "ongoing analysis"
     of the world. There are stylistic and thematic parallels
     with Rossellini's film Stromboli; in both "knowledge breeds
     guilt." An accompanying note ("Agricolapalkinto Juhani
     Jaskarille") observes that Juhani Jaskari won the Agricola
     prize for this translation. Appended to a summary of Under
     the Volcano is a list of former prizewinners and a photo-
     graph of Jaskari.

29   LÓPEZ RUÍZ, JUVENAL. "La risa del demonio." Revista Imagen
     (Caracas), no. 48 (1 ra. época), pp. 16-17.
           Explores the relation between Under the Volcano and Dark
     as the Grave, between the mescal visions in the latter book
     and the utterances about life and death, between Lowry and
     other writers including Borges, and the importance of the
     colour white.

1969

30   LOWRY, MARGERIE. "Nota Introductoria" in Malcolm Lowry,
       <u>Ultramarine</u>. Translated by Alfonso Llanos. Caracas:
       Monte Avila Editores, pp. 7–10.
           Translation of 1962.B23.

31   MUDRICK, MARVIN. "Must We Burn Mme. de Beauvoir?" <u>The Hudson</u>
       <u>Review</u>, 21, no. 4 (Winter), 757–58.
           In the midst of a review article, condemns <u>Under the Vol-</u>
       <u>cano</u> and <u>Dark as the Grave</u> for lacking depth, credible dia-
       logue, grammatical accuracy, "and any creditable form of
       mental activity."

32   NIMMO, D. C. "Lowry's Hell." <u>Notes and Queries</u>, 16, no. 7
       (July), 265.
           A note on the Hamilton, Ontario, reference in Chapter 10
       of <u>Under the Volcano</u>, suggesting that the Hamilton (known
       locally as the "To Hell and Back") Railway allusion helps
       establish the Consul's hellish mental landscape.

33   PAUL, ANTHONY. "L'être et le néant." <u>The Financial Times</u>
       (26 June), p. 10.
           Finds <u>Dark as the Grave</u> interesting as autobiography.

34   PURDY, AL. "Perle Epstein." <u>The Five Cent Review</u> (Montreal),
       1, no. 3 (October), 11–12.
           Memoir--ignoring the book under review--of meeting Lowry
       in the mid-1950s.

35   RIPATTI, AKU-KIMMO. "Alkoholistin loppu" [The end of an
       alcoholic]. <u>Kainuun Sanomat</u> (Kajaani, Finland) (30 March),
       p. 5.
           Recapitulates Lowry's difficulties getting <u>Under the</u>
       <u>Volcano</u> published; finds its central theme to be the decline
       of Western culture.

36   ROPER, GORDON. Review of <u>Dark as the Grave Wherein My Friend</u>
       <u>is Laid</u>. <u>University of Toronto Quarterly</u>, 38, no. 4
       (July), 356–57.
           Passing mention of the novel, with its "awesome strug-
       gle," and of <u>Lunar Caustic</u>, in a survey of the previous
       year's work ("Letters in Canada").

37   ROSENLUND, JARKKO. "Klassikot" [Classics]. <u>Turun Päivälehti</u>
       (Turku, Finland) (21 March), p. 11.
           A brief review of <u>Under the Volcano</u>, finding the novel
       dramatic and autobiographical. Identifies the U.S.A. as
       Lowry's homeland.

38 SHORTER, KINGSLEY. "Lowry's Private Trip." <u>The New Leader</u>,
    52 (15 September), 14–16.
        Though Epstein's book identifies many symbols in <u>Under
    the Volcano,</u> <u>Dark as the Grave</u>--"a variorum edition of
    Lowry's interminable dialogue with himself"--provides a
    clearer sense of the novel's genesis. Yet it irritates,
    like <u>Lunar Caustic</u>, because of its posturing. The Cabbal-
    ism was Lowry's attempt to resolve the confusion/antithesis
    between subject and object, but it does not deliver him from
    the "prison of the self." Despite its "powerful visionary
    sense of nature," <u>Under the Volcano</u> remains solipsistic.

39 SUNDQVIST, HARRY. "Humaltuneen purren matka" [Drunken boat's
    trip]. <u>Suomenmaa</u> (Helsinki) (16 August).
        A laudatory review of <u>Under the Volcano</u>, focusing on
    the poetry of the language and alcoholism.

40 SUVIOJA, MIKA. "Klassiko omalla vuosisadallaan" [A classic
    in his time]. <u>Etelä-Suomen Sanomat</u> (Lahti, Finland),
    (16 February).
        Provides a biographical summary and a laudatory review
    of <u>Under the Volcano</u>, exploring the volcano symbolism
    briefly.

41 TOYNBEE, PHILIP. "Under the Weather." <u>The Observer</u>
    (29 June), p. 24.
        A review, finding that despite its virtues, <u>Dark as the
    Grave</u> is over-written and boring.

42 WHITLEY, JOHN. "Scenes from Suburban Life." <u>The Sunday
    Times</u> (29 June), p. 55.
        Finds <u>Dark as the Grave</u> important despite its longueurs
    and sloppiness.

43 WIDMER, ELEANOR. "The Drunken Wheel: Malcolm Lowry and <u>Under
    the Volcano</u>" in <u>The Forties: Fiction, poetry, drama.</u>
    Edited by Warren French. Deland, Fla.: Everett Edwards,
    pp. 217–26.
        Finds the fusion of the author with his work to be the
    chief fascination of Lowry, who tries to "transcend the
    spectre of death by magic." Though eclecticism weakens
    <u>Under the Volcano</u>, it remains a powerful rendering of the
    failure of the Consul in all his guises.

44 WOODCOCK, GEORGE. "Malcolm Lowry's Occult Vision." <u>Toronto
    Daily Star</u> (14 June), p. 15.
        A general summary of Lowry's publications, commenting
    on the state of criticism, and querying some of Perle
    Epstein's conclusions in <u>The Private Labyrinth of Malcolm
    Lowry</u>.

1969

45   ZERAFFA, MICHEL. <u>Personne et personnage: le romanesque des</u>
      <u>années 1920 aux années 1950</u>. Paris: Editions Klincksieck,
      pp. 321, 328-29, 343-58, 363.
         Discusses <u>Under the Volcano</u>, along with works by
      Malraux, Sartre, Céline, McCullers, and Greene, in a long
      chapter entitled "Réduction à l'existence." Contrasts
      Lowry's world-view with Joyce's in <u>Ulysses</u>, and shows how
      the form of Lowry's novel represents a regression "from Us
      to I," from being to having. Comments further on the Con-
      sul's character and on the pressures that govern his life.

<u>1970 A BOOKS</u>

1   ANDERSEN, GLADYS MARIE. "A Guide to <u>Under the Volcano</u>."
      Ph.D. dissertation, University of the Pacific (Stockton,
      Cal.), 670 pp.
         A cross-referenced alphabetical list of literary and
      other symbols, motifs, and allusions, together with a con-
      cordance keying these to the 1965 Lippincott and 1966
      Signet editions of <u>Under the Volcano</u>.

2   CORRIGAN, MATTHEW. "Phenomenology and Literary Criticism:
      A Definition and an Application." Ph.D. dissertation,
      State University of New York (Buffalo), 337 pp.
         An exploration of Edmund Husserl's notions of conscious-
      ness, with an application of these (pp. 205-99) to Lowry's
      works and his development of a "new" novel form.

3   CULLIS, TARA. "A Structural Analysis of the Wheel Symbolism
      in Malcolm Lowry's <u>Under the Volcano</u>." Graduating Essay,
      The University of British Columbia, 37 pp.
         Examines traditional uses of wheel symbolism and their
      application to Lowry's novel.

4   DODSON, DANIEL B. <u>Malcolm Lowry</u>. Columbia Essays on Modern
      Writers 51. New York and London: Columbia University
      Press, 48 pp.
         A brief outline biography is followed by brief summa-
      tions and judgments of <u>Ultramarine</u> (which is less tech-
      nically interesting than Aiken's work); <u>Lunar Caustic</u>
      (which also uses "contrapuntal dialogue"); <u>Under the Vol-</u>
      <u>cano</u>; <u>Selected Poems</u> (where the "wounded soul" is "more
      audible, less articulate"); <u>Hear Us O Lord</u> (each story
      being separately summarized, and each character considered
      one of Lowry's <u>personae</u>); <u>Dark as the Grave</u> (which is a
      disappointment, but shows Lowry abandoning his use of
      <u>persona</u>). It alludes to the manuscripts but does not use

them. A brief, highly selective bibliography completes the volume.

About the short stories it is observed that Lowry was "careless with fact," and that in "The Forest Path to the Spring" he saw "deeper" than "bland" Wordsworthian pantheism. "The Bravest Boat" is praised as a "love idyll."

The longest section, on Under the Volcano, contains a plot summary, followed by a summary of several elements in the novel: numerological references, animal symbolism, animism, Edenic and Dantesque patterns, and character. Drunkenness is seen as a correlative to the drunkenness of the world--a world self-condemned to impotence and presided over by evil.

Reprinted: 1976.B5.

5   EARLY, LEONARD ROY. "Endless Voyages: A Study of the Protagonist in Malcolm Lowry's Fiction." Ph.D. dissertation, University of Saskatchewan, 127 pp.

An attempt, by examining theme and technique in Hear Us O Lord, Under the Volcano, Lunar Caustic, and Dark as the Grave, to suggest the outlines of "The Voyage That Never Ends" and its main theme: a "desperate affirmation of free will against the immense weight of the past."

6   RAMSAY, ROBIN. "The Impact of Time and Memory in Malcolm Lowry's Fiction." Master's thesis, The University of British Columbia, 89 pp.

Uses the theories of Ortega and J. W. Dunne in an attempt to examine some of the "shapes" reality took for Lowry-- through premonition, coincidence, recurrence, telepathy, e.g.--and considers his literary adaptations of serialism.

7   RIDDELL, JOHN A. "Malcolm Lowry: The Voyage that Never Ends." Master's thesis, Dalhousie University, 99 pp.

Traces the Dantesque idea of "voyage" through Lowry's works.

1970 B SHORTER WRITINGS

1   ABE, YUKIKO. "Higeki--Malcolm Lowry no baai" [Tragedy--in Malcolm Lowry's Work], in her Gendai Eibungaku no Shosoo [Aspects of Modern English Literature]. Tokyo: Kooseisha-Kooseikaku, pp. 47-64.

Asserts that although the conditions for tragedy (conflicts between love and morality or love and law) are absent from modern life, tragedy can still be written by writers like Lowry, Eliot, and Joyce. Technique is the key.

1970

Lowry's Consul is caught between affirming and rejecting love, his inner tragedy intensified by outer conditions, until a noble death is his only salvation. He had classical heroic qualities. Fiction is made to seem more real than reality.

2   ADAMS, PHOEBE. Review of October Ferry to Gabriola. The Atlantic, 226 (December), 126.
A brief notice claiming the novel is "worth reading."

3   ALLEN, BRUCE D. "Only the Torso of a Masterpiece." Library Journal, 95, no. 18 (15 October), 3488.
Brief review of October Ferry to Gabriola.

4   BENHAM, DAVID. "Lowry's Purgatory: Versions of Lunar Caustic." Canadian Literature, no. 44 (Spring, pp. 28-37.
A comparison of the two versions that went into the making of Lunar Caustic: "The Last Adress" and "Swinging the Maelstrom," supplying an explication and tracing the shift from solipsism to human interaction.
Reprinted: 1971.A5.

5   BOURNIQUEL, CAMILLE. "Librairie du Mois." L'Esprit, 12 (December), 985-87.
A summary review of the French translation of Dark as the Grave, pointing out the autobiographical details behind the book and exploring the novel's poignancy.

6   BUCKEYE, ROBERT. Review of Epstein's The Private Labyrinth of Malcolm Lowry. Dalhousie Review, 49 (Winter), 574-75.
A dismissal of Epstein's work, concerning itself mostly with Lowry's critical comments on his own work and with the musicality of his style.

7   CHURCHILL, R. C. "English-Canadian Literature" in George Sampson, The Concise Cambridge History of English Literature. Third edition. Cambridge: Cambridge University Press, p. 750.
Lowry wrote well about dipsomaniacs.

8   CORRIGAN, MATTHEW. "Malcolm Lowry, New York Publishing, & the 'New Illiteracy.'" Encounter, 35, no. 1 (July), 82-93.
A critical account of the publication of Dark as the Grave, attacking the New York editorial preconceptions which did not recognize Lowry's loss of interest in the traditional novel form. The novel as published thus represents concretely the frustrations of the modern writer. The tensions in the novel arise in part from conflict with

publishers, as did many of Lowry's tensions, recorded in his letters. The case of Lowry is then used as the basis for an attack upon the "new illiteracy"—the failure of intelligence and taste—which too often shapes current publishing in America.

9 _____. "A Noble Failure by a Corrupted Mystic." The New York Times Book Review (25 October), pp. 5, 54.
Lowry's failure with October Ferry to Gabriola is of more interest than more recent easy successes, because it documents the failure of a certain kind of consciousness.

10 COSTA, RICHARD HAUER. "Malcolm Lowry and the Addictions of an Era." The University of Windsor Review, 5, no. 2 (Spring), 2-10.
An account of Under the Volcano, pointing to its humour, its humanistic existentialism, its concern for alienated man, and other reflections of its time. The material is incorporated in 1972.A2.

11 _____. "Malcolm Lowry's 'Paradiso.'" The Nation, 211 (26 October), 408-09.
A summary of October Ferry to Gabriola, acknowledging its flaws of incompleteness but finding it a "worthy antiphon" to Lowry's "Inferno."

12 DURRANT, GEOFFREY. "Death in Life: Neo-Platonic Elements in 'Through the Panama.'" Canadian Literature, no. 44 (Spring), pp. 13-27.
Draws upon the writings of Thomas Taylor the Platonist—the chief English source for the ideas of Proclus, Porphyry, and others—to illustrate how Lowry's stories of the voyage of the soul can be read in a Neo-Platonic context. A careful, detailed exegesis follows, annotating Lowry's use of directional, numerical, and visual symbolism; tracing the significance of the parallels with the Ancient Mariner, Ulysses, and Cupid and Psyche stories; and probing the distinctions being made between material and spiritual worlds, the actions of the intellect and the senses, and the voyage to enlightenment.
Reprinted: 1971.A5.

13 EPSTEIN, PERLE. "Swinging the Maelstrom: Malcolm Lowry and Jazz." Canadian Literature, no. 44 (Spring), pp. 57-66.
Reviews Lowry's enthusiasm for jazz and Bix Beiderbecke, then recounts the references to jazz in his work and the frequent "musical techniques" he uses: refrain, aria, onomonopoeic effects, discord, cutting contests. The

1970

individual viewpoints of Hugh, Geoffrey, and Yvonne are
compared to "improvisations of soloists."
Reprinted: 1971.A5.

14 GASS, WILLIAM H. "In Terms of the Toenail: Fiction and the
Figures of Life" in New American Review, 10. Edited by
Theodore Solotaroff. New York and Toronto: New American
Library, Signet; London: New English Library, pp. 51-68.
In a context involving Hamlet, Beckett, and Pierre
Menard, discusses Under the Volcano's subjectivity. The
novel constructs, does not describe, a world; it shows,
and does not say, its meaning. Even its literal language
performs a figurative function, and the novelist's world
becomes a metaphorical model of everyday reality.
Reprinted: 1970.B15; 1972.B15.

15 _____. "In Terms of the Toenail: Fiction and the Figures of
Life" in Fiction and the Figures of Life. New York:
Knopf, pp. 55-76.
Reprint of 1970.B14.

16 HARRISON, DICK. "The American Adam and the Canadian Christ."
Twentieth Century Literature, 16, no. 3 (July), 164-65.
The end of Under the Volcano can be read as potentially
redemptive or irrevocably Faustian. The ambiguity relates
to major themes in English Canadian literature.

17 HERMANS, WILLEM FREDERIK. "Lowry, aandoenlijke epigoon"
[Lowry, the pathetic imitator] in his Van Wittgenstein tot
Weinreb Het sadistische universum 2 [From Wittgenstein to
Weinreb - The Sadistic Universe 2]. Amsterdam: De Bezige
Bij, pp. 132-39.
Largely a summary of events in Lowry's life, as revealed
in his letters, to show Lowry wrestling with his recognition of his unsteady position as a writer. Like all imi-
tators, Lowry goes through elaborate arguments to exonerate
himself from the accusation of influence. Compares Under
the Volcano with Charles Jackson's The Lost Weekend.

18 JONES, JOSEPH and JOHANNA JONES. Authors and Areas of Canada.
People and Places in World-English Literature, no. 1.
Austin: Steck-Vaughn, pp. 40-41.
Brief biobibliographical item, with photograph.

19 LEECH, CLIFFORD. "The Shaping of Time" in The Dramatist's
Experience with Other Essays in Literary Theory. London:
Chatto & Windus; New York: Barnes & Noble, pp. 87-107.
Reprint of 1968.B32.

20   LILLQUIST, HOLGER. "Se Faustus' undergång." <u>Nya Argus</u>,
      pp. 200-04.
          Swedish review, summarizing <u>Under the Volcano</u>, comparing
      it with Joyce's and Faulkner's, and exploring its cinematic
      technique and political message.

21   LORENZ, CLARISSA. "Call It Misadventure." <u>The Atlantic</u>, 225,
      no. 6 (June), 106-112.
          The author recalls first meeting Lowry in 1929, when she
      was married to Conrad Aiken; she notes her diary entries
      concerning him, and comments on his athletic ability, his
      shyness with women, his knowledge of nature, and his
      "oedipal problems." Further memories of meeting him again
      in Spain, in 1933, recount his romance with Jan Gabrial and
      his continuing friendship with Aiken.
          Reprinted: 1975.A3. Translated: 1974.B56.

22   LOWRY, MALCOLM. "Two Letters." <u>Canadian Literature</u>, no. 44
      (Spring), pp. 50-56.
          Letters to Albert Erskine (1946) containing emendations
      to Chapter V of the manuscript of <u>Under the Volcano</u>, and to
      David Markson (1951), then a student at Columbia University,
      commenting on the influences on his work.
          Reprinted: 1971.A5.

23   LOWRY, MARGERIE. "Editor's Note" in her edition of Malcolm
      Lowry, <u>October Ferry to Gabriola</u>. New York and Cleveland:
      World Publishing, pp. 335-36.
          Notes on the writing of the novel and on two unfinished
      themes in the book: the character of the McCandless and
      the motivation for Ethan's move.
          Reprinted: 1971.B18. Translated: 1974.B58.

24   MOORE, DENNIS JAMES. "The Transformations of 'Billy Budd.'"
      Ph.D. dissertation, Northwestern University, 209 pp.
          On pp. 74-89, uses <u>Lunar Caustic</u>, with its "lyric
      agonies," as one example of a modern variation of Melville's
      work.

25   MORENO, CARLOS MARTÍNEZ. "Prólogo" to his translation of
      Malcolm Lowry, <u>Lunar Caustic</u>. Montivideo: Editorial
      Alfa, pp. 7-16.
          Recounts the publishing history of the novella, bio-
      graphical details concerning the writer, and suggests
      Artaud, Beckett, and Mann as the frame of references for
      readers of the book to keep in mind.

26   NADEAU, MAURICE. Preface to Malcolm Lowry, <u>Sombre comme la</u>
      <u>tombe où repose mon ami</u>. Paris: Editions Denoël, pp. i-vi.

1970

Sketches the biographical background to the novel, and traces Wilderness's descent and return.

27　NEW, WILLIAM H. "Lowry, the Cabbala and Charles Jones." Canadian Literature, no. 43 (Winter), pp. 83–87.
　　　A brief review of the interest in hermeticism and the occult in Vancouver in the period immediately preceding Lowry's arrival, by way of commenting on Epstein's book on Lowry's Cabbalism, and the metaphysical quests of his later writing.
　　　Reprinted: 1972.B28.

28　＿＿＿＿. "Lowry's Reading: An Introductory Essay." Canadian Literature, no. 44 (Spring), pp. 5–12.
　　　A survey of works that Lowry read and of ways in which these "objects read" entered the subjectivity with which Lowry rendered experience. Quotations from Annie Besant which appear in the manuscript of "The Ordeal of Sigbjørn Wilderness" are reproduced to illustrate what Lowry intended by Wilderness's multiple identities.
　　　Reprinted: 1971.A5.

*29　REGER, MURIEL. "Lowry's Quahnahuac Today." Vistas (The News, Mexico City) (31 May), pp. 2–4.
　　　Unlocatable. Cited by Gunn (item 1974.B44).

30　SERREAU, GENEVIÈVE. "Le Retour aux sources." La Quinzaine Littéraire, no. 105 (1–15 November), pp. 9–10.
　　　A review of the French translation of Dark as the Grave, tracing some of the autobiographical parallels and commenting on the anguish the book arouses.

31　SHEPPARD, R. Z. "Interrupted Journey." Time, 96 (9 November), 88.
　　　A review of October Ferry to Gabriola, finding it untamed and convoluted.

32　STURM, TERRY. "Frank Sargeson's 'Joy of the Worm.'" Landfall, 24, no. 1 (March), 33–38.
　　　Passing reference to Under the Volcano, as a stylistic counterpart to Sargeson's novel, The Hangover.

33　TIESSEN, PAUL G. "Malcolm Lowry and the Cinema." Canadian Literature, no. 44 (Spring), pp. 38–49.
　　　Reviews Lowry's interest in film and his two attempts at screen-writing, then proceeds to demonstrate his adaptations of cinematic technique in Under the Volcano: visual

rhythms, long-shot and close-up contrasts, camera-eye symbols. The relation between the wheel images and the motion
picture reel itself is examined, and the connection between
method, metaphor and meaning is affirmed.
Reprinted: 1971.A5.

34 WOODCOCK, GEORGE. "The Absorption of Echoes." <u>Canadian Liter-
ature</u>, no. 44 (Spring), pp. 3-4.
An editorial introducing a special Lowry issue of the
journal, focussing on "absorption" as a literary quality.

35 _____. <u>Canada and the Canadians</u>. London: Faber & Faber;
Toronto: Oxford University Press, pp. 252, 255-56.
Passing reference to Lowry's work in a commentary on
modern Canadian culture, affirming that Lowry's handling
of Canadian landscapes was as original as his handling
of Mexican ones.
Reprinted: 1973.B35.

36 _____. "Four Facets of Malcolm Lowry" in his <u>Odysseus Ever
Returning: Essays on Canadian Writers and Writing</u>.
Toronto: McClelland & Stewart, New Canadian Library no. 71,
pp. 56-75.
Reprint of items 1958.B2; 1961.B60, B61; with a commentary on <u>Dark as the Grave Wherein My Friend Is Laid</u>
(first broadcast on CBC radio, 1968) tracing the biographical background to the work, outlining its strengths and
weaknesses, finding parallels in Gide, and finally condemn-
ing its "regressive" artistic "solipsism." The last section is reprinted: 1971.A5.

37 WRIGHT, TERENCE. "'Under the Volcano': The Static Art of
Malcolm Lowry." <u>Ariel</u>, 1, no. 4 (October), 67-76.
Sees the Joycean element of stasis as <u>Under the Volcano</u>'s
most interesting technical feature. The Consul's fall is
not to be seen as process, but as a contemplation of a
spiritual state. No moral judgment is invited. The structure can be seen as a series of scenes rather than as a
narrative process, and the characters are looked at rather
than lived with. The symbols further emphasize pattern,
and the Mexican landscape is important as a setting in
which the illusion of life and Lowry's demand for an aesthetic response are both possible.

<u>1971 A BOOKS</u>

1 ALBAUM, ELVIN. "La Mordida: Myth and Madness in the Novels
of Malcolm Lowry." Ph.D. dissertation, State University
of New York (Stony Brook), 254 pp.

1971

> Considers Lowry's poetic and redemptive, visionary fictions as ritual encounters, drawing on theories of Eastern and Western mysticism.

2   HOWARD, BENJAMIN WILLIS. "Malcolm Lowry: The Ordeal of Bourgeois Humanism." Ph.D. dissertation, Syracuse University, 286 pp.
> Observes that though Lowry is thematically repetitive—the dissertation examines the published work from <u>Ultramarine</u> to <u>October Ferry to Gabriola</u>—this testifies to his moral fidelity to the values he felt had gone from the world.

3   NEW, WILLIAM H. <u>Malcolm Lowry</u>. Canadian Writers No. 11. Toronto: McClelland and Stewart, 64 pp.
> A biographical chapter, disputing some but not all of the Lowry myths, is followed by four chapters on the Lowry canon and a selective bibliography. On the whole, emphasizes Lowry's literary forms and the intellectual background to his work. Uses the integrated structure of <u>Hear Us O Lord</u> as a model of Lowry's cyclical designs and his concern for multiple shifts of identity. Sees puns and names as significant elements in these concerns. Alludes to the development of his technique from the early stories through to <u>Lunar Caustic</u> and the poems, and considers the paradoxical simultaneity of heaven and hell throughout Lowry's writings. A chapter on <u>Under the Volcano</u>, tracing a number of its motifs and suggesting the importance of the allusions and the humorous elements, is followed by a chapter on the later novels, which emphasizes Lowry's experiments with perception and his weaving together of fact and fiction. A closing chapter describes the unpublished manuscripts in The University of British Columbia collection, and briefly summarizes several of the stories, "The Ordeal of Sigbjørn Wilderness" and "La Mordida."

4   SILVERMAN, CARL MARK. "A Reader's Guide to <u>Under the Volcano</u>." Ph.D. dissertation, State University of New York (Buffalo), 120 pp.
> A chapter by chapter commentary on the novel.

5   WOODCOCK, GEORGE, ed. <u>Malcolm Lowry: The Man and His Work</u>. Vancouver: The University of British Columbia Press, Canadian Literature Series No. 3, ix + 174 pp.
> Collects seventeen essays, with some of Lowry's letters and poems, all but five of which first appeared in <u>Canadian Literature</u>, nos. 6, 8, 9, 26, and 44. There are notes on the text and the contributors, an inexact note on Lowry's life, and a selective bibliography. Item 1961.B61 is given

a subtitle "A Note on Lowry's Stories"; item 1961.B39 is
given a new subtitle, "The Critic as Correspondent"; "Art
as the Writer's Mirror: Literary Solipsism in Dark as the
Grave" is the new title given to the reprint of the fourth
section of item 1970.B36. Matthew Corrigan's "The Writer
as Consciousness: A View of October Ferry to Gabriola"
appeared simultaneously in Canadian Literature, 48, under
the title "Lowry's Last Novel." Like the three previously
unpublished essays (by Carey, Kilgallin, and Thomas), it is
listed separately; See 1971.B6-B7, B14, B32.

1971 B SHORTER WRITINGS

1   ANON. "Lowry's Attempt at a Cosmic Novel." The Times Liter-
      ary Supplement (27 August), p. 1020.
          Passing over George Woodcock's Malcolm Lowry, the review
      finds October Ferry to Gabriola turgid, uninventive, and
      derivative.

2   BAREHAM, T[ERENCE]. "Paradigms of Hell: Symbolic Patterning
      in Under the Volcano" in On the Novel: A present for Walter
      Allen on his 60th birthday from his friends and colleagues.
      Edited by B. S. Benedikz. London: J. M. Dent & Sons,
      pp. 113-27.
          Asserts that Lowry's "intellectual" and "tragic" master-
      piece is an artist's attempt to make meaning out of life's
      randomness. Symbol is important for understanding charac-
      ter and appreciating the coherence of the plot. The drunk-
      enness establishes a sense of disorientation. Symbols like
      the ravine, garden, dog, tower, and wheel impinge on each
      other and carry multiple implications, amplifying the book's
      meaning as the scenes change.

3   BEECHING, JACK. "The Last Romantic?" The Times Educational
      Supplement (24 September), p. 15.
          Though October Ferry to Gabriola requires "effort of
      good will" from the reader, it pales other fiction and
      still demonstrates Lowry's "integrity" as a romantic writer
      expressing the crisis of his age.

4   CALDER-MARSHALL, ARTHUR. "Lowry, Clarence Malcolm" in Dic-
      tionary of National Biography 1951-60. Edited by E. T.
      Williams and Helen M. Palmer. London: Oxford University
      Press, pp. 654-56.
          A solid, short biographical summary.

1971

5   CALZADILLA, JUAN. "Ultramarina." <u>Revista Nacional de Cultura</u> (Caracas), 197 (April, May, June), 111–12.
    A review of the Spanish translation of the novel (which records the modifications Lowry made to the text), pointing out relationships between Lowry and Hilliot.

6   CAREY, MAURICE J. "Life with Malcolm Lowry," edited by Anthony R. Kilgallin, in <u>Malcolm Lowry: The Man and His Work</u>. Edited by George Woodcock. Vancouver: The University of British Columbia Press, pp. 163–70.
    Lowry's Vancouver landlord recalls their first encounter there. Some details about this period in his life are at variance with those Lowry later communicated and those accepted by Day.

7   CORRIGAN, MATTHEW. "Lowry's Last Novel." <u>Canadian Literature</u>, no. 48 (Spring), pp. 74–80.
    Acknowledges that <u>October Ferry to Gabriola</u> is flawed, but admires its power. Shaped like a vortex, the novel animates a drama "between present and past consciousness." Lowry's later work is thus thematically retrospective, locating terror not in present threats but in recognition of the significance of the past. The present is then "underlived," which is dangerous for a writer unless he is a phenomenologist. To read Lowry properly is to recognize his effort to render a vision of a higher order than is usual in modern literature. Printed simultaneously in: 1971.A5.

8   COSTA, RICHARD HAUER. "<u>Pietà</u>, <u>Pelado</u>, and 'The Ratification of Death': The Ten-Year Evolvement of Malcolm Lowry's <u>Volcano</u>." <u>Journal of Modern Literature</u>, 2, no. 1 (September), 3–18.
    Traces the textual development of <u>Under the Volcano</u>, working towards a picture of the four principals as "interacting forces."
    Incorporated in 1972.A2.

9   DAY, DOUGLAS. "Prefazione" to Malcolm Lowry, <u>Buio come la tomba dove giace il mio amico</u>. Translated by Attilio Veraldi. Milan: Arnoldo Mondadori Editore, pp. 7–25.
    Translation of 1968.B17.

10 DENNIS, NIGEL. "Eviction from Eden." <u>Sunday Telegraph</u> (29 August).
    An account of theme and emotion as Lowry's forte—and of "houses" as his "heroes and heroines"—as most recently evidenced in <u>October Ferry to Gabriola</u>. Like many writers

of the 1930s and 1940s, he is difficult to read, though his
concern for psychology has the "charm of intense feeling."

*11 DOYEN, VICTOR. "Malcolm Lowry" in English Literature in the
     Twentieth Century. Edited by Herman Servotte. Antwerp:
     De Nederlandsche Boekhandel, pp. 89–94.
        Unlocatable. Cited in Brian O'Kill's checklist (see
     p. xix).

 12 HAWORTH, DAVID. "Huge and Sad." New Statesman, 82 (27 August),
     276.
        Lowry's October Ferry to Gabriola is summarized, and
     described as a "fine romantic thing."

 13 HOWARD, MICHAEL S. Jonathan Cape, Publisher. London:
     Jonathan Cape, pp. 141, 210–12.
        Recounts Lowry's publishing history with Cape, noting
     that William Plomer had been the reader for Under the Vol-
     cano and quoting from Plomer's comments on Lowry's defensive
     letter to Cape about this novel.

 14 KILGALLIN, ANTHONY R. "The Long Voyage Home: October Ferry
     to Gabriola" in Malcolm Lowry: The Man and His Work.
     Edited by George Woodcock. Vancouver: The University of
     British Columbia Press, pp. 78–87.
        Traces the composition of the novel, identifying allu-
     sions and possible sources; explains Lowry's use of cabbal-
     istic and technical psychoanalytic terms; finds "redundant
     exposition" to be its worst flaw, and "the development of
     the process of redemption" its greatest achievement.

 15 _____. "Malcolm Lowry" in his The Canadian Short Story.
     Toronto: Holt, Rinehart and Winston, pp. 83–84.
        Headnote to "Strange Comfort Afforded By The Profession."

 16 LAWRENCE, VINCENT. "Ah Wilderness!" The Irish Press
     (28 August), p. 12.
        A review appreciating the "potential of words" which
     October Ferry to Gabriola reveals, a "worthy monument to
     the troubled genius" of its author.

 17 LE D[OZE], G[AËLLE]. "Post-Scriptum Malcolm Lowry." L'Esprit,
     n.s. 1 (January), pp. 115–18.
        A reflection on various sides of Lowry's character--his
     drunkenness and humour included--together with comments on
     French opinions about Lowry, based in part on a conversa-
     tion with Michel Polac.

1971

18   LOWRY, MARGERIE. "Editor's Note" in her edition of Malcolm
        Lowry, October Ferry to Gabriola. London: Jonathan Cape;
        New York, London, and Scarborough, Ont.: New American
        Library, Plume, pp. 335-36.
            Reprint of 1970.B23.

19   MARSH, JAN. "Demonic Day." New Society, 18, no. 465
        (26 August), p. 385.
            A review praising the "movement and texture and clarity"
        of October Ferry to Gabriola, which causes a powerful "dis-
        ruption and coherence" inside a reader's mind.

20   NYE, ROBERT. "A Modern Extension of the Divine Comedy." The
        Guardian (Manchester) (26 August), p. 9.
            A generally approving review of October Ferry to
        Gabriola, commenting on the "density of Lowry's working
        methods.

21   NYLINDER, ÅKE. "Malcolm Lowry." Horisont, pp. 109-12.
            A review of the Swedish translation of Under the Volcano,
        considering mainly the Consul's loneliness and metaphysical
        questioning. The Consul is a victim of "the death of the
        heart." Explores the historical setting: the significance
        of the date vis-à-vis the Battle of Ebro during the Spanish
        Civil War.

22   OHM, VIVECA. "Malcolm Lowry's Troubled Ghost Stalks Academic
        Precincts." The Vancouver Sun, "Leisure" supplement
        (3 September), pp. 4A-5A.
            An account of Lowry's life and Lowry criticism based on
        an interview with Tony Kilgallin.

23   PERROTT, ROY. "Boozer's Gloom." The Observer (29 August),
        p. 23.
            A brief review of October Ferry to Gabriola, approving of
        of its "sardonic Lowryisms" and grand descriptions, though
        acknowledging it as a "draft" version.

24   SCOTT, JACK. "Lowry: More Evidence for Our Claim." Victoria
        Daily Times (31 July), p. 13.
            A review of Woodcock's Malcolm Lowry, reflecting on
        British Columbia's claims to the novelist.

25   _____. "This Is Lowry at the Full Power of His Talent."
        Victoria Daily Times (23 January), p. 12.
            A brief, laudatory review of October Ferry to Gabriola.

26   SCOTT, MICHAEL MAXWELL. "Recent Fiction." <u>Daily Telegraph</u>
     (26 August), p. 6.
         A complimentary short review of <u>October Ferry to</u>
     <u>Gabriola</u>.

27   SNOW, C. P. "Wolfe's Clothing." <u>Financial Times</u>
     (2 September), p. 10.
         A review of <u>October Ferry to Gabriola</u>, praising the
     editing but noting Lowry's lack of a "gift for construction."
     Often boring, the novel still shows a "dramatic visual
     sense." Like all of Lowry's work, it is a "dithyramb."
     Lowry's romantic lack of corruption--and the helplessness
     associated with it--is what attracts a coterie to him.

28   SPENCER, SHARON. <u>Space, Time and Structure in the Modern</u>
     <u>Novel</u>. New York: New York University Press, pp. 7-8.
         Contrasts the Consul with Robert Musil's Ulrich in <u>The</u>
     <u>Man Without Qualities</u>, pointing to the fineness of Lowry's
     evocation of Mexico, yet his concentration on one central
     character.

29   STARRS, ROY. "...And a New Insight into Lowry, the B.C.
     Squatter." <u>The Vancouver Sun</u>, "Leisure" supplement
     (13 August), p. 30A.
         A descriptive review of Woodcock's <u>Malcolm Lowry</u>.

30   SYMONS, JULIAN. "Dispossession." <u>Sunday Times</u> (29 August),
     p. 23.
         Finds <u>October Ferry to Gabriola</u> an unsatisfactory but
     remarkable book, in which the long flashbacks and symbolic
     themes--despite the personal details that intrude upon uni-
     versality--reveal Lowry's "genius."

31   TAYLOR, CHET. "Dissonance and Digression: The Ill-fitting
     Fusion of Philosophy and Form in Lawrence Durrell's
     <u>Alexandria Quartet</u>." <u>Modern Fiction Studies</u>, 17, no. 2
     (Summer), 167-79.
         Passing reference (p. 171) to the Consul's finding
     destruction at the leading edge of awareness. The context
     is a discussion of Durrell's character Darley in <u>Justine</u>
     and <u>Clea</u>.

32   THOMAS, HILDA. "Lowry Letters" in Malcolm Lowry: <u>The Man and</u>
     <u>His Work</u>. Edited by George Woodcock. Vancouver: The Uni-
     versity of British Columbia Press, pp. 103-09.
         Observes that the letters demonstrate several things:
     that Lowry himself was healthier than the Consul and must
     not be identified with him alone; that <u>Under the Volcano</u>

1971

was planned; that Lowry's style developed as part of his attempt to evolve a form "appropriate to a new approach to reality." The letters also provide a way of measuring the posthumous work against the author's intention.

33 WAUGH, AUBERON. "Auberon Waugh on New Novels." <u>Spectator</u>, 227 (4 September), 344–45.
A dismissal of <u>October Ferry to Gabriola</u> as a 'sixth former' book, not about dispossession or love, but merely a description of a bus trip by a man named Eltham [sic].

34 WHITE, JOHN J. <u>Mythology in the Modern Novel: A Study of Prefigurative Techniques</u>. Princeton: Princeton University Press, p. 8.
A footnote pointing to Lowry's urge to create new myths out of old ones.

1972 A BOOKS

1 CONSIDINE, RAYMOND HOWARD. "Malcolm Lowry's Major Prose Fiction." Ph.D. dissertation, University of Tennessee, 192 pp.
Examines each of Lowry's major prose works in the light of his Dantesque scheme for "The Voyage that Never Ends."

2 COSTA, RICHARD HAUER. <u>Malcolm Lowry</u>. New York: Twayne, 208 pp. Twayne's World Authors Series 217.
Follows the Twayne series format in providing a chronology, extensive notes, a selective but annotated bibliography, and an index. Incorporates some of the material Costa published in earlier articles. A four-page note on the poetry appears at the beginning of the "Notes" section. An introduction and nine chapters trace Lowry's career as a fiction writer, with two main concerns: the process by which <u>Under the Volcano</u> emerged from its short story version and the three drafts that preceded the published book, and the artistic concerns of Lowry's years in Canada. The events of the first part of Lowry's life are told quickly, incorporated into an account of the "symbiosis" that links Lowry (through Aiken) to Joyce. Modelling his work upon Aiken's but learning from it as well, Lowry finally surpassed Aiken in his portrait of the Consul. Playing games with time and space, <u>Under the Volcano</u>'s contrapuntal methods create a circular book, carrying the major themes with their symbolic correlates. Comparing the versions of the novel, declares that in the published work the Consul is triumphant in his fall, hope being always the necessary condition and Lowry being a comedian with a tragic mask.

Contrasts the later work--marred by "sycophantic chat-
ter"--with Under the Volcano to show that the writer was
never again far enough from his fictional alter egos.
Classifies the later short stories by setting--not in relation to each other--though asserts explicitly that Lowry is
not a "regional" writer. Regards "Gin and Goldenrod" as
the finest "anecdotal" story and "The Forest Path to the
Spring"--"antiphon to the demonic voices"--the best of the
late stories. Compares the attitudes toward Nature with
those of Thoreau.
 Chapter 8 provides a "coda," calling Lowry's life "archetypal" and pointing to the advantages of a Jungian response
to his work, particularly the images involving time and
memory--the "haunting by images portending doom." Chapter
9 comments on the individuality of Lowry's accomplishments,
but also affirms the tonal and intellectual connection between him and his age.

3 HARRISON, KEITH. "Under the Volcano and October Ferry to
 Gabriola: The Weight of the Past." Ph.D. dissertation,
 McGill University, 253 pp.
 Suggests that the idea of "the past" works as an ordering
 thematic principle; also reflects on the function of Freudianism, alcoholism, allusion, Marxism, and Indian traditions
 in Lowry's work.

4 KNOLL, JOHN FRANCIS. "Malcolm Lowry and the Cinema." Ph.D.
 dissertation, St. Louis University, 149 pp.
 An inexact biographical account is followed by a consideration of Lowry's works as "verbalized silent films"
 and an examination of the thematic significance of the
 references to particular films in Lowry's fiction and
 poetry.

1972 B SHORTER WRITINGS

1 ADELMAN, IRVING and RITA DWORKIN. The Contemporary Novel: A
 Checklist of Critical Literature on the British and American Novel Since 1945. Metuchen, N. J.: Scarecrow Press,
 pp. 326-28.
 A selective list of critical commentaries (including
 some reviews and theses), divided into categories entitled
 "General," "Ultramarine," and "Under the Volcano." Cutoff
 date is 1968 for periodicals and 1969 for books.

2 ANON. Review of October Ferry to Gabriola. Tygodnik
 Powszechny (Cracow), 34, p. 6.

1972

Asserts that the central characters, dreaming of mankind's golden age and of blessed lands, find in their flight from themselves and others only a wild, forbidding, and inhospitable island.

3   BARNES, JIMMY WEAVER. "Fiction of Malcolm Lowry and Thomas Mann: Structural Tradition." Ph.D. dissertation, University of Arkansas, 212 pp.
An exploration (using Joseph Campbell's monomyth) of parallel structures in Lowry and Mann, linking Under the Volcano with The Magic Mountain, "Elephant and Colosseum" with "Tonio Kröger," Dark as the Grave with Dr. Faustus, etc. Finds Mann often humorous, but Lowry nearly always serious and tragic.

4   BRADBROOK, MURIEL. Literature in Action. London: Chatto & Windus, pp. 178–87.
Humour for Lowry was a way of conquering terrors; Canada became for him a landscape "of the heart" where unity was possible. Canada's literary tradition of "analysis, diffidence and humour" provided Lowry with an environment in which he could discover his strengths and work out his mythology.

5   BRADBURY, MALCOLM. "The Novel" in The Twentieth Century Mind: History, Ideas, and Literature in Britain. Volume 3: 1945–1965. Edited by C. B. Cox and A. E. Dyson. London and New York: Oxford University Press, pp. 332–36.
Durrell, Beckett, and Lowry are the three most important experimental novelists of the period. All expatriates, they are concerned with the relation between creative force and life. Lowry's quandary--how to allow modernist ironies to limit romanticism--prevented him from completing many of his works. Yet he wrote well on the agonies of the quest.

6   BYGRAVE, MIKE. "Under the Volcano: A Study of Malcolm Lowry's Novel." Time Out, no. 121 (9–15 June), pp. 38–41.
Finds the novel autobiographical and un-English; Lowry is a critic not an artist, rejecting Europe but unable to accept America.

7   CARSTENSEN, FEDERICO BREHM. "La Cábala en 'Bajo el volcán.'" La Palabra y el Hombre, no. 2 (April–June), 40–45.
Explains the signs and symbols of the novel, based on a summary of Perle Epstein's commentary on the Zohar. Sees Laruelle's motive as seeking to save Geoffrey in part to recapture lost innocence for himself.

8   COGSWELL, FRED. "Chaos the Route to Paradise." <u>Journal of</u>
    <u>Canadian Fiction</u>, 1, no. 3 (Summer), 92.
       A review of New's <u>Malcolm Lowry</u>, reflecting on the need
    for contemporary writers to turn back from "magic" to "value
    and science and reason."

9   COSTA, RICHARD HAUER. "The Northern Paradise: Malcolm Lowry
    in Canada." <u>Studies in the Novel</u>, 4, no. 2 (Summer), 165-72.
       Briefly describes the events of Lowry's life in Canada,
    then indicates how Lowry's vision of the Northern Paradise--
    Canada perceived as fictional landscape rather than as a
    Commonwealth nation, except in the letters--"teeters toward
    hell" in <u>October Ferry to Gabriola</u>. <u>Under the Volcano</u> re-
    mains, however, Lowry's single masterpiece.

10 DAY, DOUGLAS. "Preface" to Malcolm Lowry, <u>Dark as the Grave</u>
    <u>Wherein My Friend Is Laid</u>. Edited by Douglas Day and
    Margerie Lowry. Harmondsworth: Penguin, pp. 5-18.
       Reprint of 1968.B17.

11 ENRIGHT, D. J. "Art Shares Its Bread: On Malcolm Lowry" in
    his <u>Man Is an Onion: Reviews and Essays</u>. London: Chatto
    & Windus, pp. 20-25.
       Reprint of 1967.B16.

12 FORRESTER, VIVIANE. "Toujours la quête éperdue." <u>La</u>
    <u>quinzaine littéraire</u>, no. 145 (July 16-31), pp. 7-8.
       Summarizes <u>October Ferry to Gabriola</u>, stressing the
    Adamic quest theme, and noting that for the first time
    Lowry's female character becomes a prisoner suffering
    anxiety.

13 GALAVIZ, JUAN MANUEL. "Las 25 estaciones de Malcolm Lowry."
    <u>La Palabra y el Hombre</u>, no. 1 (January-March), pp. 36-47.
       Asserting that in <u>Under the Volcano</u> and <u>Dark as the</u>
    <u>Grave</u> the face of Mexico is shown in alcohol, describes
    the 25 bars (their names associated with heaven or hell)
    which the various characters visit, and the circumstances
    under which they do so. ["Estaciones" carries associations
    with "stops" (i.e. bars), "seasons" (i.e. ages of man),
    and "stations" (as in "of the Cross").]

14 GARZILLI, ENRICO. <u>Circles Without Center: Paths to the Dis-</u>
    <u>covery and Creation of Self in Modern Literature</u>.
    Cambridge: Harvard University Press, pp. 135-38, 147.
       In a commentary on the relation between literary form
    and characters' sense of their own identity, the Consul's
    situation is seen as the case of a man who sees himself as

1972

an outcast, unable to abandon this identity without losing
himself. Symbolic and real elements in the novel are
specified.

15 GASS, WILLIAM H. "In Terms of the Toenail: Fiction and the
Figures of Life" in <u>Fiction and the Figures of Life</u>. New
York: Random House, Vintage Books, pp. 55–76.
Reprint of 1970.B14.

16 GUERARD, ALBERT J. "The Illuminating Distortion." <u>Novel</u>, 5,
no. 2 (Winter), 101–21.
An essay on fictional moments of odd behaviour and
strange response which reveal an author's or a character's
"forbidden psycho-sexual games," using scenes in versions
of <u>Under the Volcano</u> to show Geoffrey's latent desires for
homosexual and incestual relationships.

17 HEWITT, DOUGLAS. <u>The Approach to Fiction: Good and Bad Readings of Novels</u>. London: Longman group, p. 79.
Uses <u>Under the Volcano</u> as an example of a "fantastic"
work that nonetheless creates a sense of "credibility."

18 HUTCHISON, ALEXANDER. Review of Criticism. <u>Malahat Review</u>,
no. 22 (April), pp. 126–27.
A short, generally unfavourable review of Woodcock's
<u>Malcolm Lowry</u>.

19 LEARMONT, MARINA. "Modern Classics." <u>Books and Bookmen</u>, 17
(March), ix–xi.
A brief descriptive review of <u>Dark as the Grave</u>.

20 McCONNELL, FRANK D. "Lowry, Malcolm." <u>Collier's Encyclopedia</u>,
vol. 15. Crowell-Collier Educational Corp., p. 60.
A brief, inexact account of Lowry's life and work.

21 McMULLEN, LORRAINE. "Malcolm Lowry's 'The Forest Path to the
Spring.'" <u>The Canadian Fiction Magazine</u>, no. 5 (Winter),
pp. 71–77.
A commentary on symbol and theme which focusses on cyclic
flow, cyclic structure, and the idea of rebirth.

22 MAKOWIECKI, STEFAN. "An Analysis of Humour in the Works of
Malcolm Lowry." <u>Studia Anglica Posnaniensia: An International Review of English Studies</u>, 4, no. 1–2, 195–201.
Lowry's humour is less that of character and situation
than that of language, as in puns, deliberate misspellings,
and elaborate conceits. The more subtle humour of irony is
also present. The role of humour is to supply a sense of

naturalness, a reminder that Geoffrey is man as well as symbol.

23 MORLEY, PATRICIA A. The Mystery of Unity: Theme and Technique in the Novels of Patrick White. Montreal and London: McGill-Queen's University Press, pp. 50, 104, 150-51.
    Compares aspects of Under the Volcano with aspects of The Living and the Dead and Voss.

24 NEW, WILLIAM H. "The Canadian Short Story: Introduction." WLWE, 11, no. 1 (April), 7-9.
    Brief mention of Lowry in a short essay introducing a special issue of the journal, devoted to Canadian short fiction.

25 _____. "Gabriola: Malcolm Lowry's Floating Island." The Literary Half-yearly, 13, no. 1 (January), 108-18.
    Examines the techniques at work in October Ferry to Gabriola, including Lowry's use of literary allusion, his transformation of local signs and names into symbols, his imagery, and his Neoplatonic use of directions. Emphasizes the novel's exploration of the "contraries of the mind's eye."
    Revised: 1972.B26.

26 _____. "Gabriola: Malcolm Lowry's Floating Island" in his Articulating West. Toronto: New Press, pp. 196-206.
    Revision of 1972.B25.

27 _____. "Introduction" to Articulating West. Toronto: New Press, pp. xi-xxvi.
    Explores the symbolic landscapes represented by "East" and "West" in Canadian writing. Lowry is one of a number of writers whose works are used as examples.

28 _____. "Lowry, the Cabbala and Charles Jones" in his Articulating West. Toronto: New Press, pp. 189-95.
    Reprint of 1970.B27.

29 _____. "Modern Fiction" in Read Canadian: A Book about Canadian Books. Edited by Robert Fulford, David Godfrey, and Abraham Rotstein. Toronto: James Lewis & Samuel, pp. 219-27.
    Hear Us O Lord is seen as one of the key works of twentieth century Canadian fiction. Process is more important than character; chaos and paradise are seen as being necessarily in tension.

1972

30 NYE, ROBERT. "Books--A Warning to Health." New Statesman,
       84 (14 April), 498.
          Passing approval of the paperback reprint of Dark as the
       Grave.

31 PIDANCET-LAUDE, CORINNE. "Deux miroirs d'un même texte."
       Critique (Paris), 28 (November), 1015-16.
          Finds that, because of themes and characters, October
       Ferry to Gabriola mirrors Under the Volcano. The first,
       however, a conversationally simple account of a real jour-
       ney, differs from the symbolic and intellectually structured
       account of an interior journey.

32 PILOT, MARIAN. "Malcolm Lowry." Tygodnik Kulturalny, no. 42,
       p. 5.
          After a brief biographical summary, suggests that the
       events of October Ferry to Gabriola (flight from civiliza-
       tion, quest for an unattainable land), parallel the domi-
       nant patterns in Lowry's life.

33 RAAB, LAWRENCE. "The Two Consuls: Under the Volcano."
       Thoth, 12, no. 3 (Spring/Summer), 20-29.
          Suggests that the Consul is a kind of anti-tragic figure,
       eliciting neither pity nor fear, but exhaustion. The idea
       of tragedy, however, pervades the book. As the Consul
       takes the shape of --is--the book, readers are made aware
       of a "second" Consul, for whom values still have meaning
       and tragedy is not unreal.

34 ROBERTSON, ANTHONY. Review of New's Malcolm Lowry. West
       Coast Review, 7, no. 1 (June), 56-57.
          A critique of the book, claiming that Lowry is not a
       Canadian writer.

35 SKORODENKO, V. "Mal'kol'm Lauri." Foreword to Malcolm Lowry,
       U podnozhiya vulkana, Rasskazy, Lesnaya tropa k rodniku.
       Moscow: Progress (Mastera sovremennoy prozy: Kanada--
       "Masters of Modern Prose: Canada"--series), pp. 5-14.
          Asserts that Lowry was one of a few Western writers who
       understood and revealed the moral disintegration of per-
       sonality in the bourgeois world, the social sickness de-
       riving from social structure rather than from biology or
       metaphysics. Lowry found in Canada an approach to his
       ideal of health. After a brief biography, an analysis of
       Under the Volcano emphasizes Lowry's trust in history. He
       "wrote about abominations without forgetting the greatness
       of man."
          See also: 1974.B9.

1973 A BOOKS

1   BAXTER, EDITH LORRAINE. "The Mexican Setting in Under the
     Volcano." Master's thesis, The University of Alberta,
     109 pp.
        Argues that Lowry not only used details of Mexican
     geography and history in his novel but also built them into
     his symbolic structure. Mexican mythology—with its
     unique attitudes to death—offers the key to understanding
     the Consul, who becomes a true Mexican "sacrificial hero."

2   COMBS, JUDITH O. Malcolm Lowry, 1909-1957: An Inventory of
     His Papers in The Library of The University of British
     Columbia. Reference Publication No. 42. Vancouver: The
     University of British Columbia, 24 pp.
        Lists incoming and outgoing letters; poetry, prose, and
     music manuscripts; notes, notebooks, financial records,
     photographs, memorabilia, and miscellany. Lowry's criti-
     cism of Philipe Thoby-Marcelin is listed, but criticism of
     Lowry's work is not. An introduction provides a brief
     biographical account, a description of the inventory, and
     an outline of the process by which the collection went to
     The University of British Columbia. This last outline does
     not appear in the first (withdrawn) version of the guide,
     although the title, date, and the inventory itself remain
     unchanged.

3   DAY, DOUGLAS. Malcolm Lowry: A Biography. New York:
     Oxford University Press, xiii + 483 pp.
        Appended to the biography are a chronology and a selec-
     tive bibliography; the book is indexed and illustrated with
     photographs. The "official" biographer of Lowry was to
     have been Conrad Knickerbocker, who died in 1966, and whose
     notes (along with Margerie Lowry's papers) were then made
     available to Douglas Day, resulting in this biocritical
     study. The nine chapters and epilogue to a degree follow
     the structure of Under the Volcano, opening with Lowry's
     death, then moving backwards in time in order to account
     for it. The focus is on Lowry's less attractive side, his
     egotism, alcoholism and sexual anxieties, and on the accom-
     plishment of Under the Volcano.
        Chapters 2-5 comprise an essentially chronological
     account of Lowry's childhood, family relations and school
     life; his Cambridge affiliations, tense friendship with
     Conrad Aiken, and marriage to Jan Gabrial; his residence
     in Spain, New York, and Mexico; and the writing of Ultra-
     marine, "In Ballast to the White Sea," and Lunar Caustic.
     Chapters 6-9 continue the chronology, briefly describing

1973

the Canadian residence (though focussing more on the trips
to Mexico, Haiti and Europe), but interrupting the narrative
to provide an extended commentary on the making and meaning
of Under the Volcano. Summarizing its different versions,
Day claims it as "the greatest religious novel of this century," isolating what he calls the cthonic, human, political,
and magical levels of meaning, the last of which he does not
consider Lowry to have been serious about. The later works-
in-progress are briefly described; the short story "meditations" comprising Hear Us O Lord from Heaven Thy Dwelling
Place are considered almost all failures. The epilogue,
making some reference to Jung, returns to the Freudian position adumbrated earlier in the book when Day calls Lowry a
"classic oral-compulsive," explaining the fictional concerns
and the failure to complete the later works in terms of the
neuroses he identifies in the man.
Reprinted: 1975.A1.

*4   DOYEN, VICTOR. "Fighting the Albatross of Self." Ph.D. dis-
sertation, Université de Louvain, 341 pp.
Cited in correspondence from Doyen.

5   KILGALLIN, TONY. Lowry. Erin, Ontario: Press Porcépic,
226 pp. + a loose errata and addenda sheet.
Three chapters, illustrated by reprints of hermetic and
other symbolic designs, are followed by two appendices:
a checklist of the "magical library" of Charles Stansfeld-
Jones, and a list of 100 authors whose works Lowry appre-
ciated. The first chapter is biographical, its particular
feature being a series of verbatim quotations, based on
interviews and communications, from various people who knew
Lowry: Cambridge classmates, his doctor, Vancouver friends,
Stansfeld-Jones's widow, and a number of English, American,
and Canadian writers. The portrait of Maurice Carey,
Lowry's Vancouver landlord, is more sympathetic than that
offered by Day. The two succeeding chapters are exigetical,
relating Ultramarine and Under the Volcano to short stories
written for The Fortnightly or during the 1930s, and fol-
lowing the narrative line of each novel, identifying along
the way the geographic, cabbalistic, and literary allusions
and the standard symbolic associations implied by Lowry's
language. Alludes to Aiken's involvement in the writing of
Ultramarine, and traces the process of writing and rewriting
Under the Volcano. The account of Under the Volcano's
cinematic technique (reference is made to the theory and
practice of Eisenstein, Murnau, and others), together with
the account of Lowry's allusive technique, implies the symbolic dimensions of the author's work.

102

1973 B SHORTER WRITINGS

1   ALVAREZ, A. "Malcolm Lowry." The New York Times Book Review
    (4 November), pp. 3, 18, 20.
        Much of Lowry's anguish derived from being a writer,
    though, conscious only of himself, Lowry lacked a subject
    for his writing. Besides "for someone as dedicatedly...
    suicidal..., success was literally intolerable." A review
    of Day's biography by way of recapitulating Lowry's life.

2   BRADBURY, MALCOLM. "Malcolm Lowry as Modernist" in his Pos-
    sibilities. London, Oxford, and New York: Oxford Univer-
    sity Press, pp. 181-91.
        Reclaims Lowry as an English novelist, whose experimenta-
    tion and cosmopolitanism relate him to Beckett and Durrell.
    Behind these traits lies his individualistic romanticism,
    against which he introduces his note of tragedy. When
    modernism and romanticism diverge, irony is left. His
    incomplete efforts to explore the "principle of creativity"
    are traced.

3   B[RUCCOLI], M. J. "Malcolm Lowry's Film Treatment for Tender
    Is the Night" in Fitzgerald/Hemingway Annual 1972. Edited
    by Matthew J. Bruccoli and C. E. Frazer Clark, Jr. Dayton,
    Ohio: The National Cash Register Co., p. 337.
        A note indicating that the Lowry version expands but
    remains faithful to the Fitzgerald version, in another
    idiom.

4   BUITENHUIS, PETER. "Into One Tormented Mind." The Globe and
    Mail (Toronto) (15 December), p. 33.
        Reflections on the relation between an artist's life and
    work, by way of reviewing Kilgallin's and Day's studies.

5   BUSCH, FREDERICK. "But this is what it is to live in hell:
    William Gass's 'In the heart of the heart of the country.'"
    Modern Fiction Studies, 19, no. 1 (Spring), 97-108.
        Examines Gass's comments on Lowry's work, and finds the
    ferris wheel scene in Under the Volcano to lie behind Gass's
    portrait of hell in his Indiana short story.

6   COSTA, RICHARD HAUER. Review of Criticism. Modern Fiction
    Studies, 18, no. 4 (Winter), 612-18.
        Praise, in the context of a longer review, for Daniel
    Dodson's monograph and the memoirs collected in George
    Woodcock's Malcolm Lowry.

1973

7   CROSS, RICHARD K.   "Malcolm Lowry and the Columbian Eden."
    Contemporary Literature, 14, no. 1 (Winter), 19-30.
        Connects the Eden theme--the identification of Geoffrey
    with Adam, Eridanus with Paradise, Primrose Wilderness with
    Eve--with the tradition of American romance, including
    Melville and Faulkner.

8   DRABIKOWSKI, MAREK.   "Skorpion czyli jeszcze słówko o Konsulu"
    [The Scorpion, or One Word More about the Consul].   Więź,
    16, no. 7-8 (July-August), 221-24.
        Places Lowry among the great modern humanist writers.
    One theme of Under the Volcano is that of self-destruction,
    embodied in the image of the scorpion and the disintegrating
    rock.

9   GASS, WILLIAM H.   "Malcolm Lowry's Inferno."   The New York
    Review of Books, 20, no. 19 (29 November), 26-27.
        First of a two-part evocative commentary on--or recrea-
    tion of--Lowry's life.   Observes that drunkenness was pro-
    tection for Lowry against charges of weakness he could not
    face, which at the same time gave him, like Lear's fool,
    license to speak truth or lie.

10 _____.   "Malcolm Lowry's Inferno: II."   The New York Review
    of Books, 20, no. 20 (13 December), 28-30.
        Second of two parts.   A commentary on recent criticism,
    rejecting attempts to put formal limits on Lowry's books.
    Every journey in his books is a "spatial metaphor for
    'going in,'" and the works "have no boundaries."

11 GOMES LEITE, MAURÍCIO.   "Viagem Através do Vulcão" [A Trip
    through the Volcano].   Minas Gerais Suplemento Literário,
    no. 369 (22 September), pp. 1-5.
        An introduction to Lowry's life and works, translating
    extracts from reviews and from Under the Volcano, and pro-
    viding a bibliography, a list of the principal alcoholic
    beverages mentioned in Under the Volcano, and, in twelve
    numbered sections, brief accounts of symbols and patterns.
    Mentions in particular the importance of alcohol, Cabbala,
    the landscape, film (draws parallels with Godard, Bunuel,
    Losey, and Resnais), and the relation between Under the
    Volcano, Lowry's life, and his later fiction.

12 GRACE, SHERRILL E.   "Under the Volcano: Narrative Mode and
    Technique."   Journal of Canadian Fiction, 2, no. 2 (Spring),
    57-61.
        The fusion and function of the immediate and esoteric
    levels shape the novel's meaning.   Implied author, cryptic
    narrator, and major characters all contribute narrative

perspectives. The abrupt chapter distinctions intentionally interrupt traditional narrative flow, several scenes creating sensations of stasis which in turn illuminate the Consul's spiritual dilemma.

13 HACKING, NORMAN. "Malcolm Lowry: A Great Drunk?" The Province (Vancouver) (19 December), p. 40.
    An account of Lowry's life—a Greek tragedy of a man pursued by a demon—by way of review of Day's biography.

14 HOGG, JAMES. "A Look in the Volcano." The Vancouver Sun, "Leisure" supplement (23 November), p. 35A.
    A review of Day's biography, finding "compassion" for the "violent, debauched, half-demented creature" who is its subject.

15 KAZIN, ALFRED. "Bright Book of Life: American Novelists and Storytellers from Hemingway to Mailer. Boston and Toronto: Little, Brown, pp. 18-19, 296.
    Asserts that Under the Volcano is a novel of twentieth century political hell and the triumph of evil and that, by its poetic narrative rhythms, it is linked with the tradition of "epic novel." Lowry's theme, his political intelligence, shows in the conjunctions of his style: the link between the physical and moral worlds in a cosmic unity.
    Reprinted: 1974.B48.

16 KILGALLIN, TONY. "The Beaver and the Elephant." The Times Literary Supplement (26 October), p. 1300.
    Passing mention of Lowry in a general survey of Canadian writing.

17 KIRSCH, ROBERT. "The High Cost of Heightened Sensibility." Los Angeles Times (28 October), pp. 52, 62.
    Lowry, like Richard Wright and Eugene O'Neill, shared an obsession about writing to discover order and an equally obsessive imaginative memory that colours the facts of their own lives.

18 KNICKERBECKER [sic], CONRAD [KNICKERBOCKER]. "Malcolm Lowry i zewnętrzny krąg Piekła" [Malcolm Lowry and the Outer Circle of Hell]. Translated by J. L. Literatura na świecie, no. 11, pp. 128-29.
    Translation of 1963.B18.

19 KNICKERBOCKER, CONRAD. "Malcolm Lowry e il cerchio esterno dell'Inferno" in Malcolm Lowry, Caustico Lunare. Translated by Vincenzo Mantovani. Milan: Arnoldo Mondadori Editore, pp. 7-10.
    Translation of 1963.B18.

1973

20   LEHMANN-HAUPT, CHRISTOPHER. "Life in the Infernal Machine."
     The New York Times (8 November), p. 45.
         Asserts that Lowry's life--a "high-wire act in hell"--
     is well dramatized by Day's biography; Day's concern for
     Cocteau reflects Lowry's fascination with him.

21   McNEILL, C. G. "A Memory of Malcolm Lowry." American Review
     17: the magazine of new writing. Toronto, New York, and
     London: Bantam Books, pp. 35-39.
         Comments on Lowry's physique and phobias (anthropoid
     calluses and varicose veins caused by standing to dictate,
     he avers) by the doctor who attended him in Dollarton.
     Reprinted: 1975.B18.

22   MARKS, JASON. "The 'Hell in Paradise' of Malcolm Lowry." The
     New York Times (14 October), pp. 8, 11.
         A brief account of Lowry's composition of Under the Vol-
     cano serves as a preface to a descriptive evocation of a
     trip through Cuernavaca, tracing the Consul's footsteps.
     Advice about visiting Cuernavaca is appended (the article
     appears in the "Travel and Resorts" section).

23   MELLARD, JAMES M. "On Lowry: A Lifelong Search for Homes
     and Fathers." Chicago Tribune (4 November), sec. 7, p. 11.
         A summary, based on Day's biography, of the "Adamic"
     nature of Lowry's life.

24   NEWLOVE, DONALD. "Malcolm Lowry." The Village Voice Literary
     Supplement, 18 (8 November), 33-34.
         An emotionally charged account of Lowry's life, based
     on the biography by Donald Day [sic].

25   PAZ, OCTAVIO. "Landscape and the Novel in Mexico" in his
     Alternating Current. Translated by Helen R. Lane. New
     York: Viking, pp. 14-16.
         Translation of 1967.B29. Reprinted: 1974.B73.

26   PREYER, ROBERT. "Malcolm Lowry." Book World (The Washington
     Post), 7, no. 42 (28 October), 1, 8-9.
         Review of Donald [sic] Day's biography, claiming that it
     shows "respect and forbearance" throughout, that its "clin-
     ical profile" is helpful, but that the "model" literary
     criticism does not account for the "pain" of actually
     reading Lowry.

27   S., M. "Lowry i pisarze na szcycie" [Lowry and Writers at the
     Top]. Literatura, 46 (15 November), 6.

1973

Mentions Lowry's complex personality and Day's biography, and speaks of Under the Volcano as a "paradoxical reply" to Ulysses.

28 SCOTT, JACK. "More of the Hot Glare of Autopsy." Victoria Times (3 November), p. 22.
    A summary of some of the interviews in Kilgallin's Lowry.

29 SHEPPARD, R. Z. "The Misadventurer." Time, 102 (29 October), 84.
    Disputes Day's claim that Under the Volcano is the century's greatest religious novel--complaining about its self-absorption and "interior decorator's use of mysticism"--but finds it the greatest about alcoholism.

30 SMITH, A. J. M. "Malcolm Lowry 1909-1957" in The Canadian Century: English-Canadian Writing Since Confederation. The Book of Canadian Prose. Volume 2. Edited by A. J. M. Smith. Toronto: Gage, pp. 525-26.
    Biographical headnote to "Through the Panama."

31 TAYLOR, CHET. "The Other Edge of Existential Awareness: Reading of Malcolm Lowry's Under the Volcano." Literary Half-Yearly, 14, no. 1 (January), 130-50.
    Does not find any optimism, freedom, or transcendence at the end of the novel. There is no communication; the only possible concept of tragedy is an ironic one; and the only real problem is that of suicide.

32 WALSH, WILLIAM. Commonwealth Literature. London: Oxford University Press, pp. 84-85.
    Expatriates Lowry and Brian Moore illustrate the theme of the displaced person in Canadian fiction.

33 WATERSTON, ELIZABETH. Survey: A Short History of Canadian Literature. Toronto: Methuen, pp. 137-38.
    Expatriate Lowry had a major impact on Canadian writing.

34 WHITE, KAYCE. "Vancouver Was Eden." The Vancouver Sun (24 November), p. 46.
    An interview with Douglas Day, in which he observes that Conrad Knickerbocker "was totally absorbed by Lowry's personality" whereas he himself "became disdainful" of the writer.

35 WOODCOCK, GEORGE. Canada and the Canadians. Second edition. London: Faber & Faber; Toronto: Oxford University Press, pp. 254, 257-58.
    Reprint of 1970.B35.

107

1973

36   _____. Malcolm Lowry, in Supplement to <u>The Oxford Companion</u>
<u>to Canadian History and Literature</u>. Edited by William Toye.
Toronto, London, and New York: Oxford University Press,
pp. 219-20.
    Brief biocritical account.

1974 A BOOKS

1   BRADBROOK, M. C. <u>Malcolm Lowry: His Art and Early Life, a</u>
<u>study in transformation</u>. Cambridge: Cambridge University
Press, xiii + 170 pp.
    The prologue and six chapters of this book, dealing with
the effect of Lowry's early life on his work, are followed
by: an epilogue on Cambridge University at the time Lowry
was there (pp. 123-32); a summary of his letter to Jonathan
Cape [<u>See</u> 1965.A1] (pp. 133-37); reprints of "A Rainy Night"
and "Satan in a Barrel," two of Lowry's early stories published first in <u>The Fortnightly</u> (Leys School) (pp. 138-50);
extensive notes and an index. Two maps, of the Liverpool
and Vancouver areas, are also included, as is a chronology
and translations (p. ix) from some of the Norwegian poems
of Nordahl Grieg.
    Asserting the importance of biographical information as
a measure of the way Lowry transformed history into art,
the book provides details of Lowry's early family life and
school experience and shows how actual events turned into
recurrent fictional ones. His early sea voyage was magni-
fied, under the influence of Conrad Aiken and Nordahl Grieg,
into a series of visionary voyages and demonic storm scenes.
The early "Satan in a Barrel" relates clearly to the Faustian sensibilities of <u>Under the Volcano</u>. The personae of
the later novels and stories represent not disguises of the
self but simultaneous, though distinguishable, features of
the "integrated self." Residence in England later became
exile for him--<u>October Ferry to Gabriola</u> reveals how much
Canada had become Lowry's home. In <u>October Ferry</u>, England
and Cambridge represent hell, just as Mexico had earlier.
The Peter Cordwainer incidents in the book are drawn from
Lowry's memory of Paul Fitte's suicide in Cambridge in 1929.
The images of terror that lodged themselves in Lowry's memory led to his multilayered prose and constant revelation
of coincidences. A substantial claim is made for the quality of the later works.
    The epilogue describes The Tripos papers Lowry wrote,
points to his association with Charlotte Haldane, and mentions some of the people who were speaking or writing at
Cambridge at the time: Rosamund Lehmann, I. A. Richards,
Jacob Bronowski, and William Empson.

2   DECK, LAURA M.   "Myth as Metaphor: The Odyssey of Malcolm
     Lowry."   Ph.D. dissertation, Denison University (Granville,
     Ohio), 147 pp.
          A consideration of Lowry's use of myth--archetypes,
     oppositions, a supernatural universe, a spiralling sense
     of time and place--in his characterization of Wilderness,
     Trumbaugh, Plantagenet, and Firmin, and his rendering of
     their voyages.   An appendix (pp. 99-138) contains the
     transcript of an interview with Margerie Lowry on such
     subjects as Lowry's attitudes to myth and religion.

3   GRACE, SHERRILL E.   "The Voyage that Never Ends: Time and
     Space in the Fiction of Malcolm Lowry."   Ph.D. dissertation,
     McGill University, 186 pp.
          Argues that an opposition between Lowry's need for time
     (flow) and fear of space (static enclosure) informs his
     work, and affects the systems of order and movement (the
     images of wheel, ferryboat, borders) into which he recur-
     rently inquires.

*4 MAKOWIECKI, STEFAN.   "Malcolm Lowry and the Lyrical Convention
     of Fiction."   Ph.D. dissertation, University of Poznán,
     approx. 155 pp.
          Cited in correspondence from Makowiecki.

5   O'KILL, BRIAN LAWRENCE.   "A Stylistic Study of the Fiction of
     Malcolm Lowry."   Ph.D. dissertation, Cambridge University
     (Trinity College), 224 pp.
          Extended stylistic commentary on the novels and the
     early and late short stories, analyzing rhythm, syntax,
     lexicon, grammar, punctuation, and euphony.   An appendix
     (pp. 196-206) analyses Lowry's revisions of a single pas-
     sage of "Elephant and Colosseum."

1974 B SHORTER WRITINGS

1   AIKEN, CONRAD.   "Hambo ici et là."   Translated by Clarisse
     Francillon.   Les lettres nouvelles, 2-3 (May-June),
     pp. 263-79.
          Translation of excerpts from 1952.A1.

2   ALGREN, NELSON.   Malcolm Lowry.   The Critic (Chicago), 32
     (May-June), 63-66.
          By way of reviewing Day's biography, recounts the dramatic
     highlights of Lowry's engagement with Mexico, quotes from
     Rimbaud and Lowry, and finds that Under the Volcano ("an evo-
     cation of hell on earth") typifies Lowry's realization that
     his commitment to writing was his own maquina infernal.

1974

3   ANDERSON, DON and STEPHEN KNIGHT. "Introduction" to their
    edition <u>Cunning Exiles: Studies of Modern Prose Writers</u>.
    Sydney and London: Angus & Robertson, pp. 6–8.
      Mentions how Lowry, the exile, wrote of intellectual
    isolation in a "formally adventurous" way.

4   ANON. "Lowry, (Clarence) Malcolm." <u>The New Encyclopaedia
    Britannica</u>, Micropaedia, vol 6. Chicago, London, and
    Toronto: Encyclopaedia Britannica, pp. 362–63.
      A summary biographical entry, referring to the cinematic
    technique of <u>Under the Volcano</u>. Cross-references to vols.
    10 (p. 1222 "Western literature") and 13 (pp. 280 ff.) of
    the Macropaedia (the latter in Anthony Burgess's article,
    "Novel," being the more helpful) produce a series of pas-
    sing references to <u>Under the Volcano</u> as a "cult" and "sym-
    bolic" novel.

5   ANON. "The Mythopoetics of Mescal." <u>The Times Literary
    Supplement</u> (19 April), pp. 417–18.
      An account of Lowry's life, focussing on his Cambridge
    years and the composition of <u>Under the Volcano</u>, criticizing
    Day's and Kilgallin's commentary on Lowry's English
    background.

6   ANON. ["Your Reviewer."] "Malcolm Lowry." <u>The Times Liter-
    ary Supplement</u> (10 May), p. 503.
      A letter, in response to item 1974.B16, outlining the
    facts of Paul Fitte's suicide as he sees them, and noting
    that Lowry did not mention the suicide to his friends in
    the subsequent decade.

7   ANON. ["Your Reviewer."] "Malcolm Lowry." <u>The Times Liter-
    ary Supplement</u> (24 May), p. 558.
      A letter, in response to item 1974.B17, suggesting that
    Lowry gave desired evidence at the inquest into Paul Fitte's
    death, and that later stories were invented.

8   ANON. ["Your Reviewer."] "Malcolm Lowry." <u>The Times Liter-
    ary Supplement</u> (21 June), p. 671.
      A letter disputing the point made in item 1974.B61.

9   AUSTIN, PAUL W. "Russian Views of Lowry." <u>Canadian Litera-
    ture</u>, no. 62 (Autumn), pp. 126–28.
      A commentary on Russian translations of <u>Under the Volcano</u>
    and some of the stories, isolating V. Skorodenko's article
    (1972.B35) for summary, showing its "sophistication" and
    its "political bias."

10 BAREHAM, TERENCE. "After the Volcano: An Assessment of
    Malcolm Lowry's Posthumous Fiction." Studies in the Novel,
    6, no. 3 (Fall), 349-62.
       An attempt to demonstrate the structural and thematic
    integrity of Dark as the Grave and October Ferry to Gabriola.

11 BAXTER, CHARLES MORLEY. "Black Holes in Space: The Figure of
    the Artist in Nathanael West's Miss Lonelyhearts, Djuna
    Barnes' Nightwood, and Malcolm Lowry's Under the Volcano."
    Ph.D. dissertation, State University of New York (Buffalo),
    197 pp.
       In a chapter entitled "The Triumph of Humpty Dumpty:
    Shattered Art in Under the Volcano," considers each of the
    four main characters in relation to artistic theory, and
    likens Lowry's novel to Shelley's Alastor.

12 _____. "A Self-Consuming Light: Nightwood and the Crisis of
    Modernism." Journal of Modern Literature, 3, no. 5 (July),
    1175-87.
       Suggests that Modernism has resulted in a closed universe
    in which the novel only talks about its own isolation,
    "technical lavishness" increasing "in direct proportion to
    the narcissism of the work." Djuna Barnes' Nightwood pro-
    vides an extended illustration. Finds Lowry's character
    Firmin to be like Matthew O'Connor in Nightwood: a "priest"
    who "rises to delirium and silence." Lowry and Barnes are
    both isolated writers, preoccupied with the occult, reaching
    toward values only to find the demonic and the feverish.

13 BINNS, RONALD. "Lowry: Volcanic Man Not Dampened by Dollar-
    ton Rains." The Ubyssey (Vancouver), Page Friday supple-
    ment, 56, no. 9 (27 September), 4-5.
       An introductory survey of Lowry's life and work (with
    photographs of three of Lowry's Vancouver residences),
    concentrating on his Canadian sojourn and his images of
    Canada. Makes use of material in unpublished letters.

14 _____. "Wrestling with Lowry." The Vancouver Sun, "Leisure"
    supplement (18 October), p. 32A.
       A review of Kilgallin's book, asserting that Lowry
    "constructed his novels around the principle of deliberate
    ambiguity." See also: 1974.B52.

15 BOOTH, WAYNE, C. A Rhetoric of Irony. Chicago and London:
    The University of Chicago Press, p. 209.
       Refers to the tragedy of Under the Volcano, the novel's
    ironies being limited by the "human importance of the char-
    acters," by the fact that "caring is never discounted."

1974

16   BRADBROOK, M. C. "Malcolm Lowry." <u>The Times Literary Supple-</u>
      <u>ment</u> (3 May), p. 477.
            A letter to the editor, pointing out that Lowry's char-
      acter Cordwainer is based on Fitte's and another student's
      suicide; also notes that the later works are akin to the
      <u>nouveau roman,</u> and that his youthful experience remained
      alive in his imagination.

17   _____. "Malcolm Lowry." <u>The Times Literary Supplement</u>
      (17 May), p. 527.
            A letter, in response to item 1974.B6, quoting
      1929.B2.

18   _____. "Not in Mexico." <u>New Statesman</u>, 87 (5 April), 481.
            A review of Day's and Kilgallin's books, developing into
      a commentary on Lowry's later use of the <u>nouveau roman</u> and
      his traumatic responses to events from his childhood and
      youth.

19   BRADBURY, MALCOLM. "Lowry's Curse." <u>The Guardian</u>
      (Manchester), 110 (27 April), 20.
            An approving review of Day's biography, despite some
      concern about Lowry's true stature.

20   CALDER-MARSHALL, ARTHUR. "Portrait-montage de Malcolm Lowry."
      Translated by Clarisse Francillon. <u>Les lettres nouvelles</u>,
      no. 2-3 (May-June), pp. 15-23.
            Translation of 1967.B12.

21   _____ et al. "Books and Writers - Week 34." BBC Home Broad-
      cast (16 September), pp. 4-5. Produced by Dorian Cooke and
      narrated by Chris Bickerton.
            Following a discussion of Arnold Bennet, the programme
      turns to Calder-Marshall's memoir of Lowry at Cambridge.
      He disputes Bradbrook's version of Lowry's contact with
      Haldane, and doubts the "authenticity" of the later works.

22   CARROY, JEAN-ROGER. "De Melville à Lowry, et retour par nos
      abîmes." <u>Les lettres nouvelles</u>, no. 2-3 (May-June),
      pp. 123-69.
            Compares the family background of Melville and Lowry,
      then examines thematic parallels and parallel motifs in
      various works by the two writers. Particular attention is
      given to the mother and brother figures. "Axiological,
      ontological, and sexological" oppositions structure Lowry's
      world. The significance of "double" is investigated, and
      Melvillean identifications in <u>Lunar Caustic</u> noted.

23   CHRIST, RONALD. "The Grin and Gin Are There, but Not the
      Art." National Observer (Silver Springs, Md.), 13
      (26 January).
          Mixed reception of Day's perspective on Lowry.

24   CORSILLO, MARIO. "Lowry." Alive, no. 34 (Summer), p. 18.
          A review of Kilgallin's Lowry, criticizing it as "bour-
      geois," and condemning Lowry for his celebration of fascism
      and his contempt for the proletariat.

25   COSTA, RICHARD HAUER. "The Beaching of the Good Ship
      Solipsist: The Post-Volcano Malcolm Lowry." Paper read
      at Modern Language Association Seminar (28 December) in
      New York. Mimeographed.
          Applies to the later Lowry Nabokov's notion that auto-
      biography locates the central metaphors of one's life.
      Lowry's later fiction, however, is marred by his obsession
      with himself.

26   _____. "Conrad Aiken (1889–1973): The Wages of Neglect."
      Fiction International, 2/3, pp. 76–80.
          A memoir of an interview between the author and Aiken,
      during which one subject was Aiken's influence on Lowry.

27   _____. "Lowry's Forest Path: Echoes of Walden." Canadian
      Literature, no. 62 (Autumn), pp. 61–68.
          Sees the problem of Lowry's works to be that of Walden:
      the difficulty of separating the author from his fictional
      personae. The control in "The Forest Path to the Spring"
      comes from Lowry's use of a poetic pastoral mode. Lowry's
      and Thoreau's works are then compared, section by section,
      as searchers for transcendence of time and place.

28   _____. Review of Day's Biography. Comparative Literature,
      26, no. 4 (Fall), 354–58.
          A laudatory summation of Douglas Day's work.
      Condensed: 1975.B5.

29   CRESSWELL, ROSEMARY. "Malcolm Lowry's Other Fiction" in Cun-
      ning Exiles: Studies of Modern Prose Writers. Edited by
      Don Anderson and Stephen Knight. Sydney and London: Angus
      & Robertson, pp. 62–80.
          Finds that the interest of Ultramarine, Lunar Caustic,
      and Hear Us O Lord lies in their development of the themes
      and vision that are expressed in Under the Volcano, and in
      their demonstration of the "cerebral" and "literary" nature
      of Lowry's craftsmanship. Summarizes Ultramarine; suggests
      that Lunar Caustic is memorable not as social realism but

1974

for its surrealist vision and study of personal isolation; and focusses on <u>Hear Us O Lord</u>, which is a unified book "about the writing of the book," about the "psychic state that triggers the creative impulse" and the complex transformation of fact into fiction. Examines symbolic patterns, point of view, themes of love, creativity, and quest. Suggests that the use of oxymorons stylistically renders the thematic paradoxes and dualities, that the cinematic techniques are part of Lowry's rejection of conventional narrative structures, and that the mixture of musical modes aptly expresses his "permutational" and non-linear development of themes. <u>Dark as the Grave</u> emphasizes Lowry's control over the "illusion" of autobiography, which critics have misinterpreted.

30   CROSS, RICHARD K. "<u>Moby-Dick</u> and <u>Under the Volcano</u>; Poetry from the Abyss." <u>Modern Fiction Studies</u>, 20, no. 2 (Summer), 149-56.
     Explores parallels in sensibility between the two novels, finding Ishmael's "void" as the villain in both, but noting the differences which Geoffrey's irony causes.

31   _____. "<u>Under the Volcano</u>: A Book of the Dead." Paper read at Modern Language Association Seminar (28 December) in New York. Mimeographed.
     An extended commentary on links between love and death in the novel.

32   DAY, DOUGLAS. "Writing the Biography of an Unknown Genius." <u>The Chronicle of Higher Education</u>, 8, no. 18 (4 February), 11.
     Reflections on the subjective art and the craft of biographical writing, and on his own difficulties marshalling the compassion and objectivity needed to try to appreciate Lowry and, "fictively," to recreate his life.

33   DE MARGERIE, DIANE. "Correspondance et correspondances." <u>Les lettres nouvelles</u>, no. 2-3 (May-June), pp. 205-17.
     Reprint of 1969.B15.

34   DODSON, DANIEL B. "Manifest Mysteries in <u>Under the Volcano</u>." Paper read at Modern Language Association Seminar (28 December) in New York. Mimeographed.
     Suggests that the revisions of the novel may have resulted in some particular narrative ambiguities--e.g. the identity of Weber, the likelihood of Yvonne's faithlessness--but that they may be deliberate.

35 DOYEN, VICTOR. "La genèse d''Au-dessous du Volcan.'" Les
    lettres nouvelles, no. 2–3 (May–June), pp. 87–122.
        Biographical background concerning Lowry's life in Spain,
    New York, Mexico and Canada prefaces commentary on the novel.
    Lowry introduced certain elements into the novel's drafts
    after experiencing each place and reading various books:
    Aiken, Ouspensky, etc. Traces the changes in the various
    versions, the alterations in the characters, the introduc-
    tion of cabbalistic elements, the correction of Spanish
    quotations, and observes that final form expressed the
    author's uneasiness well, bringing him celebrity but not
    peace.

36 EDMONDS, DALE. "'__': A Topography of the Typography of
    Under the Volcano." Paper read at Modern Language Associa-
    tion Seminar (28 December) in New York. Mimeographed.
        Begins with an account of the correspondence between
    Lowry and Albert Erskine concerning the typography of the
    book, Lowry believing that the appearance was an important
    contributor to meaning. Examines various technical depar-
    tures from language: quoted silences, box borders, signs,
    and numbers ("666" is associated with the medical imagery/
    phobias in the book).

37 _____. "The Voyage Begins: Toward an Understanding of
    Malcolm Lowry." Journal of Modern Literature, 4, no. 1
    (September), 133–38.
        An extended review of the books by Day, Costa, and
    Kilgallin, approving of the first two.

38 ENRIGHT, D. J. "Inside the Volcano." The Listener, 91
    (11 April), 474–75.
        A review of books by Day and Kilgallin, concentrating
    on the myths that have developed around Lowry's life.

39 FARRELL, J. G. "Late Lowry." New Statesman, 88 (19 July),
    86–88.
        A review of Bradbrook's book, disagreeing with her
    claims for Lowry's later works (finding self-obsession
    rather than structure in them) and approving Day's claim
    that he was a one-book author. Acknowledges several points
    on which Bradbrook's book corrects Day's.

40 FRANCILLON, CLARISSE. "Lowry, personnage de Conrad Aiken."
    Les lettres nouvelles, no. 2–3 (May–June), pp. 261–79.
        Editorial comments on 1974.B1.

1974

41 _____ [?]. Notes. <u>Les lettres nouvelles</u>, no. 2-3 (May-June),
pp. 222, 258-59.
Notes explaining allusions in French translations of
several poems and letters.

42 GRACE, SHERRILL. "More Light on Lowry." <u>Journal of Canadian
Fiction</u>, 3, no. 1 (Winter), 105-07.
A review of books by Day, Costa, and Kilgallin, comment-
ing on the merits and shortcomings of each.

43 GRIFFITH, MALCOLM. Review of Costa and Day. <u>Western Human-
ities Review</u>, 28 (Summer), 274-77.
Claims that Lowry is a writer we turn to for a mirror
and explanation of our own lives. Distinguishes between
critic-academicians (Costa, Day when discussing the "levels"
of <u>Under the Volcano</u>) and straightforward biographical
story-tellers.

44 GUNN, DREWEY WAYNE. "The Volcano and the Barranca" in his
<u>American and British Writers in Mexico 1556-1973</u>. Austin
and London: University of Texas Press, pp. 164-80.
Using letters and Conrad Aiken's <u>Ushant</u> as major sources,
recounts Lowry's involvement with Mexico and the drafts of
<u>Under the Volcano</u>, and provides an elucidation of actual
Mexican political events during the 1930s. Critical commentary on the novels and poems is secondary to the exploration of Lowry's love-hate involvement with Mexico.

45 HAGEN, WILLIAM MORICE. "Realism and Creative Fable in
<u>Nostromo</u> and <u>Under the Volcano</u>: An Approach to Technique
and Structure." Ph.D. dissertation, University of Iowa,
205 pp.
Shows how two writers dramatize European-Latin American
contacts; for Lowry the individual consciousness provides
the moral structure of history.

46 HILL, ART. "The Alcoholic on Alcoholism." <u>Canadian Litera-
ture</u>, no. 62 (Autumn), pp. 33-48.
Avers that above all, <u>Under the Volcano</u> is about drunkenness, and finds the Consul totally consistent with what
is known about alcoholics, including "the inspired duplic-
ity of the alcoholic mind." Reviews various critical re-
sponses, rejecting Day's assertion that Lowry was essentially
happy and also all attempts to interpret only at a symbolic
level, asserting the credibility of the Consul's everyday
world, including his unclear motivation and his vagueness
about his past.
Reprinted: 1975.B16.

47 HOCHSCHILD, ADAM. "The Private Volcano of Malcolm Lowry."
    Ramparts, 12, no. 8 (March), 45-48.
        In part a review of Day's biography, in part a rejection
    of William Gass's claim (1973.B9-10) that Lowry is not po-
    litical, praises Lowry's work because it reaches for a full
    human response and not just for the intellectual delight of
    verbal play. Also provides a biographical summary, and
    observes that Under the Volcano's greatness is of a psy-
    chological kind.

48 KAZIN, ALFRED. Bright Book of Life: American Novelists and
    Storytellers from Hemingway to Mailer. London: Secker &
    Warburg, pp. 18-19, 296.
        Reprint of 1973.B15.

49 KIDD, ANDREW. "Complaint Holds Up Biography of Sussex Writer."
    Evening Argus (Brighton) (10 January).
        A brief account of Lowry's life and death.

50 ____. "A Golden Boy Retreats to Die." Evening Argus
    (Brighton) (18 April).
        An account of Lowry's death, based on details in Day's
    biography.

51 KILGALLIN, TONY. "Malcolm Lowry." The Times Literary Supple-
    ment (9 August), p. 858.
        A rejection of points made in item 1974.B5 and an
    announcement that Jan Gabrial is still living.

52 ____. "Retort!" The Vancouver Sun (22 November), p. 30A.
        Reply to item 1974.B14, asserting the contradictoriness
    of much of Lowry's private life.

53 KIM, SUZANNE. "Les oeuvres de l'adolescence." Les lettres
    nouvelles, no. 2-3 (May-June), pp. 69-86.
        Revision of 1965.B14.

54 KLINCK, CARL F. and R. E. WATTERS. "Malcolm Lowry" in Cana-
    dian Anthology. Edited by Carl F. Klinck and R. E. Watters.
    Third edition. Toronto: Gage, pp. 359-60.
        Updated version of 1966.B16.

55 LEWIS, R. W. B. "A Biographical Work of Art." The Virginia
    Quarterly Review, 50, no. 3 (Summer), 441-44.
        An elegantly complimentary review of Day's "meditative"
    biographical process, which implicitly accepts his judg-
    ments of Lowry's life and work. Finds Lowry's later works,
    with their "obscurely foreign-language titles," muddled and
    forgettable.

1974

56 LORENZ, CLARISSA. "Appelez ça accident." Translated by
    Clarisse Francillon. Les lettres nouvelles, no. 2-3
    (May-June), pp. 49-66.
        Translation of 1970.B21.

57 LOWRY, MARGERIE. "Introductory Note" to Malcolm Lowry, Ultra-
    marine. Revised edition. Harmondsworth: Penguin,
    pp. 7-10.
        Reprint of 1962.B23.

58 _____. "Nota della curatrice" in Malcolm Lowry, Il Traghetto
    per Gabriola. Translated by Vincenzo Mantovani. Milan:
    Arnoldo Mondadori Editor, pp. 375-77.
        Translation of 1970.B23.

59 LUCKETT, RICHARD. "On a Dead Volcano." Spectator, 232
    (11 May), 574-75.
        Locates some of the errors in Day's biography and adds
    anecdotal material concerning Lowry at Cambridge. Finds
    Lowry's life to be characterized by shyness, fear, alco-
    holic thirst, and a child-mother relationship with women.
    Expresses suspicion of "the Lowry cult."

60 MacSKIMMING, ROY. "Day on Lowry: A Distinctly Petty View."
    Saturday Night, 89, no. 4 (April), 38, 40.
        Complains that Day does not deal compassionately with
    Lowry's weaknesses and waste of genius.

61 MALEY, F. W. "Malcolm Lowry." The Times Literary Supplement
    (31 May), p. 586.
        A letter suggesting that Under the Volcano was never a
    best seller.

62 MENANO, ANTÓNIO AUGUSTO. "Um Escritor Maldito – Malcolm
    Lowry" [A Damned writer – Malcolm Lowry]. Minas Gerais
    Suplemento Literario (Brazil), 16 (March), 11.
        Identifies several strands of Under the Volcano: saga
    of solitude; romance about alcoholism; study of jealousy,
    of destiny as the imperative coordinate of life; political
    philosophy. The Consul represents the insurmountable rup-
    ture between heroes and the world. A note to the article
    indicates that this is a reprint from an offset publication,
    Escora (Coimbra, Portugal), 2, undated (unlocated).

63 MERCIER, VIVIAN. "Malcolm Lowry." Commonweal, 99, no. 17
    (1 February), 445-46.
        Considers Day's biography to perform "nursemaid" ser-
    vices to a "bad" novelist.

64   MEYERS, JEFFREY. "<u>Angst</u> and Art." <u>Critical Quarterly</u>, 16,
        no. 4 (Winter), 370–77.
            A review of works on Kafka, Lowry, and Mann, which
        approves of Douglas Day's placing him in the tradition of
        the <u>poête maudit</u>, and compares his art to Kafka's, thriving
        on a self-destructive impulse.

65   MOSS, JOHN. <u>Patterns of Isolation in English Canadian Fiction</u>.
        Toronto: McClelland & Stewart, pp. 17, 21–23, 33, 36.
            Brief reference to Lowry's ability to match tone with
        his sense of exile. Lowry had a "garrison" sensibility,
        and wrote as an insider.

66   MUGGERIDGE, MALCOLM. "Books." <u>Esquire</u>, 81, no. 4 (April),
        14.
            By way of reviewing Day's biography, decides that "drunks
        and religious maniacs belong in the same limbo."

67   NADEAU, MAURICE. Introduction, "Chronologic," and "Ouvrages
        de Malcolm Lowry publiés en français." <u>Les lettres
        nouvelles</u>, no. 2–3 (May–June), pp. 5–12.
            Data concerning Lowry and the contributors to this spe-
        cial Lowry issue of the magazine.

68   NEW, W. H. "Lowry By Day." <u>Canadian Literature</u>, no. 61
        (Summer), pp. 100–02.
            A review of Day's biography, questioning its commentary
        on the Canadian years, its Freudianism, and its critical
        premises, while praising its detail on Lowry's Spanish
        connections.

69   NOXON, GERALD. "Le Jeune Malcolm." <u>Les lettres nouvelles</u>,
        no. 2–3 (May–June), pp. 24–30.
            Translation of 1964.B33.

70   O'KILL, BRIAN. "Malcolm Lowry." <u>The Times Literary Supple-
        ment</u> (26 April), p. 447.
            A letter criticizing the <u>TLS</u> review (item 1974.B5) of
        Day's biography, pointing to certain errors in both the
        biography and the review. Emphasizes particularly that
        the published short story "Under the Volcano" is not the
        first (1936) version of the novel.

71   OLSON, STANLEY. "A Lush Talent?" <u>Books and Bookmen</u>, 19,
        no. 9 (June), 86–88.
            Finds Lowry fortunate in his biographer, and Day unfor-
        tunate in his subject, for Lowry's work has probably been
        overrated.

1974

72 PAGNOULLE, CHRISTINE. "Par-delà les miroirs." <u>Les lettres</u>
   <u>nouvelles</u>, no. 2-3 (May-June), pp. 170-83.
   Beginning with the final chapter of <u>Under the Volcano</u>,
   focusses on the theme of identity in the novel, examining
   Geoffrey's relationships with Hugh, Blackstone, and others.
   The images of the dog (anagram of god), fall, and ascension
   are considered. Based on a study presented to the University of Liège in 1972.

73 PAZ, OCTAVIO. "Landscape and the Novel in Mexico" in his
   <u>Alternating Current</u>. Translated by Helen R. Lane. London:
   Wildwood House, pp. 14-16.
   Reprint of 1973.B25.

74 POWNALL, DAVID E. <u>Articles on Twentieth Century Literature:</u>
   <u>An Annotated Bibliography 1954 to 1970</u>. New York: Kraus-
   Thomson Organization, pp. 2386-96.
   Lists 42 items on Lowry (L956-L998).

75 PURDY, AL. "Lowry: A Memoir." <u>Books in Canada</u>, 3, no. 1
   (January-February), 3-4.
   Recollection of visiting Lowry with Downie Kirk and
   Curt Lang, and appreciating the novelist's "attractive"
   personality.

76 RUSSELL, JOHN. "A Fugitive from Pride." <u>Modern Age</u>, 18,
   no. 2 (Spring), 211-13.
   An approving summary of Day's biography.

77 SAVAGE, MEREDYTH. "After Douglas Day: <u>Lowry</u> and Tony
   Kilgallin." <u>Prism International</u>, 13, no. 3 (Spring),
   107-16.
   Contrasts Kilgallin's "symbolistic and analytic" approach
   to Lowry with Day's "gestalt...outlook," referring to spe-
   cific differences in information and judgment.

78 STERN, JAMES. "Ma première rencontre avec Malcolm Lowry."
   Translated by Françoise and Tony Cartano. <u>Les lettres</u>
   <u>nouvelles</u>, no. 2-3 (May-June), pp. 31-48.
   Reprint of 1968.B46.

79 TIESSEN, PAUL. Introduction and Notes to his edition of
   Malcolm and Margerie Lowry, "A Few Items Culled From What
   Started Out To Be a Sort of Preface to a Film-Script."
   <u>White Pelican</u>, 4, no. 2 (Spring), 2-5, 19-20.
   Editorial notes concerning the genesis of the film-
   script, theories of film-making, and the condition of
   the manuscript on which this edition is based. The Lowry
   preface itself appears on pp. 5-18.

80   TOYNBEE, PHILIP. "Message in a Bottle." <u>The Observer</u>
      (7 April), p. 36.
         Observes, in a review of Day's biography, that humility
      and false pride characterize the lives of Lowry, Fitzgerald,
      and Dylan Thomas. Day's Freudianism is attacked; Lowry's
      alcoholism is considered at moderate length.

81   VEITCH, DOUGLAS W. "The Fictional Landscape of Mexico: Read-
      ings in D. H. Lawrence, Graham Greene and Malcolm Lowry."
      Ph.D. dissertation, Université de Montréal, 366 pp.
         Asserts that the general response to Mexico is one of
      alienation and isolation, and that writers relate a land
      of extremes to metaphysical explanations. Lawrence works
      with archetypal journeys; Greene recognizes the limitations
      of the human condition; Lowry shuttles between these expan-
      sive and truncated views, identifying the landscape extremes
      with basic human contradictions. The three treatments to-
      gether provide a fictional landscape of Mexico.

82   WALKER, RONALD GARY. "Blood, Border, and <u>Barranca</u>: The Role
      of Mexico in the Modern English Novel." Ph.D. dissertation,
      University of Maryland, 409 pp.
         Examines Lowry's use of a Mexican setting in a context
      involving Lawrence, Huxley, Greene, and Waugh. Lowry's
      symbolic landscape is richest.

83   WEST, REBECCA. "Great Thirst for Love." <u>Sunday Telegraph</u>
      (London) (7 April).
         As a review of Day's and Kilgallin's books, supplies a
      critique of Day's comments on Lowry's politics--pointing to
      his reaction against Haldane's leftwing views. Also
      attacks the general overestimation of Lowry's prose (which
      "combines the rhythms of garrulity and asthma") but defends
      their judgment of <u>Under the Volcano</u> because its universal
      theme demands readers' identification with the Consul.

84   WOODCOCK, GEORGE. "The Myth of Malcolm Lowry." <u>Commentary</u>,
      57, no. 3 (March), 71-73.
         Reflections on the way in which Lowry's life was trans-
      formed into a kind of myth, on the reasons for this change,
      and on the difficulties of writing his biography. Adds a
      corrective note, on the London pubs Lowry frequented in
      the 1930s, to Day's account of the period.

85   _____. "Suffering Terminal Genius." <u>Books in Canada</u>, 3,
      no. 1 (January/February), 2-3.
         In reviewing Day's and Kilgallin's books, explores the
      "strange case" of the artist transformed into the hero and

1974

the "miracle" of self-liberation represented by <u>Under the Volcano</u>.

86　YACOUBOVITCH, R. I.　"Cassure, canal, baranquilla."　<u>Les lettres nouvelles</u>, no. 2-3 (May-June), pp. 184-204.
An examination of the style of "Through the Panama."
Independent simultaneous phrases create logical equivalences; puns, alliteration, and rhythm are techniques for humour and/or logical shifts; proper names, and mixtures of British and Canadian English allow other "telegraphed" meaning.

<u>1975 A BOOKS</u>

1　DAY, DOUGLAS.　<u>Malcolm Lowry</u>.　New York:　Dell, Laurel Editions, 444 pp.
Reprint of 1973.A3.

2　KOERBER, BETTY TURNER.　"Humor in the Work of Malcolm Lowry."
Ph.D. dissertation, University of California at Los Angeles, 191 pp.
Observes that Lowry was a tragicomic, not a tragic, writer, whose comic method is influenced by the cinema.
His linking of humour with his own personality led to humorous passages occurring in his work when he was attempting to reconcile opposites or preserve himself against disintegration.　His techniques recur from his early school stories to his late work, but they mesh completely with form and theme only once, in <u>Under the Volcano</u>.

3　LOWRY, MARGERIE, ed.　<u>Malcolm Lowry:　Psalms and Songs</u>.　New York and Scarborough, Ontario:　New American Library, Meridian, 308 pp.
An anthology, with a preface explaining the selection; a biographical note; and a brief bibliography of the English-language editions of Lowry's works.　The anthologized pieces include <u>Lunar Caustic</u>, five early Lowry stories (including "June the 30th, 1934," not published elsewhere), and four later ones (including "Enter One in Sumptuous Armour," not published elsewhere).　They are brought together with twelve memoirs and commentaries.　Of the secondary works, only those by A. C. Nyland and Norman Matson--and the English version of Clarisse Francillon's work--are previously unpublished.　C. G. McNeill's memoir is retitled.
<u>See</u> 1975.B14, B18, B19, B27.

4   ST. PIERRE, PAUL MATTHEW. "The Quest Motif in Malcolm Lowry's
    Novel, <u>Hear Us O Lord from Heaven Thy Dwelling Place</u>."
    Graduating essay, The University of British Columbia, 69 pp.
        Argues the unity of the book by investigating multiple
    quest analogues and demonstrating the ways in which Lowry
    has interrelated them.

5   TIBBETTS, BRUCE HAMILTON. "Malcolm Lowry's Long Night's Jour-
    ney Into Day: The Quest for Home." Ph.D. dissertation,
    University of Tulsa, 169 pp.
        Sees the quest for home (both physical and spiritual)
    as the central image in Lowry's work, and traces it through
    his published fiction. Characters tempted away from home,
    exiled from home, or unable to leave for home all find them-
    selves facing crises.

1975 B SHORTER WRITINGS

1   BALDESHWILER, EILEEN. "The Uses of Wilderness." Paper read
    at Modern Language Association Seminar (29 December) in
    San Francisco. Mimeographed.
        Finds the character of Wilderness interesting because
    he is an "emblem" of Lowry's concern for man-as-writer.
    Lowry's capacity for metaphor--the visionary nightmares of
    burning houses and ships in storms as well as the attempts
    to express musical integration--is one of his greatest
    strengths.

2   BINNS, RONALD. "Lowry's Anatomy of Melancholy." <u>Canadian</u>
    <u>Literature</u>, no. 64 (Spring), pp. 8-23.
        Lowry's <u>Ultramarine</u> blends the "modernist psychological"
    and "proletarian realist" traditions in fiction for various
    ends, among which is a "dramatic analysis" of Hilliot's
    melancholy which derives from and comments upon Lowry's own
    sense of himself as author. The "arcane medical rhetoric"
    and the fabric of metaphor support this theme, and reveal
    that the novel is in fact quite tightly structured.

3   BOULTON, MARJORIE. <u>The Anatomy of the Novel</u>. London and
    Boston: Routledge & Kegan Paul, pp. 136-37.
        Brief mention of <u>Under the Volcano</u> in a commentary on
    uses of landscape in fiction. The real Mexico becomes the
    symbolic alien world of an alienated man, in which amusing
    linguistic misunderstandings represent a world of
    non-communication.

1975

4   CORRIGAN, MATTHEW. "Malcolm Lowry: The Phenomenology of
    Failure." Boundary 2, 3, no. 2 (Winter), 407–42.
        Explores the extent to which Lowry failed to appeal to
    his age and critics' failure immediately to recognize his
    talent reflects preconceptions about language and literary
    form. Lowry's mental splitting of reality is discussed
    (the critical method reflects the technique of "Through the
    Panama"), as is his recurrent failure to deal objectively
    with his fear of consciousness. Moral and aesthetic quests
    coalesce in his repeated drive for completed style and
    thought, but the man himself always intervened. The Dantean
    model and traditional senses of novel form defeated him.
    The narratives break down into moments of stasis, reflect-
    ing on themselves--the best late works being the novellas.
    Modern fiction's focus on the "vehicle" of the story line
    alters the sense of narrative, which Lowry, trying to make
    story out of consciousness, failed quite to establish. His
    "predilection for self-realization" undermined action in
    his works, yet the failure provides a clear statement
    "against our age" which is itself part of his accomplishment.

5   COSTA, RICHARD HAUER. Review of Day's Biography. South
    Atlantic Quarterly, 74, no. 2 (Spring), 269–70.
        A briefer version of 1974.B28.

6   DAHLIE, HALLVARD. "Lowry's Debt to Nordahl Grieg." Canadian
    Literature, no. 64 (Spring), pp. 41–51.
        Demonstrates the parallel passages in Ultramarine and
    The Ship Sails On, and refers to a number of Lowry's simple
    literal borrowings. What is significant is Lowry's trans-
    formation of Grieg's realism into a "complex aesthetic."
    Lowry's comic vision is also contrated with Grieg's "bleak
    determinism."

7   _____. "Malcolm Lowry's Ultramarine." Journal of Canadian
    Fiction, 3, no. 4, 65–68.
        Ultramarine's blending of realistic and comic modes
    reflects the duality in Lowry's view of man. His tech-
    nique juxtaposes notions of individual isolation and com-
    munity structure. An explication of the novel follows.

8   _____. "New Direction in Canadian Fiction" in Commonwealth
    Literature and the Modern World. Edited by Hena
    Maes-Jelinek. Brussels: Didier, 1975, pp. 169–74.
        Lowry's comic vision finds expression in later Canadian
    writers, like Kroetsch, Godfrey, Cohen. Their rejection
    of conventional realism and their search for new modes of
    expression relate to Lowry's own.

9 _____. "On Nordahl Grieg's The Ship Sails On." The International Fiction Review, 2, no. 1 (January), 49–53.
Mentions Lowry in the context of an analysis of Grieg's
novel.

10 DONALDSON, GEORGE. "A Life of Malcolm Lowry." Cambridge
Quarterly, 6, no. 4, 376–91.
A brief biography, applying Johnsonian criteria to Day's
biography, locating its strengths and weaknesses.

11 DURRANT, GEOFFREY. "Aiken and Lowry." Canadian Literature,
no. 64 (Spring), pp. 24–40.
A study of the indebtedness of Ultramarine to Blue Voyage, of Lowry's adaptation of Aiken's use of the Ulysses,
Psyche, and Narcissus myths, and of their consistency with
Neoplatonic interpretations. The study reveals more independence from Aiken and more craftsmanship than early
criticism suggested.

12 _____. "A Classical Myth Transformed – Lowry's 'The Forest
Path to the Spring.'" Paper read at Modern Language Association Seminar (29 December) in San Francisco.
Mimeographed.
Suggests that reading Lowry's work in the context of its
literary tradition may be a better approach than pursuing
its autobiographical elements. The classical influences
upon Wordsworth and Coleridge are used to illuminate the
Eridanus references, the path symbolism, and the philo-
sophic/directional polarities of Lowry's story. Sweden-
borgian paths and correspondences also reveal metaphysical
depths. No hermetic knowledge is required to appreciate
the story; what is needed is a readiness to sympathize with
Lowry's uncontemporary, traditional vision of nature as a
language of the spiritual world.

13 EDMONDS, DALE. "Mescallusions, or the Drinking Man's Under
the Volcano." Paper read at Modern Language Association
Seminar (29 December) in San Francisco. Mimeographed.
A catalogue of Geoffrey's alcoholic intake, with two
appendices: one specifying date, place, beverage, amount,
and circumstances; the other listing 72 alcoholic beverages
mentioned in the novel. A third appendix [not seen] was to
have contained definitions of mescal.

14 FRANCILLON, CLARISSE. "My Friend Malcolm" in Malcolm Lowry:
Psalms and Songs. Edited by Margerie Lowry. Translated by
Suzanne Kim. New York and Scarborough, Ontario: New Amer-
ican Library, Meridian, pp. 87–96.
Translation of 1960.B8.

1975

15   GRACE, SHERRILL E. "Malcolm Lowry's Magic Realism: The Study
       of an Aesthetic." Paper read at Modern Language Associa-
       tion Seminar (29 December) in San Francisco. Mimeographed.
            Considers Lowry's "protean" view of life and art, using
       "Ghostkeeper" as the main example.

16   HILL, ART. "The Alcoholic on Alcoholism: Lowry's Unique
       Achievement in Under the Volcano" in The Canadian Novel in
       the Twentieth Century. Edited by George Woodcock. Toronto:
       McClelland & Stewart, New Canadian Library No. 115,
       pp. 87-102.
            Reprint of 1974.B46.

17   JOHNSON, JAY. "Under Malcolm Lowry." Essays on Canadian
       Writing, no. 2 (Spring), pp. 67-69.
            A review, contrasting Kilgallin's and Bradbrook's
       approaches to Lowry, applauding Bradbrook's explanation of
       fictional transformation.

18   McNEILL, C. G. "Malcolm Lowry Visits the Doctor" in Malcolm
       Lowry: Psalms and Songs. Edited by Margerie Lowry. New
       York and Scarborough, Ontario: New American Library,
       Meridian, pp. 102-05.
            Reprint of 1973.B21.

19   MATSON, NORMAN. "Second Encounter" in Malcolm Lowry: Psalms
       and Songs. Edited by Margerie Lowry. New York and
       Scarborough, Ontario: New American Library, Meridian,
       pp. 97-101.
            An evocative memoir of meeting Lowry twice--in 1934 and
       then twenty years later in Paris--and of being impressed by
       his solitariness and his artistic commitment.

20   MORRIS, WRIGHT. About Fiction: Reverent Reflections on the
       Nature of Fiction with Irreverent Observations on Writers,
       Readers, & Other Abuses. New York: Harper & Row,
       pp. 171-72.
            Finds Mexico appropriate for Under the Volcano: modern,
       romantic, full of contrasts.

21   MULLER, C. H. Review of Bradbrook's Malcolm Lowry. Unisa
       English Studies, 9, pp. 53-54.
            A summary of the book's contents, questioning Lowry's
       quality but complimenting the study of his Cambridge years.

22   NEW, WILLIAM H. Among Worlds: An Introduction to Modern Com-
       monwealth and South African Fiction. Erin, Ontario: Press
       Porcépic, pp. 117, 119-21, 183, 248.

Lowry's exploration of dualities, exemplified primarily
in the short stories and <u>October Ferry to Gabriola</u>, takes
his characters in pursuit of an order which had intrinsic
meaning. A brief introductory bibliography is appended.

23 _____. "Some Comments on the Editing of Canadian Texts" in
<u>Editing Canadian Texts: Papers given at the Conference on</u>
<u>Editorial Problems University of Toronto November 1972</u>.
Edited by Francess G. Halpenny. Toronto: Hakkert,
pp. 24–28.
Comments on various kinds of editorial problems. Refers
to Lowry's manuscripts and his symbolic use of placenames.

24 _____, comp. <u>Critical Writings on Commonwealth Literature:</u>
<u>A Selective Bibliography to 1970, with a List of Theses and</u>
<u>Dissertations</u>. University Park and London: Pennsylvania
State University Press, pp. 165–69, 299–300.
Lists these and major critical and biographical works.
Omits most reviews.

25 NEW, WILLIAM H. and H. J. ROSENGARTEN. "Malcolm Lowry" in
their <u>Modern Stories in English</u>. New York: Crowell;
Toronto: Copp Clark, p. 255.
Headnote to "Strange Comfort Afforded by the Profession."

26 _____. "Strange Comfort Afforded by the Profession" in their
<u>Instructors Manual for "Modern Stories in English</u>." New
York: Crowell, pp. 29–30.
Brief notes toward an explication of the story. Reference is made to the story's multiple internal translations,
its humour, and its concern with fragmented identities.

27 NYLAND, A. C. "Malcolm Lowry: The Writer" in <u>Malcolm Lowry:</u>
<u>Psalms and Songs</u>. Edited by Margerie Lowry. New York and
Scarborough, Ontario: New American Library, Meridian,
pp. 139–84.
Reprint of Chapter II of 1967.A8. In three sections
("The Apprentice," "The Journeyman," "The Master"), surveys Lowry's schoolboy writings in <u>The Leys Quarterly</u>, his
writings of the 1930s, and the poems, <u>Under the Volcano</u>,
and <u>Hear Us O Lord</u>. Traces early adumbrations of Lowry's
characteristic themes, and shows how Lowry experimented
with traditional styles, literary forms, and punctuation
conventions.

28 POTTINGER, ANDREW. "Volcanic Vagueness." <u>Canadian Literature</u>,
no. 64 (Spring), pp. 122–24.

1975

A critique of Bradbrook's criticism, claiming it fails
to distinguish between fiction about the author's life and
fiction about failure to find meaning in the past.

29   RAINE, KATHLEEN. <u>The Land Unknown</u>. London: Hamish Hamilton,
      pp. 51–52, 69–70.
          References to Lowry at Cambridge, in the context of a
      chapter on <u>Experiment</u> (pp. 40–58), contrasting Lowry's "in-
      articulate, profound feeling and intuitive insight" with
      William Empson's impressive articulateness. Reflects on
      Lowry's genius and his vulnerability, and on the "gift of
      access to the universal" which in <u>Ultramarine</u> and <u>Under the
      Volcano</u> he sought to express.

30   READ, MICHAEL. "Life's Great Conflagration." <u>Southern Review</u>
      (Adelaide), 11, pp. 257–66.
          A critique of Day's psychonalytic approach to Lowry and
      and elucidation of Lowry's medical problems, this review
      traces events in Lowry's life, recommends a Jungian rather
      than a Freudian approach to his work, and explores the
      "gnostic" element in his character which is also adduced
      by Bradbrook and Birney. It bears upon the portrait of the
      Consul. Day's critical perspective on the relation between
      life and art is unsatisfactory, but Bradbrook's book pro-
      vides a corrective answer.

31   RICHEY, CLARENCE W. "'The Ill-Fated Mr. Bultitude': A Note
      upon an Allusion in Malcolm Lowry's <u>Under the Volcano</u>."
      <u>Notes on Contemporary Literature</u>, 3, no. 3, pp. 3–5.
          A note elucidating Lowry's reference to F. Anstey's
      [Thomas Anstey Guthrie's] <u>Vice Versa</u> in Chapter 6 of <u>Under
      the Volcano</u>, and on its aptness regarding Hugh's situation.

32   SLADE, CAROLE. "<u>Under the Volcano</u> and Dante's <u>Inferno I</u>."
      <u>The University of Windsor Review</u>, 10, no. 2 (Spring–Summer),
      44–52.
          Examines the implications of Dante's first tercet (life
      as a journey, the self in a moral landscape, hope for re-
      demption) and traces their modulation in the geography,
      symbolism and characterization of Lowry's book. Finds
      Jacques to be not a main character because he is not, like
      the three key figures, associated with Dantesque language.

33   SPARIOSU, MIHAI. "Malcolm Lowry and the Enactment of Fiction:
      <u>The Voyage that Never Ends</u>." Paper read at Modern Language
      Association Seminar (29 December) in San Francisco.
      Mimeographed.
          Referring to cinematic, theatrical (role-playing), sym-
      bolic, tragic, and comic elements in <u>Under the Volcano</u> and

128

Dark as the Grave, suggests that Lowry understood that
literature is "play" but that "enacting one's own fiction"
is dangerous.

1976 A BOOKS

1   BRITTAIN, DONALD and JOHN KRAMER. <u>Volcano: An Inquiry into
     the Life and Death of Malcolm Lowry</u>. Narrated by Donald
     Brittain, with words of Malcolm Lowry spoken by Richard
     Burton. Produced by Donald Brittain and R. A. Duncan.
     90 min. First broadcast on the Canadian Broadcasting
     Corporation television network, April 7.
        Made on location in Canada, England, and Mexico, the
     film interviews 44 people about Lowry, and quotes exten-
     sively from <u>Under the Volcano</u>. Focussing on <u>Under the
     Volcano</u>, it essentially follows the structure of Douglas
     Day's biography. The National Film Board news release
     about the film contains capsule information on Lowry,
     Brittain, Burton, and Kramer.
        The film was nominated for an Academy Award in 1977, in
     the Feature Documentary category. Entered also in the 19th
     American Film Festival (New York, 1977), it won first prize
     in the feature length arts category.

2   BUBBERS, LISSA PAUL. "The Poetry of Malcolm Lowry in Relation
     to the Fiction." Master's thesis, York University (Toronto),
     88 pp.
        Argues that Lowry's envisioned poetic collection "The
     Lighthouse Invites the Storm" parallels and clarifies the
     prose cycle "The Voyage that Never Ends." Explores the
     multiple personae of both, the systems of aesthetics, and
     the symbolic dualities which are resolved into Lowry's con-
     cept of a cyclical universe.

3   DOROSZ, KRISTOFER. <u>Malcolm Lowry's Infernal Paradise</u>.
     Uppsala: Acta Universitatis Upsaliensis, Studia Anglistica
     Upsaliensia 27, 166 pp.
        A 1976 doctoral dissertation at the University of
     Uppsala. Attempts to locate the moral cause at the heart
     of <u>Under the Volcano</u>, the <u>Gestalt</u> "order" of the book's
     many levels. Draws on the theories of the Polish philos-
     opher Roman Ingarden (an appendix summarizes them,
     pp. 156–58), which finds aesthetic value in "metaphysical
     qualities." The elements of black magic and demonic in-
     version suggest "infernal paradise" as a central preoccupa-
     tion. Themes of ascent (images of height, birds, wings)
     are associated with flight and fall; cabbalistic doctrine
     associates ascent with light and darkness, which Lowry

1976

presents equivocally; thirst and drink suggest the polarities of the waste land; Faustian, Promethean, and Zoharic
metaphysics make the Consul an "eternal" prisoner on earth,
a black magician by archetype; love and guilt are inter-
connected; life and the garden are "contaminated by death";
and paradoxically--salvation and freedom being illusions--
it is in his responsibility for the evil with which the
novel's universe is permeated that the Consul's "greatness"
lies. The overabundance of ambiguous details mars the
artistry of the novel, though it remains "one of the greatest novels of the century." The analyses of particular
themes and image patterns reveal the "poetic story" which
gives coherence to the whole. A brief bibliography follows,
together with an index to discussions of the novel's "major
themes."

4 MILLER, DAVID. <u>Malcolm Lowry and the Voyage that Never Ends</u>.
London: Enitharmon Press, 55 pp.
After a brief biographical account, traces Lowry's
"epic," "The Voyage that Never Ends," from <u>Ultramarine</u>
(a basic mythical structure involving descent), to <u>Under
the Volcano</u> (the infernal descent into existential hell),
to <u>Lunar Caustic</u> (which locates a purgatory in hellish New
York surroundings, and finishes with "fear in full focus"
but also with a resolution), to <u>Dark as the Grave</u> and <u>La
Mordida</u> (which salvage mysticism out of terror), to <u>In
Ballast to the White Sea</u> and <u>Eridanus</u> (The Forest Path to
the Spring) and <u>October Ferry to Gabriola</u> (which are
briefly summarized). The frontispiece shows the first page
of the typescript of "La Mordida."

5 SLEMON, STEPHEN GUY. "Lowry's Journal Form: Narrative Technique and Philosophical Design." Master's thesis, The
University of British Columbia, 128 pp.
Shows how the structure of Lowry's later fiction--with
emphasis on "Ghostkeeper" and the manuscript version of
<u>Dark as the Grave</u>--gives rise to his themes. The "journal
form," adumbrated in "Through the Panama" and <u>Under the
Volcano</u>, develops into a "new form" which reconciles Lowry's
borrowings from Ortega and J. W. Dunne. Extensive consideration is given to serialism, the ramifications of Lowry's
notebooks, and static and kinetic notions of time and
narrative method.

1976 B SHORTER WRITINGS

1   ARAC, JONATHAN. "The Form of Carnival in Under the Volcano."
    Paper read at Modern Language Association Seminar
    (26 December) in Chicago. Mimeographed.
        Examines the "carnivalization" characteristic of
    Menippean satire, where humorous forms and mention of
    laughter deliberately have no funny effects. Applies
    Mikhail Bakhtin's notion of "reduced laughter" to Under
    the Volcano, finding formal and thematic elements--e.g.,
    journalistic components, parodic use of other genres, con-
    trast, fantasy, social incongruity, intellectual serious-
    ness, underworld naturalism--which provide generic unity.
    Carnival celebrates the process of change. Lowry's allu-
    sions should be read for the internal design they create
    rather than as references to external realities.

2   BAREHAM, TONY. "The Englishness of Malcolm Lowry." Journal
    of Commonwealth Literature, 11, no. 2 (December), 134-49.
        Examines the Englishness of Lowry's birth, background,
    and training, and shows how English attitudes (to wilder-
    ness, pubs, and alienation from his homeland) affected his
    rendering of character and landscape. Asserts that inter-
    preting the ironies and schisms of his writing is impossible
    without an appreciation of his English experience.

3   BRADBROOK, M. C. "Narrative Form in Conrad and Lowry" in
    Joseph Conrad: A Commemoration. Papers from the 1974
    International Conference on Conrad. Edited by Norman
    Sherry. London: Macmillan; New York: Barnes and Noble,
    pp. 129-42.
        Explores a number of parallels between Lowry and Conrad,
    showing how each writer's sense of his foreignness and his
    need to belong results in intense fictional renderings of
    "interior journey." Emphasizes each writer's development
    of new fictional structures--"including structural ab-
    sences"--in order to reevaluate the last works of both.
    Compares Ultramarine with Youth, Under the Volcano with
    Nostromo, and attempts to show how October Ferry to
    Gabriola and the stories of Hear Us O Lord illuminate the
    configurations of Victory and The Shadow-Line. In both
    writers one discovers the reality of attitudes built on
    illusion, and "haunted" voyages of characters with anguished
    memories, expressed by means of the open symbolic struc-
    tures that Lowry called "Aeolian."

4   DAHLIE, HALLVARD. "Malcolm Lowry and the Northern Tradition."
    Studies in Canadian Literature, 1, no. 1 (Winter), 105-14.

1976

> Citing Lowry's references to the North and Norway, demon-
> strates how Lowry relates to what the historian W. L. Morton
> calls the "northern character" in Canada. Lowry's ability
> to render the real landscape mythologically contributed im-
> portantly to the development of Canadian writing, yet
> Lowry--cf. Kroetsch and Atwood--remains an outsider to this
> landscape.

5 DODSON, DANIEL B. "Malcolm Lowry" in <u>Six Contemporary British Novelists</u>. Edited by George Stade. New York: Columbia University Press, pp. 115-64.
Reprint of 1970.A4.

6 FEE, MARGERY and RUTH CAWKER. "Lowry, Malcolm" in their <u>Canadian Fiction: An Annotated Bibliography</u>. Toronto: Peter Martin Associates, pp. 70-71.
A list of Lowry's published book-length works and of book-length criticism concerning his work, with brief eval- uations and descriptive annotations.

7 GRACE, SHERRILL. "Malcolm Lowry and the 'Reel' World." Paper read at Modern Language Association Seminar (26 December) in Chicago. Mimeographed.
Asserts that films influenced Lowry thematically, sty- listically, and epistemologically--the technical influence not being the most important. Recounts the impact of vari- ous films, particularly <u>The Cabinet of Dr. Caligari</u> and other German Expressionist films, on Lowry's early stories, the <u>Tender Is the Night</u> script, <u>Under the Volcano</u>, and <u>October Ferry to Gabriola</u>.

8 GRACE, SHER[R]ILL D. "Outward Bound." <u>Canadian Literature</u>, no. 71 (Winter), pp. 73-79.
Argues for greater attention to be paid to <u>Ultramarine</u>. Shows how the circular structure of the book is reinforced by images of circles and circling, and how the geographic and spiritual voyages are always required to break out of equilibrium into flux.

9 HOLT, LEIGH and RONALD WALKER. "Faustus to Firmin: An Approach to Teaching <u>Under the Volcano</u>." Paper read at Modern Language Association Seminar (26 December) in Chicago. Mimeographed.
An account of the advantages to teaching <u>Under the Vol- cano</u> together with Marlowe's <u>Dr. Faustus</u>. Both involve "the recognition of love's worth and availability" and the realization that it will never be requested. Both lead to an investigation of heroism and a valuation of contemporary human consciousness.

10   KNELMAN, MARTIN. "Lowry's Inferno." <u>Weekend Magazine</u>
      (Montreal), 26 (3 April), 21-22.
          An account of the disasters in Lowry's life, and the
      "diabolical," "melancholy," "threatening and demonic" world
      of <u>Under the Volcano</u>, turns into an appreciative commentary
      on Donald Brittain's National Film Board film about Lowry's
      life.

11   McPHERSON, HUGO. "Fiction 1940-1960" in <u>Literary History of</u>
      <u>Canada</u>. Edited by Carl F. Klinck. Second edition.
      Volume 2. Toronto: University of Toronto Press, pp. 229-30.
      Slight revision of 1965.B20.

12   MAKOWIECKI, STEFAN. "Symbolic Pattern in <u>Under the Volcano</u>."
      <u>Kwartalnik Neofilologiczny</u>, 23, no. 4, 455-63.
          Finds that attempts to trace single themes (Faustian,
      Dantesque, e.g.) fail to explain the novel's complex struc-
      ture. What should be stressed instead is the fact that all
      the symbols give rise to the principle of antithesis, the
      coexistence of opposites. The "positive ambiguity" of the
      novel derives from the thematic design, which in turn is
      based not on association and counterpoint, but on "radia-
      tion" and synthesis.

13   NEW, WILLIAM H. "Fiction" in <u>Literary History of Canada</u>.
      Edited by Carl F. Klinck. Second edition. Volume 3.
      Toronto: University of Toronto Press, pp. 234, 274-77.
          Comments on Lowry's fiction, largely in connection with
      the problem of form in his later works, in the context of
      a survey of Canadian fiction between 1960 and 1973.

14   _____. Malcolm Lowry, in <u>Contemporary Novelists</u>. Second
      edition. Edited by James Vinson. London: St. James
      Press; New York: St. Martin's Press, pp. 1591-92.
          A brief survey of major themes (the fluidity of time
      and memory, the nature of creation, the alternation between
      fear and harmony), focussing on <u>Hear Us O Lord</u> and <u>Under</u>
      <u>the Volcano</u>. Prefaced (pp. 1590-91) by the editor's
      biographical and bibliographical notes on Lowry.

15   _____. "A Note on Romantic Allusions in <u>Hear Us O Lord</u>."
      <u>Studies in Canadian Literature</u>, 1, no. 1 (Winter), 130-36.
          Lowry's sympathy with the ideas raised by Coleridge's
      "The Aeolian Harp" and Wordsworth's <u>The Prelude</u> affected
      the form of <u>Hear Us O Lord</u>. The poems help clarify the
      relation between form and meaning. Wordsworth's "Elegiac
      Stanzas..." provides another guide to the ethical and
      sensory perceptions which Lowry takes as his subject.

1976

16 PHELAN, MAURICE. "Under the Volcano: The Dantean Design."
    Paper read at Modern Language Association Seminar
    (26 December) in Chicago. Mimeographed.
        Examines the Dantean structure that organizes Under the
    Volcano, a pattern which casts Laruelle in the role of the
    Neutrals, Juan Cerillo in that of the Heavenly Messenger;
    the dying Indian is a version of Montefeltro, Yvonne's
    letters a "humorous correlative" of the Counterfeiters. A
    chapter-by-chapter analysis of the novel suggests other
    parallels, the conclusion being that the Consul at the end
    is still "continuing his journey toward the light."

17 POTTINGER, ANDREW J. "The Consul's 'Murder.'" Canadian
    Literature, 67 (Winter), 53-63.
        A study of the narrator's subjective/objective rendering
    of events in Under the Volcano, rejecting symbolic meanings
    in favour of a literal reading, with the intent of focussing
    on the Sartrian moral dilemmas of the final chapter: the
    conflict involved in judging a person, under pressure of
    time, while alienated from him.

18 SEYMOUR-SMITH, MARTIN. "Lowry, Malcolm" in his Who's Who in
    Twentieth Century Literature. London: Weidenfeld and
    Nicolson, pp. 217-18.
        A brief biocritical entry, stressing Lowry's alcoholism
    and the balance between symbolism and convincing realistic
    detail in Under the Volcano.

19 SLADE, CAROLE. "'What About Female Readers?': The Character
    of Yvonne in Under the Volcano." Paper read at Modern
    Language Association Seminar (26 December) in Chicago.
    Mimeographed.
        Asserts that Yvonne is "an individualized character who
    resists definition in a traditional female role," whose
    language is nonetheless not distinguishable from that of
    Geoffrey and Hugh. She is embarked upon her own journey,
    like Geoffrey and Wilderness.

20 STADE, GEORGE. "Introduction" to his edition of Six Contempo-
    rary British Novelists. New York: Columbia University
    Press, pp. vii-x.
        Mentions the importance of appreciating the Joycean
    imitation in Under the Volcano.

21 TIESSEN, PAUL. "Introduction" to Malcolm Lowry and Margerie
    Bonner Lowry, Notes on a Screenplay for F. Scott Fitzgerald's
    "Tender Is the Night." Bloomfield Hills, Mich., and
    Columbia, S. C.: Bruccoli Clark, pp. v-xix.

An account of the writing of the script (1947–1950) and
of Twentieth Century-Fox's rejection of it in 1951. Quotes
from a number of Lowry's unpublished letters to Frank Taylor
(of MGM, and later Twentieth Century-Fox). Points to the
stylistic parallels between the screenplay and <u>Under the
Volcano</u> and suggests possibilities for comparison of characters (Dick Diver and the Consul) and the manner of resolv-
ing thematic tensions.

22   _____. "Malcolm Lowry as Film Theorist." Paper read at a
        joint session of the Association of Canadian University
        Teachers of English and the Film Studies Association of
        Canada (27 May) in Quebec City.
        A conservative call for a definition of what literary
        critics mean by the term "cinematic." Eisenstein-like
        close-ups and film's mechanical pace differ from literary
        images and movements. Film may have been a model for <u>Under
        the Volcano</u>, but it does not necessarily follow that the
        novel will be cinematic. Lowry's comments on the force of
        film images are exemplified in his "Tender Is the Night"
        script, which would be, in his sense, a "cinematic" <u>film</u>.

23   WOOD, BARRY. "The Edge of Eternity." <u>Canadian Literature</u>,
        no. 70 (Autumn), pp. 51–58.
        Finds "circle-centre patterns" important in "The Forest
        Path to the Spring" as guides to the mystical core of the
        work. Identifies the spring with the timeless present
        (epitomizing eternity), and considers the path to and from
        it to represent spatially the connection with sequential
        time, past and future. Tao images and music are associated
        with the "total fusion of opposites at the still point."

24   WOODCOCK, GEORGE. Review of <u>Psalms and Songs</u>. <u>The Vancouver
        Sun</u>, "Leisure" supplement (2 January), p. 29A.
        A brief review.

Index

Abe, Yukiko, 1970.B1
About Fiction: Reverent Reflec-
    tions on the Nature of Fic-
    tion with Irreverent
    Observations on Writers,
    Readers, & Other Abuses,
    1975.B20
Abrahams, William, 1966.B29
"The Absorption of Echoes,"
    1970.B34
Adams, Phoebe, 1961.B1; 1970.B2
Adelman, Irving, 1972.B1
"After Douglas Day: Lowry and
    Tony Kilgallin," 1974.B77
"'After the Volcano...,'" 1961.B37
"After the Volcano," 1968.B36
"After the Volcano: An Assess-
    ment of Malcolm Lowry's Post-
    humous Fiction," 1974.B10
"Against the Spell of Death,"
    1964.B8
"Agricola-palkinto Juhani
    Jaskarille," 1969.B28
Aguilera-Malta, Demetrio, 1964.B1
"Ah Wilderness," 1971.B16
Aiken, Conrad,
--as author, 1952.A1; 1961.B2-B3;
    1967.B1; 1968.B1
--as subject, 1952.B4, B6;
    1961.B7; 1962.B20, B27;
    1964.B13; 1966.B14; 1967.B1,
    B13-14, B43; 1968.B51;
    1970.B21; 1972.A2; 1973.A3;
    1974.B26, B40; 1975.B11
"Aiken and Lowry," 1975.B11
"The Albatross of Self," 1962.B29
Albaum, Elvin, 1971.A1
Albérès, R. M., See Marill, René

"The Alcoholic on Alcoholism,"
    1974.B46
"The Alcoholic on Alcoholism:
    Lowry's Unique Achievement in
    Under the Volcano," 1975.B16
Alcoholism, 1960.B1, B6, B16;
    1962.B21; 1963.B24; 1969.B23;
    1970.B7; 1972.B13; 1973.B11,
    B29; 1974.B46; 1975.B13
Aldridge, John W., 1956.B1
Algren, Nelson, 1974.B2
"Alkoholistin loppu," 1969.B35
Allen, Bruce D., 1970.B3
Allen, Trevor, 1967.B2
Allen, Walter, 1947.B1; 1964.B3-5
"Aller seelentag im amerikanischen
    Roman," 1957.B10
All My Sins Remembered, 1964.B15
Alternating Current, 1973.B25
Alvarez, A., 1973.B1
"Am einbrechenden Kraterrand,"
    1964.B20
"The American Adam and the Cana-
    dian Christ," 1970.B16
American and British Writers in
    Mexico 1556-1973, 1974.B44
"American Literature," 1948.B2
Among Worlds: An Introduction to
    Modern Commonwealth and South
    African Fiction, 1975.B22
"An Analysis of Humour in the
    Works of Malcolm Lowry,"
    1972.B22
The Anatomy of the Novel, 1975.B3
"...And a New Insight into Lowry,
    the B.C. Squatter," 1971.B29
"Angst and Art," 1974.B64
Andersen, Gladys Marie, 1970.A1

137

Anderson, Don, 1974.B3, B29
Andrianne, René, 1963.B1
"A nos amis," 1949.B1
"Another Room in Hell," 1968.B48
"Answer to the Sphinx," 1961.B7
"Appelez ça accident," 1974.B56
The Approach to Fiction, 1972.B17
Arac, Jonathan, 1976.B1
"Armonajan oppaaski," 1968.B33
Arrowsmith, J. E. S. "Fiction-I,"
    1933.B4
"Art as the Writer's Mirror:
    Literary Solipsism in Dark as
    the Grave," 1971.A5
Articles on Twentieth Century
    Literature: An Annotated
    Bibliography 1954 to 1970,
    1974.B74
"The Art of Poetry IX: Conrad
    Aiken: an interview,"
    1968.B1
Ascherson, Neal, 1963.B7
"Aspects of the Absurd in Modern
    Fiction, with Special Refer-
    ence to Under the Volcano and
    Catch 22," 1969.B4
"Aspects of the Quest in the
    Minor Fiction of Malcolm
    Lowry," 1966.A3
Astre, Georges-Albert, 1951.B1
Atkins, Elizabeth, 1969.B4
"Auberon Waugh on New Novels,"
    1971.B33
"Au-delà de l'enfer," 1962.B15
"Au-dessous du volcan" (Estang),
    1961.B32
"Au-dessous du volcan" (Sigaux),
    1950.B8
"Au-dessous du volcan" (Sigaux),
    1960.B15
"'Au-dessous du volcan' aurait pu
    être écrit par Baudelaire,"
    1950.B5
"Au-dessous du volcan, dix ans
    après," 1961.B59
Austin, Paul W., 1974.B9
"Author Dead 5 Years, Book Wins
    Literary Prize," 1962.B2
Authors and Areas of Canada,
    1970.B18
"Autobiography and Novel,"
    1968.B27

"Avant-propos," 1959.B7
"Avant-propos à l'édition
    américain," 1976.B18
"Avec Malcolm Lowry (1909-1957),"
    1960.B16

B., J., 1959.B2
B., M. J., 1973.B3
Bakhtin, Mikhail, 1976.B1
Baldeshwiler, Eileen, 1975.B1
Bannerman, James, 1966.B2
Bareham, Terence, 1971.B2; 1974.B10
Bareham, Tony, 1976.B2
Barnes, Djuna, 1974.B11-12
Barnes, Jim, 1969.B5
Barnes, Jimmy Weaver, 1972.B3
Baro, Gene, 1961.B15
Barucca, Primo, 1961.B16
Barzun, Jacques, 1947.B6
Bates, Lewis, 1969.B6
Baur, Joseph, 1952.B1
Baxter, Charles Morley,
    1974.B11-12
Baxter, Edith Lorraine, 1973.A1
"The Beaching of the Good Ship
    Solipsist: The Post-Volcano
    Malcolm Lowry," 1974.B25
Be All My Sins Remembered,
    1965.B6
Beattie, Munro, 1962.B6
Beattie, Toddy, 1947.B7
Beauregard, Mario, 1964.B26
"The Beaver and the Elephant,"
    1973.B16
Beeching, Jack, 1971.B3
"Before the Volcano," 1963.B36
Benedikz, B. S., 1971.B2
Benham, David S., 1969.A1;
    1970.B4
Berl, Emmanuel, 1963.B8
"Besides the Volcano," 1967.B42
Besterman, Theodore, 1968.B6
"Bewährungfrist vor dem Tode,"
    1966.B20
Bibliography, 1961.B22-23, B34;
    1962.B11; 1964.B9; 1968.A7,
    B6, B17, B53; 1970.B18;
    1972.B1; 1973.A2; 1974.B67,
    B74; 1975.B22, B24; 1976.B6,
    B14
Bickerton, Chris, 1974.B21

"Bid and Made," 1968.B38
Bieńkowski, Zbigniew, 1964.B7
Binns, Ronald, 1974.B13-14;
    1975.B2
"Biographical Note on Malcolm
    Lowry," 1961.B42
"A Biographical Work of Art,"
    1974.B55
Biography, See Lowry, Malcolm
Birney, Earle,
--as author, 1953.B1; 1961.B6,
    B17-23, B25; 1962.B6-11;
    1964.B8-9; 1968.B6, B31
--as subject, 1962.B36
"Birney Discusses Malcolm Lowry,"
    1962.B36
"Black Holes in Space: The Fig-
    ure of the Artist in
    Nathanael West's Miss
    Lonelyhearts, Djuna Barnes'
    Nightwood, and Malcolm
    Lowry's Under the Volcano,"
    1974.B11
Black, Paul J., 1966.A1
"Blood, Border, and Barranca:
    The Role of Mexico in the
    Modern English Novel,"
    1974.B82
Boatwright, James, 1962.B12;
    1967.B6
Bonnefoi, Geneviève, 1960.B2
"Books," 1974.B66
"Books and Things," 1947.B13
"Books and Writers - Week 34,"
    1974.B21
"Books - A Warning to Health,"
    1972.B30
"Book Talk," 1947.B17
Booth, Wayne C., 1974.B15
"Boozer's Gloom," 1971.B23
Boulton, Marjorie, 1975.B3
Bourniquel, Camille, 1970.B5
Bowles, Paul, 1958.B1
Brace, Gerald Warner, 1947.B21
Brachvogel, H. H., 1957.B2
Bradbrook, Muriel, 1972.B4;
    1974.A1, B16-18; 1976.B3
Bradbury, Malcolm, 1962.B13;
    1972.B5; 1973.B2; 1974.B19
Braem, Helmut, 1957.B3; 1969.B7
"The Bravest Boat," 1965.B24;
    1969.B10, See also, Hear Us

O Lord from Heaven Thy Dwelling
    Place; Lowry, Malcolm, short
    fiction
Breit, Harvey, 1957.B4; 1960.B3-4,
    1965.A1, B3
Breza, Henryk, 1964.B10
Bright Book of Life, 1973.B15
Brittain, Donald, 1976.A1, B10
Bromige, David, 1968.B9
Brooke-Rose, Christine, 1967.B9
Bruccoli, Matthew J., 1973.B3
Brumm, Ursula, 1958.B1
Bryden, Ronald, 1969.B9
Bubbers, Lissa Paul, 1976.A2
Buckeye, Robert, 1970.B6
Buckler, Ernest, 1962.B14
Budrecki, Lech, 1964.B11
Buitenhuis, Peter, 1973.B4
Burek, Tomasz, 1964.B12
Burgess, Anthony, See Wilson,
    John Anthony Burgess
Burroughs, William, 1965.B17;
    1967.B26
Burton, Richard, 1976.A1
Butson, Barry, 1967.A2
"But this is what it is to live
    in hell: William Gass's 'In
    the heart of the heart of the
    country,'" 1973.B5
Bygrave, Mike, 1972.B6

Cabbala, 1960.B1; 1964.B21, B31;
    1967.A4, B17, B27; 1968.A4;
    1969.A5, B38; 1970.B27;
    1972.B7; 1973.B11; 1976.A3
"Cabbalistic Elements in Malcolm
    Lowry's Under the Volcano,"
    1967.A4
Cabau, Jacques, 1962.B15; 1963.B10
"Cain Shall Not Slay Abel Today,"
    1968.B23
Calder-Marshall, Arthur, 1967.B12;
    1971.B4; 1974.B20-21
"Call It Misadventure," 1970.B21
Calzadilla, Juan, 1971.B5
"Cambridge Poetry," 1930.B1
"Cambridge Tragedy. Student
    Found Dead. Gas Filled Room,"
    1929.B1
Canada and the Canadians, 1970.B35
Canadian Fiction: An Annotated
    Bibliography, 1976.B6

Canadian literature, 1952.B5; 1961.B46; 1965.B19; 1967.B39; 1968.B37; 1970.B7, B16, B18, B36; 1971.B24; 1972.B4, B24, B27, B29; 1973.B16, B32-33; 1974.B65; 1975.B8, B22; 1976.B4

The Canadian Novel in the Twentieth Century, 1975.B16

"Canadian Poetry and Fiction," 1963.B21

"The Canadian Short Story: Introduction," 1972.B24

Canadian Writers; écrivains canadiens, 1967.B40

"Canadian Writing and 'The Great Theme,'" 1952.B5

"Canadian Writing: Present Declarative," 1965.B19

Carey, Maurice J., 1971.B6

Carroy, Jean-Roger, 1960.B5; 1965.B4, B18; 1974.B22

Carstensen, Federico Brehm, 1972.B7

Cartano, Françoise and Tony, 1974.B78

Casari, Laura Elizabeth Rhodes, 1967.A3

"Cassure, canal, barranquilla," 1974.B86

Castelnau, Marie-Pierre, 1961.B24

Catastrophe and Imagination: An Interpretation of the Recent English and American Novel, 1957.B6

"Cates Park Plaque to Honor Writer," 1961.B12

Cathelin, Jean, 1961.B25

Cawker, Ruth, 1976.B6

Chalker, John, 1968.B8

Chandler, George, 1962.B16

"Chaos the Route to Paradise," 1972.B8

Chapelan, Maurice, 1968.B9

Chavardès, Maurice, 1961.B26; 1962.B17; 1963.B11

Chittick, V. L. O., 1964.B13

Chociłowski, Jerzy, 1964.B14

Christ, Ronald, 1974.B23

Christella Marie, Sister, 1965.B5

Churchill, R. C., 1970.B7

Churchill, Victor Alexander Spencer, Viscount, 1964.B15

Circles Without Center, 1972.B14

Clark, Cecil, 1966.B4

Clark, Eleanor, 1947.B8

"A Classical Myth Transformed – Lowry's 'The Forest Path to the Spring,'" 1975.B12

Clements, Robert J., 1968.B10

Cluny, Claude Michel, 1966.B5

Cogswell, Fred, 1968.B12; 1972.B8

"Cold Ash," 1961.B54

Coleman, John, 1968.B11

Coleridge, S. T., 1976.B15

"The Collected Poetry of Malcolm Lowry," 1969.A4

Colombo, John Robert, 1963.B13; 1966.B6

Combs, Judith O., 1973.A2

Commonwealth Literature, 1973.B32

Commonwealth Literature and the Modern World, 1975.B8

"Complaint Holds Up Biography of Sussex Writer," 1974.B49

"Connaissez-vous Malcolm Lowry?," 1962.B25

Connolly, Francis X., 1947.B9

Conrad, Joseph, 1974.B45; 1976.B3

Conrad Aiken, 1962.B20

Conrad Aiken: A Life of His Art, 1962.B27

"Conrad Aiken: An Interview," 1968.B51

"Conrad Aiken (1889-1973): The Wages of Neglect," 1974.B26

Conron, Brandon, 1967.B40

Considine, Raymond Howard, 1972.A1

"The Consul's 'Murder,'" 1976.B17

The Contemporary Novel, 1972.B1

Contemporary Novelists, 1976.B14

Cook, Bruce, 1968.B12

Cooke, Dorian, 1974.B21

"Correspondance et correspondances," 1974.B33

Corrigan, Matthew, 1966.B7; 1968.B13-14; 1970.A2, B8-9; 1971.B7; 1975.B4

Corsillo, Mario, 1974.B24

Costa, Richard Hauer,
--as author, 1966.B8-9;

1967.B13-14; 1968.A2, B15-
16; 1970.B10-11; 1971.B8;
1972.A2, B9; 1973.B6;
1974.B25-28
--as subject, 1966.B9
"Cotton Broker's Death,"
1945.B2
Cox, C. B., 1972.B5
Crawford, John, 1969.B10
Creative Writing in Canada,
1961.B46
Cresswell, Rosemary, 1974.B29
Critical Writings on Commonwealth
Literatures, 1975.B24
Criticism, 1960.B14, B20-21;
1961.B59; 1969.B44; 1970.A2-
3; 1973.B10; 1974.B9, B67;
1975.B4; 1976.B2, See also
names of individual critics
Crosby, John, 1947.B10
Cross, Richard K., 1973.B7;
1974.B30-31
Cuddon, J. A., 1969.B11
Cullis, Tara, 1970.A3
Cunning Exiles: Studies of Mod-
ern Prose Writers, 1974.B3,
B29
"Cyclopean Author-Critic
Shredded," 1969.B25

Dahlie, Hallvard, 1975.B6-9;
1976.B4
"Dans notre courrier...de Mme
Vve Malcolm Lowry," 1960.B10
"Dans un chambre forte de
Vancouver un romancier
déchiffre les inédits de
Malcolm Lowry," 1961.B25
"Dans un village mexicain brûlé
de soleil et de passions...
'Au-dessous du volcan' ou le
testament du génie, la
grandiose confession du Kafka
américain: Malcolm Lowry,"
1959.B2
Dark as the Grave Wherein My
Friend Is Laid,
--general studies, 1968.B17;
1969.B29; 1970.B8, B26, B36;
1971.A3; 1974.B10; 1975.B1,
B33; 1976.A5

--reviews, 1968.B3, B5, B12-14,
B16, B22, B24-25, B27, B30,
B36, B38, B45, B47-48;
1969.B3, B6, B8, B11, B18-19,
B26, B31, B33, B36, B41-42;
1970.B5, B30; 1972.B19, B30
d'Astorg, Bertrand, 1950.B1
Davenport, John, 1961.B28;
1965.B7
Davidson, Margaret Normanton,
1969.A3
Day, Douglas, 1964.B16-17;
1967.B12; 1968.B17; 1972.A3;
1973.B34; 1974.B32; 1976.A1
"Day of a Dead Man," 1961.B56
"Day on Lowry: A Distinctly
Petty View," 1974.B60
"Dazzling Disintegration,"
1947.B34
Deacon, William Arthur, 1947.B11
"Dead B.C. Writer Declared
Genius," 1967.B4
"Death in Life: Neo-Platonic
Elements in 'Through the
Panama,'" 1970.B12
"Death of the Optimist," 1968.B3
Deck, Laura M., 1974.A2
"Delirium," 1947.B15
De Margerie, Diane, 1974.B33,
See also Fernandez, Diane
"De Melville à Lowry, et retour
par nos abîmes," 1974.B22
"Demonic Day," 1971.B19
Dempsey, David, 1962.B18
Dennis, Nigel, 1971.B10
"Deux miroirs d'un même texte,"
1972.B31
"Die Verwüstung des Gartens,"
1963.B37
"Dipso to Dachau," 1965.B1
"Dispossession," 1971.B30
"Dissonance and Digression: The
Ill-fitting Fusion of Philos-
ophy and Form in Lawrence
Durrell's Alexandria Quartet,"
1971.B31
Dobbs, Kildare, 1961.B29
"Dödens triumf," 1962.B41
Dodson, Daniel, 1970.A4; 1974.B34
"Dollarton Had a Wild Genius,"
1960.B19

"The Dollarton Squatter: Reminiscences of Lowry," 1966.B22
Donaldson, George, 1975.B10
Donoghue, Denis, 1966.B10
"Dormez-vous? A Memoir of Malcolm Lowry," 1962.B33
Dorosz, Kristofer, 1976.A3
"Down to the Sea to Prove Himself a Man Among Men," 1962.B14
"The Downward Flight of a Soul," 1947.B30
Doyen, Victor, 1968.A3; 1969.B14; 1971.B11; 1973.A4; 1974.B35
Drabikowski, Marek, 1973.B8
"Drunkards and Insane Interest Jittery World," 1947.B11
"Drunken Nightmare of the Damned," 1947.B18
"The Drunken Wheel: Malcolm Lowry and Under the Volcano," 1969.B43
Duncan, R. A., 1976.A1
Durrant, Geoffrey, 1970.B12; 1975.B11-12
Durrell, Lawrence, 1971.B31
Dworkin, Rita, 1972.B1
Dyson, A. E., 1972.B5

E., See Electorowicz, Leszek
Early, Leonard Roy, 1970.A5
Easton, T. R., 1969.A4
"The Echoing Ego," 1961.B57
"'Ecoute notre voix ô Seigneur!,'" 1962.B38
"Ecoute notre voix, ô Seigneur, par Malcolm Lowry," 1963.B1
Edelstein, J. M., 1961.B30; 1962.B19; 1964.B18
"The Edge of Eternity," 1976.B23
"Editor's Note," 1970.B23
Edmonds, Dale H., 1965.A2, B8; 1967.B15; 1968.B20, 1974.B36-37; 1975.B13
Egeland, Kjølv, 1953.B2
"Ein Höllisches Paradies," 1952.B3
"Ein mythischer Roman," 1957.B2
Elektorowicz, Leszek, 1961.B31; 1964.B19
"The Element Follows You Around, Sir!," 1965.B1; 1967.B15,

See also October Ferry to Gabriola
"Elements Towards a Spatial Reading of Malcolm Lowry's Under the Volcano," 1969.B14
"Elephant and Colosseum," 1974.A5
"Eliot, Joyce & Lowry," 1965.B12
"El Jardin de Etla," 1964.B26
"El volcán de Quauhnáhuac," 1964.B37
"The Ending is the Beginning," 1964.B15
"Endless Voyages: A Study of the Protagonist in Malcolm Lowry's Fiction," 1970.A5
"Engines Sing Frere Jacques," 1961.B29
"English-Canadian Literature," 1970.B7
"The Englishness of Malcolm Lowry," 1976.B2
Enright, D. J., 1967.B16; 1974.B38
"Epitaph for Romantic Imagination," 1962.B22
Epstein, Perle Sherry, 1967.A4; 1968.B21; 1969.A5; 1970.B13; 1972.B7
"Eräs kärsimysh istoria," 1969.B21
Estang, Luc, 1961.B32
"European Literary Scene," 1968.B10
"Europe's Day of the Dead," 1967.B43
"Eviction from Eden," 1971.B10

"Fame Comes Too Late to a New Brighton Writer," 1963.B26
Farrell, J. G., 1974.B39
"The Fate of the Consul," 1960.B1
Fauchereau, Serge, 1967.B22
"Faust and Under the Volcano," 1965.B13
"Faustus to Firmin: An Approach to Teaching Under the Volcano," 1976.B9
"February 19, 1947," 1969.B15
Fee, Margery, 1976.B6
Fernandez, Diane, 1969.B15, See also De Margerie, Diane

"A Few Items Culled From What Started Out To Be a Sort of Preface to a Film-Script," 1974.B79

"Fiction" (New), 1976.B13

"Fiction" (Savage), 1947.B29

"Fiction" (Verschoyle), 1933.B8

"Fiction-I," 1933.B4

"Fiction 1940-1960," 1965.B20

"The Fictional Landscape of Mexico: Readings in D. H. Lawrence, Graham Greene and Malcolm Lowry," 1974.B81

"Fiction Chronicle," 1947.B16

"Fiction of Malcolm Lowry and Thomas Mann: Structural Tradition," 1972.B3

"Fighting the Albatross of Self," 1973.A4

Film, 1952.B8; 1965.B26; 1968.A6; 1969.A3, B28; 1970.B33; 1972.A4; 1973.B3, B11, B20; 1974.B29, B79; 1975.A2; 1976.A1, B7, B21-22

"First Supplement to Malcolm Lowry Bibliography," 1962.B11

Fitte, Paul, 1929.B1-2; 1974.B6-7, B16-17

Fitzgerald, F. Scott, 1973.B3; 1976.B7, B21-22

"Five Signallings in Darkness," 1962.B7

Fleischmann, Wolfgang Bernard, 1969.B7

Flint, R. W., 1947.B12

Forces in Modern British Literature 1885-1956, 1956.B2

"The Forest Path to the Spring," 1966.A3; 1968.A4; 1972.B21; 1974.B27; 1975.B12; 1976.B23, See also, Hear Us O Lord from Heaven Thy Dwelling Place; Lowry, Malcolm, short fiction

"Foreword" to "Twelve Poems by Malcolm Lowry," 1962.B8

"The Form of Carnival in Under the Volcano," 1976.B1

"Forord," 1949.B3

Forrester, Viviane, 1972.B12

The Forties: Fiction, poetry, drama, 1969.B16

Fouchet, Max-Pol, 1950.B2; 1960.B6; 1967.B17

"Four Facets of Malcolm Lowry," 1970.B36

"Four Novels," 1947.B19

"Fragments from Beyond," 1968.B24

Francillon, Clarisse,
--as author, 1950.B3, B7; 1957.B5; 1960.B8, B12; 1963.B14; 1965.B18; 1974.B1, B20, B40-41, B56; 1975.B14
--as subject, 1959.B2, 1961.B41

"Frank Sargeson's 'Joy of the Worm,'" 1970.B32

Frédérique, A.-J., 1950.B3

Fremont-Smith, Eliot, 1965.B9; 1968.B22

French, Warren, 1969.B16

"French Thoughts on Lowry," 1960.B20

Freudianism, 1973.A3

Friedman, Melvin, 1955.B1

"From Nightmare to Seredipity [sic]: A Retrospective Look at William Burroughs," 1965.B17

Frye, Northrop, 1963.B15

"A Fugitive from Pride," 1974.B76

Fulford, Robert, 1961.B34; 1972.B29

"Further Arias," 1962.B28

Gabrial, Jan, 1974.B51, See also Lowry, Malcolm

"Gabriola: Malcolm Lowry's Floating Island," 1972.B25

Gadenne, Paul, 1950.B4

Galaviz, Juan Manuel, 1972.B13

Gannett, Lewis, 1947.B13

Ganz, Raffael, 1964.B20

"Garden of Etla," 1950.B5

Garoffolo, Vincent, 1947.B14

Garzilli, Enrico, 1972.B14

Gass, William H., 1970.B14; 1973.B5, B9-10; 1974.B47

"Genius Self-Destroyed," 1967.B31

"Genom Panama," 1962.B41

Geschicte des modernen Romans, 1964.B30

Gillanders, Carol, 1968.B23

"Ghostkeeper," 1969.A5; 1975.B15; 1976.A5

Glass, Norman, 1967.B18
"Glimpses into the Life of
    Malcolm Lowry," 1961.B17
Godfrey, David, 1972.B29
"A Golden Boy Retreats to Die,"
    1974.B50
Gomes Leite, Maurício, 1973.B11
"Good Sailors Rarely Go Home,"
    1964.B34
"Gottes einsame menschen,"
    1957.B7
Grace, Sherrill E., 1973.B12;
    1974.A3, B42; 1975.B15;
    1976.B7-8
Gramigna, Guiliano, 1961.B35
"Great Circle Sailing: A Study
    of the Imagery of Malcolm
    Lowry," 1966.A2
"Great Thirst for Love," 1974.B83
Greene, George, 1966.B12
Greene, Graham, 1974.B81-82
Greene, T. E., 1967.B19
Gregor, Ian, 1968.B32
Grieg, Nordahl, 1947.B25;
    1953.B2; 1963.B31; 1975.B6,
    B9
Griffith, Malcolm, 1974.B43
"The Grin and the Gin Are There,
    but Not the Art," 1974.B23
Guerard, Albert J., 1972.B16
"A Guide to Under the Volcano,"
    1970.A1
Gunn, Drewey Wayne, 1974.B44
Guthrie, Thomas Anstey, 1975.B31

Haas, Rudolf, 1963.B16
Hacking, Norman, 1973.B13
Hagen, William Morice, 1974.B45
Haldane, Charlotte, 1949.B2
Hale, Lionel, 1947.B15
"Hambo ici et là," 1974.B1
Hannah, Pierce, 1967.B20
Hardwick, Elizabeth, 1947.B16
Harris, Wilson, 1967.B21
Harrison, Dick, 1970.B16
Harrison, Keith, 1972.A3
Harrop, Mona, 1947.B17
"Harrowing Hell," 1965.B2
Haworth, David, 1971.B12
Hays, H. R., 1947.B18
Hear Us O Lord from Heaven Thy
    Dwelling Place,

--general studies, 1961.B14, B61;
    1962.B12, B25, B31, B38;
    1963.B1; 1965.A1, B15, B24;
    1966.A3; 1967.B15, B44;
    1968.A4; 1969.A1, B10, B19;
    1970.B12; 1971.A3, B15;
    1972.B29; 1974.A5, B29, B86;
    1975.A4, B1, B26; 1976.A5, B15
--reviews, 1961.B1, B9, B15, B27,
    B29-30, B38, B44, B48, B52,
    B54-55, B57; 1962.B13, B15,
    B17, B28-29, B34, B42;
    1963.B23, See also titles of
    individual stories
"He Doesn't Like Who-Dunits But
    He Thinks Mine Are Good,"
    1947.B7
Heilman, Robert B., 1947.B19;
    1961.B36
"The 'Hell in Paradise' of Malcolm
    Lowry," 1973.B22
"Hell or Mexico?," 1969.B18
Helwe, Ulla, 1969.B17
Hemmings, John, 1969.B18
Hennecke, Hans, 1952.B2
Hermans, Willem Frederik, 1970.B17
The Hero with the Private Parts:
    Essays, 1966.B19
Hewitt, Douglas, 1972.B17
Hicks, Granville, 1965.B10;
    1968.B24
"Higeki-Malcolm Lowry no baai,"
    1970.B1
"The High Cost of Heightened
    Sensibility," 1973.B17
"High Wire to the Crater,"
    1967.B33
Hill, Art, 1974.B46
Hirschman, Jack, 1964.B21
Histoire du roman moderne,
    1962.B26
"Hitaasti kypsynyt - ponnistellan
    Iuettave," 1969.B17
Hochschild, Adam, 1974.B47
Hoel, Sigurd, 1949.B3
Hoffman, Frederick J., 1962.B20
Hogg, James, 1973.B14
"Höllenparadies der Kunst,"
    1963.B17
"Hollywood Seeks Hit Novel Writ-
    ten Here," 1947.B33
Holmström, Ragnar, 1947.B25

Holt, Leigh, 1976.B9
"Hommage à Malcolm Lowry,"
    1963.B8
"Hooking His Own White Whale,"
    1965.B16
"Horrors at Sunset," 1962.B30
Horst, Karl August, 1952.B3;
    1963.B17; 1964.B30
"Hotel Room in Chartres,"
    1967.B14
Houston, Penelope, 1969.B19
Howard, Benjamin Willis, 1971.A2
Howard, Michael S., 1971.B13
Hristić, Jovan, 1966.B13
"Huge and Sad," 1971.B12
"Humalteen purren matka,"
    1969.B39
Humboldt, Charles, 1947.B20
Humbourg, Pierre, 1950.B5
Humor, 1963.B24; 1966.B6;
    1967.A2, B1; 1972.B22;
    1975.A2, B8; 1976.B1
"Humor in the Work of Malcolm
    Lowry," 1975.A2
Husserl, Edmund, 1970.A2
Hutchinson, Jack, 1961.B37
Hutchison, Alexander, 1972.B18
Huxley, Aldous, 1974.B82

"'The Ill-fated Mr. Bultitude':
    A Note Upon an Allusion in
    Malcolm Lowry's Under the
    Volcano," 1975.B31
"Il libro dell'ebrietà," 1961.B16
"The Illuminating Distortion,"
    1972.B16
"Il romanzo dell'inferno,"
    1961.B58
"Il Vulcano di Lowry," 1961.B47
"The Impact of Time and Memory
    in Malcolm Lowry's Fiction,"
    1970.A6
"Image Fakers," 1968.B41
Imagined Worlds: Essays on some
    English Novels and Novelists
    in Honour of John Butt,
    1968.B32
"In and Out of Books: Lowry,"
    1961.B45
"In and Out of Books: Obituary,"
    1957.B4

Ingarden, Roman, 1976.A3
"Inleiding," 1966.B31
In Search of Heresy, 1956.B1
"Inside the Volcano," 1974.B38
"In Terms of the Toenail: Fic-
    tion and the Figures of Life,"
    1970.B14
"Interrupted Journey," 1970.B31
"In the Jaws of the Abyss,"
    1965.B9
"In the Wilderness," 1969.B19
"Into One Tormented Mind,"
    1973.B4
"Introduction" to Articulating
    West, 1972.B27
"Introduction" to Notes on a
    Screenplay...," 1976.B21
"Introduction" to Selected Let-
    ters of Malcolm Lowry,
    1965.B3
"Introduction" to Selected Poems
    of Malcolm Lowry, 1962.B9
"Introduction" to Six Contempo-
    rary British Novelists,
    1976.B20
"Introduction" to Under the
    Volcano, 1965.B26
"Introductory Note" to
    Ultramarine, 1962.B23
Ivănescu, Mircea, 1969.B20

"Jack Scott," 1961.B49-51
Jackson, Charles, 1965.B11;
    1966.B8; 1970.B17
Jackson, Joseph Henry, 1947.B21
Janeway, Elizabeth, 1961.B38;
    1968.B25
Jarvinen, Seppo J., 1969.B21
Jaskari, Juhani, 1969.B21, B28
Jedynak, Stanley L., 1959.B5
"Jeszcze jedna podróż do piekieł,"
    1964.B12
Jewison, Donald Bruce, 1966.A2
Johnson, Carrell, 1969.A6
Johnson, Elizabeth, 1947.B22
Johnson, Jay, 1975.B17
Jonathan Cape, Publisher,
    1971.B13
Jones, Johanna, 1970.B18
Jones, Joseph, 1970.B18
Joseph Conrad: A Commemoration,
    1976.B3

"Journey to Self-Discovery,"
     1968.B47
Journey to the Frontier: Julian
     Bell and John Cornford, their
     lives and the 1930s, 1966.B29
Joyce, James, 1933.B6; 1947.B30;
     1955.B1, B4; 1961.B56;
     1964.B13; 1965.B12, B26;
     1966.B14, B21; 1967.B14;
     1969.B45; 1970.B37; 1972.A2;
     1973.B27; 1976.B20
Jung, C. G., 1972.A2; 1973.A3
Junkola, Aapo, 1968.B26
"Juoppohullu uni ihmisestä ja
     yhteiskunnasta," 1969.B22
Jurado, Alicio, 1968.B19

K., C., 1968.B31
"Kabbala/Lowry, etc.," 1964.B21
"Kaisetsu," 1966.B14
Kalemaa, Kalevi, 1969.B22
Kangasluoma, Tuukka, 1969.B23
Kanō, Hideo, 1966.B14
Kanters, Robert, 1962.B21
Kaye, Howard, 1968.B27
Kazin, Alfred, 1973.B15
Kenner, Hugh, 1969.B24
Kidd, Andrew, 1974.B49-50
Kiely, Robert, 1968.B28
Kilgallin, Anthony R., 1965.A3,
     B12; 1966.B15; 1968.B29-30;
     1969.B25-26; 1971.B6, B14-
     15, B22; 1973.A5, B16;
     1974.B51-52
Kim, Suzanne, 1965.B14-15;
     1968.A1; 1969.B27; 1975.B14
Kirk, Downie, 1961.B39
Kirsch, Robert, 1973.B17
"Klassiko omalla vuosisadallaan,"
     1969.B40
"Klassikot," 1969.B37
Klinck, Carl F., 1955.B2;
     1965.B20; 1967.B40; 1976.B11,
     B13
Knelman, Martin, 1976.B10
Knickerbocker, Conrad,
--as author, 1962.B22; 1963.B18;
     1964.B22-23; 1965.B16;
     1966.B17; 1967.B22-23;
     1968.B31
--as subject, 1966.B17

Knight, Stephen, 1974.B3, B29
Knoll, John Francis, 1972.A4
Koerber, Betty Turner, 1975.A2
Kostelanetz, Richard, 1964.B3;
     1965.B17
Koyama, Olive, 1964.B24
Kramer, John, 1976.A1
Kunda, Bogusław Sławomir, 1967.B24
Kunitz, Stanley J., 1955.B3

L., D., See Livesay, Dorothy
L., J., 1973.B18
"La Cabala en 'Bajo el volcán,'"
     1972.B7
"La ciudad métrica de Lowry,"
     1962.B24
"La feria de los días," 1964.B39
Lafourcade, Bernard, 1962.B10
"La genèse d''Au-dessous du
     Volcan,'" 1974.B35
"Lake Lowry," 1963.B7
"La Mordida," 1976.A4
"La Mordida: Myth and Madness in
     the Novels of Malcolm Lowry,"
     1971.A1
"Landscape and the Novel in
     Mexico," 1973.B25
The Land Unknown, 1975.B29
Lane, Helen R., 1973.B25
Łapinski, Zdzisław, 1964.B25
"La risa del demonio," 1969.B29
"La rosa de los vientos," 1964.B1
"La saison des enfers," 1963.B10
The Last Great Cause: The Intel-
     lectuals and the Spanish
     Civil War, 1968.B50
"The Last Romantic?," 1971.B3
"Las 25 estaciones de Malcolm
     Lowry," 1972.B13
"Late Lowry," 1974.B39
Lawrence, D. H., 1967.B29;
     1974.B81-82
Lawrence, Vincent, 1971.B16
Learmont, Marina, 1972.B19
Leavis, F. R., 1930.B1
"Le cryptogramme Lowry," 1960.B17
"Le dernier voyage de Malcolm
     Lowry," 1962.B21
Le Doze, Gaëlle, 1971.B17
Leech, Clifford, 1968.B32
"Le feu central," 1967.B17
"The Legacy of Malcolm Lowry,"
     1961.B30

"A Legend a Little After His Own Time," 1961.B11
"Legend Grows Around Vancouver Author," 1966.B4
Lehmann, Rosamund, 1957.B6
Lehmann-Haupt, Christopher, 1973.B20
Lehtonen, Reijo, 1968.B33; 1969.B28
"Leiden, Suchen und Hoffen...," 1952.B9
"Le jardin d'Etla," 1964.B27
"Le jeune Malcolm," 1974.B69
"Le lyrisme et le mythe: de Joyce à Malcolm Lowry," 1966.B21
"Le monde au-dessous du volcan," 1960.B12
"Le Retour aux sources," 1970.B30
"Le roman," 1950.B4
"Les lettres de Malcolm Lowry," 1969.B27
"Les oeuvres de jeunesse de Malcolm Lowry," 1965.B14
"Les oeuvres de l'adolescence," 1974.B53
"L'être et le néant," 1969.B33
"Let's Ban the Myth of the Poet Drowning in Alcohol and Guilt," 1962.B39
"A Letter," 1952.B4
Levine, Norman, 1966.B18
Lewis, R. W. B., 1974.B55
"Librairie du Mois," 1970.B5
"Life in the Infernal Machine," 1973.B20
Life is a Four-Letter Word. Vol. I: Breaking In, 1966.B25
"A Life of Malcolm Lowry," 1975.B10
"Life with Malcolm Lowry," 1971.B6
"Life's Great Conflagration," 1975.B30
"The Lighthouse Invites the Storm," 1976.A2
Lillquist, Holger, 1970.B20
Lindsay, Jack, 1968.B34
Lisowski, Jerzy, 1963.B20
Literary History of Canada, 1976.B11, B13

The Literary Symbol, 1955.B4
Literature in Action, 1972.B4
Liverpool, 1963.B26
"A Liverpool of Self," 1969.A1
Liverpool writers, 1962.B16
Livesay, Dorothy, 1947.B23
Llanos, Alfonso, 1969.B30
Lloyd, Rodney Osten, 1967.A5
"A Lonely Hunter," 1966.B18
"The Long Voyage Home: October Ferry to Gabriola," 1971.B14
"A Look in the Volcano," 1973.B14
López Ruíz, Juvenal, 1969.B29
Lopos, George J., 1968.B35
"Lord Jim as Byron," 1963.B12
Lorenz, Clarissa, 1970.B21
"A Loss to Cotton," 1945.B1
"Lost, Lost, Lost," 1963.B3
The Lost Weekend, 1965.B11; 1966.B8
Lowry, Arthur Osborne, 1945.B1-2
Lowry, Malcolm,
--as author, 1950.B5-6; 1952.B4; 1961.B41; 1970.B22; 1974.B79; 1976.B21
--as subject, general biographical studies, 1947.B7; 1948.B1; 1952.A1; 1955.B2-3; 1959.B2; 1960.B1, B8, B16; 1961.B8, B11, B13, B17, B31, B37, B40, B42, B49-51; 1962.B32; 1964.B11, B13, B16-17, B23; 1965.A1, B22; 1967.B12, B40-41; 1969.B7; 1970.B17-18; 1971.B4, B17, B22; 1972.B20; 1973.A3, A5, B9, B17, B30, B36; 1974.B84; 1975.B10; 1976.B2, B10, B14, B18
--childhood and youth, 1927.B1-2; 1963.B26; 1966.B17; 1967.B34; 1974.A1
--Cambridge years, 1929.B1-2; 1949.B2; 1962.B23, B33; 1966.B17, B25, B29; 1967.B22, B28, B33; 1968.B1, B51; 1970.B21; 1974.A1, B4, B6-7, B16-17, B21, B59, B84; 1975.B29
--Europe and America, 1960.B3; 1961.B2-3, B28; 1963.B18; 1967.B22, B38; 1968.B34; 1975.B19

--later years, 1950.B3; 1957.B1,
  B5; 1960.B11, B19; 1961.B39,
  B45; 1962.B33; 1964.B15, B39;
  1965.B16; 1966.B4, B23;
  1967.B19; 1968.B29, B40;
  1969.B34; 1970.B21; 1971.B6;
  1972.B9; 1973.B21; 1974.B13,
  B75; 1975.B19
--obituaries and tributes,
  1957.B4; 1961.B10, B12, B53;
  1962.B2-3; 1963.B15, B28
--general surveys, 1963.B22-23
  B34; 1964.B22, B32; 1965.A2,
  B8, B10, B20; 1966.A2;
  1967.A3, A7-8, B27; 1968.B21,
  B48; 1969.A1; 1970.A2, A4-5,
  A7; 1971.A2-3, A5; 1972.A1-2,
  B3, B5; 1973.A3, B2, B11;
  1974.A1, A3-5, B29; 1975.B1,
  B4, B15, B22-23, B27, B33;
  1976.A2, A4, B3, B13-14
--film scripts, 1976.B7, B21-22
--journal, 1967.A4; 1969.A5;
  1976.A5
--juvenilia, 1965.B14; 1974.A1
--letters, 1961.B39; 1964.B16;
  1964.B35; 1965.A1, B3;
  1966.B6, B10, B27, B30;
  1967.B9, B16, B42; 1969.B15,
  B27; 1971.B32; 1974.B36, B41;
  1976.B21
--manuscript collection, 1961.B4-
  6, B25; 1971.A3; 1975.B23;
  1976.A5
--novels, 1968.B21; 1971.A1;
  1974.B25, B29; 1975.B4
--poetry, 1930.B1; 1953.B1;
  1961.B18-21; 1962.B7-10, B22,
  B24, B43; 1963.B12; 1964.B8;
  1968.B7, B23; 1969.A4;
  1972.A2; 1974.B41; 1976.A2
--short fiction, 1930.B2;
  1964.B40; 1965.B24; B26;
  1966.A3; 1967.B15; 1968.A4;
  1969.B10; 1970.B12; 1971.B15;
  1972.A2; 1974.B70, B86;
  1975.A3; 1976.B7, B15, B23,
  See also Aiken, Conrad; Canadian Literature; individual
  titles
Lowry, Margerie, 1947.B7;
  1957.B1; 1960.B10; 1961.B22,

  B23, B42; 1962.B9; 1965.A1;
  1968.B17, B31; 1969.B30;
  1970.B23; 1974.B79; 1975.A3;
  1976.B21
Lowry, 1973.A5
--reviews, 1973.B4; 1974.B4, B14,
  B18, B24, B37-38, B42, B77,
  B83, B85; 1975.B17
"Lowry," 1974.B24
"Lowry, Clarence Malcolm," 1971.B4
"Lowry, (Clarence) Malcolm,"
  1974.B4
"Lowry, Malcolm" (Braem), 1969.B7
"Lowry, Malcolm" (Fee and Cawker),
  1976.B6
"Lowry, Malcolm" (Kunitz),
  1955.B3
"Lowry, Malcolm" (McConnell),
  1972.B20
"Lowry, Malcolm" (Seymour-Smith),
  1976.B18
"Lowry, aandoenlijke epigoon,"
  1970.B17
"The Lowry/Aiken Symbiosis,"
  1967.B13
"Lowry: A Memoir," 1974.B75
"Lowry and Grieg," 1963.B31
"Lowry à vingt ans," 1967.B22
"Lowry by Day," 1974.B68
"Lowry i pisarze na szcycie,"
  1973.B27
"Lowry: More Evidence for Our
  Claim," 1971.B24
"Lowry, personnage de Conrad
  Aiken," 1974.B40
"Lowry Posthumous," 1969.B26
"Lowry: Posthumous, Personal,"
  1961.B15
"Lowry's Anatomy of Melancholy,"
  1975.B2
"Lowry's Attempt at a Cosmic
  Novel," 1971.B1
"Lowry's Curse," 1974.B19
"Lowry's Debt to Nordahl Grieg,"
  1975.B6
"Lowry's Forest Path: Echoes of
  Walden," 1974.B27
"Lowry's Hell," 1969.B32
"Lowry's Inferno" (Knelman),
  1976.B10
"Lowry's Inferno" (Mayberry),
  1947.B24

"Lowry's Journal Form: Narrative Technique and Philosophical Design," 1976.A5
"Lowry's Last Novel," 1971.B7
"Lowry's Letters" (Thomas), 1966.B30
"Lowry's Letters" (Thomas), 1971.B32
"Lowry's Overture as Elegy," 1968.B16
"Lowry's Private Trip," 1969.B38
"Lowry's Purgatory: Versions of Lunar Caustic," 1970.B4
"Lowry's Quahnahuac Today," 1970.B29
"Lowry's Reading: An Introductory Essay," 1970.B28
"Lowry's Subjective Equipment," 1966.B32
"Lowry's Translator, Raul Ortiz Interviewed by Centro Director," 1962.B37
"Lowry's 'Volcano' Novel Called a Modern Classic," 1965.B27
"Lowry, the Cabbala and Charles Jones," 1970.B27
"Lowry Tops at Capturing Flavor of Life by the Sea," 1961.B52
"Lowry: Volcanic Man Not Dampened by Dollarton Rains," 1974.B13
"Lowry = Volcano = Mexico =," 1965.B8
Luckett, Richard, 1974.B59
"The Luminous Wheel: A Study of Malcolm Lowry," 1967.A8
Lunar Caustic,
--general studies, 1963.B14, B18; 1966.A3; 1967.B15; 1969.A1; 1970.B4, B24-25, 1974.B22; 1975.A3
--reviews, 1963.B10-11, B33; 1968.B2, B4, B10-12, B30, B39, B41, B43-44, B49; 1969.B24, B26, B36
"Lunar Caustic," 1968.B43
"Lunar Caustic de Malcolm Lowry," 1963.B33
"'Lunar Caustic,' Le purgatoire de Malcolm Lowry," 1963.B11

"L'univers obsessionel de Malcolm Lowry: du roman aux nouvelles," 1962.B16
"A Lush Talent?," 1974.B71
Lykiard, Alexis, 1967.B25
Lytle, Andrew, 1966.B19

M., M., 1965.B22
"Maailma on puutarha eikä pelto," 1969.B28
McConnell, Frank D., 1967.B26; 1972.B20
McConnell, William,
--as author, 1960.B11; 1968.B29
--as subject, 1961.B43
McCormick, John, 1957.B6
Machleidt, Dorothea, 1966.B20
Mack, Maynard, 1968.B32
Maclean, A. D., 1965.B1
McMullen, Lorraine, 1972.B21
McNeill, C. G., 1973.B21
McPherson, Hugo, 1965.B19, B20
MacSkimming, Roy, 1974.B60
Maes-Jelinek, Hena, 1975.B8
Magee, A. Peter R., 1965.B21
Magrini, César, 1962.B24
Mahon, Derek, 1964.B29
"The Making of Under the Volcano: An Examination of Lyrical Structure, with Reference to Textual Revisions," 1969.A6
Makowiecki, Stefan, 1972.B22; 1974.A4; 1976.B12
"Malcolm," 1966.B15
"Malcolm Lowry" (Aiken), 1967.B1
"Malcolm Lowry" (Alvarez), 1973.B1
"Malcolm Lowry" (Anon.), 1967.B5
"Malcolm Lowry" (Anon.), 1974.B6
"Malcolm Lowry" (Anon.), 1974.B7
"Malcolm Lowry" (Anon.), 1974.B8
"Malcolm Lowry" (Bradbrook), 1974.B16
"Malcolm Lowry" (Bradbrook), 1974.B17
"Malcolm Lowry" (Breit), 1960.B3
"Malcolm Lowry" (Cluny), 1966.B5
Malcolm Lowry (Costa), 1972.A2
--reviews, 1974.B37, B42-43
"Malcolm Lowry" (Davenport), 1961.B28
Malcolm Lowry (Dodson), 1970.A4
--reviews, 1973.B6

"Malcolm Lowry" (Doyen),
1971.B11
"Malcolm Lowry" (Elektorowicz),
1961.B31
"Malcolm Lowry" (Enright),
1967.B16
"Malcolm Lowry" (Greene),
1967.B19
"Malcolm Lowry" (Kilgallin),
1971.B15
"Malcolm Lowry" (Kilgallin),
1974.B51
"Malcolm Lowry" (Klinck &
Watters), 1955.B2
"Malcolm Lowry" (Lykiard),
1967.B25
"Malcolm Lowry" (Maley), 1974.B61
"Malcolm Lowry" (Meijer),
1963.B24
"Malcolm Lowry" (Mercier),
1974.B63
Malcolm Lowry (New), 1971.A3
--reviews, 1972.B8, B34
"Malcolm Lowry" (New and
Rosengarten), 1975.B25
"Malcolm Lowry" (Newlove),
1973.B24
"Malcolm Lowry" (Nylinder),
1971.B21
"Malcolm Lowry" (O'Kill),
1974.B70
"Malcolm Lowry" (Parsons),
1967.B28
"Malcolm Lowry" (Pemberton),
1967.B30
"Malcolm Lowry" (Pilot),
1972.B32
"Malcolm Lowry" (Preyer),
1973.B26
"Malcolm Lowry" (Ronson),
1967.B34
"Malcolm Lowry" (Spender),
1967.B37
"Malcolm Lowry (1909-   ),"
1948.B1
"Malcolm Lowry 1909-1957,"
1973.B30
"Malcolm Lowry (1909-1957),"
1965.B22
"Malcolm Lowry (1909-1957): A
Bibliography," 1961.B22-23

"Malcolm Lowry: 1930," 1964.B33
Malcolm Lowry: A Biography,
1973.A3; 1974.B49
--reviews, 1973.B1, B4, B13-14,
B20, B23-24, B26-29; 1974.B2,
B4, B18-19, B23, B28, B37-39,
B42-43, B47, B50, B55, B59-60,
B63-64, B66, B68, B70-71,
B76-77, B80, B83, B85;
1975.B5, B10, B30
"Malcolm Lowry: A First
Impression," 1967.B38
"Malcolm Lowry: A Flat-Broke
Success," 1966.B6
"Malcolm Lowry: A Great Drunk?,"
1973.B13
"Malcolm Lowry and the Addictions
of an Era," 1970.B10
"Malcolm Lowry and the Cinema"
(Knoll), 1972.A4
"Malcolm Lowry and the Cinema"
(Tiessen), 1970.B33
"Malcolm Lowry and the Columbian
Eden," 1973.B7
"Malcolm Lowry and the Enactment
of Fiction: The Voyage that
Never Ends," 1975.B33
"Malcolm Lowry and the Lyrical
Convention," 1974.A4
"Malcolm Lowry and the Northern
Tradition," 1976.B4
"Malcolm Lowry and the Outer
Circle of Hell," 1963.B18
"Malcolm Lowry and the 'Reel'
World," 1976.B7
Malcolm Lowry and the Voyage that
Never Ends, 1976.A4
Malcolm Lowry, 1909-1957: An In-
ventory of His Papers in the
Library of The University of
British Columbia, 1973.A2
"Malcolm Lowry: A Note," 1961.B2
"Malcolm Lowry: A Reminiscence,"
1966.B23
"Malcolm Lowry as Film Theorist,"
1976.B22
"Malcolm Lowry as Modernist,"
1973.B2
"Malcolm Lowry as Novelist,"
1961.B60
"Malcolm Lowry: A Study of His
Life and Work," 1965.A2

"Malcolm Lowry: A Study of
Theme and Symbol in Under
the Volcano," 1952.A2
"Malcolm Lowry: A Study of the
Sea Metaphor in Ultramarine
and Under the Volcano,"
1967.A9
"Malcolm Lowry: A Study of the
Sea Metaphor in Under the
Volcano," 1968.B52
"Malcolm Lowry Au-dessous du
volcan," 1950.B3
A Malcolm Lowry Catalogue,
1968.A7
"Malcolm Lowry e il cerchio
esterno dell'Inferno,"
1973.B19
"Malcolm Lowry en su obra,"
1964.B35
"Malcolm Lowry et le feu
infernal," 1969.B15
"Malcolm Lowry 'Greatest Since
Joyce,'" 1960.B21
Malcolm Lowry: His Art and
Early Life, a Study in
Transformation, 1974.A1
--reviews, 1974.B39; 1975.B17,
B21, B28, B30
"Malcolm Lowry i jego
'Ultramaryna,'" 1963.B4
"Malcolm Lowry in Retrospect"
(Moore), 1965.B23
"Malcolm Lowry in Retrospect"
(Nordell), 1964.B32
"Malcolm Lowry: In Search of
Equilibrium," 1968.B21
"Malcolm Lowry: Intención de
una obra incompleta,"
1964.B40
"Malcolm Lowry i zewnętrzny
Krąg Piekła," 1973.B18
"Malcolm Lowry: Letters to an
Editor," 1964.B16
"Malcolm Lowry, New York Pub-
lishing, & the 'New Illiter-
acy,'" 1970.B8
"Malcolm Lowry: 'Pod Wulkanem,'"
1964.B25
"Malcolm Lowry, Poète Méconnu,"
1962.B10
"Malcolm Lowry, Poet of Cycles,"
1962.B43

Malcolm Lowry: Psalms and Songs,
1975.A3
--reviews, 1976.B24
"Malcolm Lowry's Drunken Divine
Comedy in Under the Volcano
and Shorter Fiction," 1967.A3
"Malcolm Lowry's Film Treatment
for Tender Is the Night,"
1973.B3
"Malcolm Lowry şi monumentul
contemporan," 1969.B20
Malcolm Lowry's Infernal Paradise,
1976.A3
"Malcolm Lowry's Inferno,"
1973.B9
"Malcolm Lowry's Inferno, II,"
1973.B10
"Malcolm Lowry's Letters,"
1967.B2
"Malcolm Lowry's Long Night's
Journey into Day," 1975.A5
"Malcolm Lowry's Magic Realism:
The Study of an Aesthetic,"
1975.B15
"Malcolm Lowry's Major Prose
Fiction," 1972.A1
"Malcolm Lowry's Mysticism in
'The Forest Path to the
Spring,'" 1968.A4
"Malcolm Lowry's Occult Vision,"
1969.B44
"Malcolm Lowry's Other Fiction,"
1974.B29
"Malcolm Lowry's 'Paradiso,'"
1970.B11
"Malcolm Lowry's Poetry,"
1961.B18
"Malcolm Lowry's 'The Forest Path
to the Spring,'" 1972.B21
"Malcolm Lowry's Troubled Ghost
Stalks Academic Precincts,"
1971.B22
"Malcolm Lowry's Ultramarine"
(Dahlie), 1975.B7
"Malcolm Lowry's Ultramarine"
(Woolmer), 1968.B53
"Malcolm Lowry's 'Under the
Volcano,'" 1958.B2
"Malcolm Lowry's Under the Vol-
cano: A Critical Reception
Study," 1966.A1

"Malcolm Lowry's Under the Vol-
cano: An Interpretation,"
1965.A4
"Malcolm Lowry's Under the Vol-
cano: or, An Introduction
to a Modern Descent into
Hell," 1968.A5
"Malcolm Lowry Tells the Story
of a Masterpiece," 1968.B12
"Malcolm Lowry: 'The Bravest
Boat,'" 1965.B24
"Malcolm Lowry - The Cinematic
Devices Used in Under the
Volcano," 1969.A3
Malcolm Lowry: The Man and His
Work, 1971.A5
--reviews, 1971.B1, B24, B29;
1972.B18; 1973.B6
"Malcolm Lowry, The Man and His
Work: The Road to Damascus,"
1967.A7
"Malcolm Lowry: The Ordeal of
Bourgeois Humanism,"
1971.A2
"Malcolm Lowry: The Phenomen-
ology of Failure," 1975.B4
"Malcolm Lowry - the Road to
Parián," 1964.B29
"Malcolm Lowry: The Voyage that
Never Ends," 1970.A7
"Malcolm Lowry: The Writer,"
1975.B27
"Malcolm Lowry: Under the Vol-
cano," 1952.B10
"Malcolm Lowry: un écrivain
'inclassable,'" 1961.B24
"Malcolm Lowry Visits the
Doctor," 1975.B18
"Malcolm Lowry - Writer,"
1963.B22
Maley, F. W., 1974.B61
"Mal'kol'm Lauri," 1972.B35
"Manifest Mysteries in Under the
Volcano," 1974.B34
"Man in Eruption," 1947.B3
Mann, Thomas, 1972.B3
Mantovani, Vincenzo, 1973.B17;
1974.B58
"Many-leveled Fiction: Virginia
Woolf to Ross Lockridge,"
1948.B3

"Ma première rencontre avec
Malcolm Lowry," 1968.B46
Marcotte, Gilles, 1962.B25
Marill, René, 1962.B26; 1966.B21
Markle, Fletcher, 1947.B10
Marks, Jason, 1973.B22
Markson, David M., 1952.A2;
1961.B44; 1964.B31; 1966.B22-
24; 1968.B36
Marsh, Jan, 1971.B19
Martin, Jay, 1962.B27
Mary Rosalinda, Sister, See
Nyland, Agnes Cecilia
"Masks and the Man: The Writer
as Actor," 1968.B13
"The Masterpiece of the Forties,"
1964.B3
Mathews, Robin, 1963.B21
Matson, Norman, 1975.B19
Matthews, Michael, 1963.B22-23
Maurey, Pierre, 1967.A7
Mayberry, George, 1947.B24
Mayne, Richard, 1962.B28
"Med Knjigami: Malcolm Lowry:
Pod ognjenikom," 1965.B25
Meetings with Poets, 1968.B34
"Mega-Prone to Catastrophe,"
1968.B25
Meijer, Henk Romijn, 1963.B24
Mellard, James M., 1973.B23
Melville, Herman, 1970.B24;
1974.B22, B30
"A Memory of Malcolm Lowry,"
1973.B21
Menano, António Augusto, 1974.B62
Mercier, Vivian, 1974.B63
"Merseyside Author," 1962.B32
"Mescallusions, or the Drinking
Man's Under the Volcano,"
1975.B13
"Mescalusions," 1967.B9
"Message in a Bottle," 1974.B80
"Mexican Pilgrimage," 1968.B28
"The Mexican Setting in Under the
Volcano," 1973.A1
"Mexico and Moscow," 1947.B32
"Mexico and Under the Volcano,"
1967.A5
Meyers, Jeffrey, 1974.B64
Miheličeva, Mira, 1965.B22
Milici, Dirk, 1968.A4
Miller, David, 1976.A4

"The Misadventurer," 1973.B29
"A Missing Link," 1968.B44
Mjöberg, Jöran, 1947.B25
"Moby-Dick and Under the Volcano;
    Poetry from the Abyss,"
    1974.B30
"Modern Classics," 1972.B18
"A Modern Extension of the Divine
    Comedy," 1971.B20
"Modern Fiction," 1972.B29
The Modern Novel, 1963.B34
The Modern Novel in Britain and
    the United States, 1964.B4
Moir, Myra, 1947.B26
Monbet, Josine, 1968.A5
Monicelli, Giorgio, 1961.B35
Monsarrat, Nicholas, 1966.B25
Montague, John, 1967.B27
Moore, Brian, 1962.B29
Moore, Dennis James, 1970.B24
Moore, Harry T., 1965.B23
Moraes, Dom, 1963.B25
"More Light on Lowry," 1974.B42
Moreno, Carlos Martínez, 1970.B25
"More of the Hot Glare of
    Autopsy," 1973.B28
"More Than Music: Glimpses of
    Malcolm Lowry," 1961.B39
Morgan, Janet B., 1952.B6
Morley, Patricia, 1972.B23
Morris, Wright, 1975.B20
"Mortal Distractions," 1947.B5
Morton, W. L., 1976.B4
Moss, John, 1974.B65
"Mucking About with H. G.,"
    1968.B11
Mudrick, Marvin, 1969.B31
Muggeridge, Malcolm, 1974.B66
Muller, C. H., 1975.B21
Music, 1966.B17; 1970.B13;
    1974.B29; 1976.B23
Musil, Robert, 1971.B28
"Must We Burn Mme. de Beauvoir?,"
    1969.B31
"My Friend Malcolm," 1975.B14
Myrer, Anton, 1960.B12
The Mystery of Unity, 1972.B23
"Myth as Metaphor: The Odyssey
    of Malcolm Lowry," 1974.A2
"Myth in Under the Volcano,"
    1964.B31

"The Myth of Malcolm Lowry,"
    1974.B84
"The Myth of Sisyphus in Under
    the Volcano," 1969.B5
"The Myth of William Blackstone
    in a Poem by Conrad Aiken,"
    1952.B6
"Mythologized Megalomania,"
    1968.B16
Mythology in the Modern Novel:
    A Study of Prefigurative
    Techniques, 1971.B34
"The Mythopoetics of Mescal,"
    1974.B5

"Nachwort," 1963.B16
"Nach zehn Jahren Arbeit ein
    Meister-Erstling," 1952.B2
Nadeau, Maurice, 1959.B7;
    1960.B14; 1970.B26; 1974.B67
"Nadmiar wrażliwości," 1968.B42
"Narrative Form in Conrad and
    Lowry," 1976.B3
Neo-Platonism, 1970.B12; 1972.B25;
    1975.B11
"Neurotic Limbo," 1961.B1
New, William H., 1968.B37;
    1970.B27-28; 1971.A3;
    1972.B24-29; 1974.B68;
    1975.B22-26; 1976.B13-15
"New Direction in Canadian
    Fiction," 1975.B8
"New Fiction" (Post Man), 1962.B34
"New Fiction" (Price), 1968.B39
Newlove, Donald, 1973.B26
"New Novels" (Allen), 1947.B1
"New Novels" (Pritchett),
    1933.B7
"New Novels," (Shuttleworth),
    1967.B35
Newton, Norman, 1952.B5; 1968.B29
Nichols, Lewis, 1961.B45
Nimmo, D. C., 1969.B32
"A Noble Failure by a Corrupted
    Mystic," 1970.B9
"Non-novels," 1967.B20
Nordahl Grieg: Fosterlandsvännen
    och Revolutionären, 1947.B25
Nordell, Roderick, 1964.B32
"The Northern Paradise: Malcolm
    Lowry in Canada," 1972.B9

"No se Puede...," 1960.B6
"Nota della curatrice," 1974.B58
"Nota Introductoria," 1969.B30
"A Note on Romantic Allusions in
    Hear Us O Lord," 1976.B15
"A Note on the Poems," 1968.B7
"Notes" (Astre), 1951.B1
"Notes" (Birney), 1961.B19
Notes on a Screenplay for
    F. Scott Fitzgerald's "Tender
    Is the Night," 1976.B21
"Notes on Current Books,"
    1963.B5
"Not in Mexico," 1974.B18
"Not Too Lost," 1961.B3
"The Novel," 1972.B5
"Novelist's Purgatory,"
    1968.B49
"Novelist Who Recorded His Own
    Self-Made Myth," 1967.B3
The Novel Now: A Student's
    Guide to Contemporary
    Fiction, 1967.B44
"The Novel of Action," 1947.B20
"Novels Back from Limbo,"
    1963.B25
Noxon, Gerald, 1947.B10;
    1964.B33
Nye, Robert, 1962.B30; 1971.B20;
    1972.B30
Nyland, Agnes Cecilia, 1967.A8;
    1975.B27
Nylinder, Åke, 1971.B21

"Obscur présent, le feu...,"
    1960.B5
October Ferry to Gabriola,
--general studies, 1965.A1;
    1967.B15; 1969.A5; 1970.B9,
    B11, B23; 1971.B7, B14;
    1972.A3, B12, B25, B31-32;
    1974.B10; 1975.B22; 1976.B7
--reviews, 1970.B2-3, B31;
    1971.B3, B10, B12, B16, B19-
    20, B23, B25-27, B30, B33;
    1972.B2
"Octubre-noviembre, 1938,"
    1964.B6
Odysseus Ever Returning,
    1970.B36
"Of Tragic Joy," 1964.B17

O'Hara, John, 1947.B29
Ohm, Viveca, 1971.B22
O'Kill, Brian Lawrence, 1974.A5,
    B70
Olson, Stanley, 1974.B71
O'Malley, Michael, 1968.B38
"On a Dead Volcano," 1974.B59
"On a Tough Idyll," 1967.B18
"Once Quite Enough. Cotton
    Broker's Son as Deckhand,"
    1927.B2
"One Great Statement," 1965.B10
"The Ones that Burn: A Memoir
    of Malcolm Lowry," 1966.B24
"On Lowry: A Lifelong Search for
    Homes and Fathers," 1973.B23
"Only the Torso of a Masterpiece,"
    1970.B3
"On Nordahl Grieg's The Ship
    Sails On," 1975.B9
"On Re-reading Under the Volcano,"
    1964.B18
"On the Day of the Dead (Some
    Reflections on Malcolm Lowry's
    'Under the Volcano')," 1954.B1
"On the Edge of the Volcano,"
    1967.B41
On the Novel, 1971.B2
"The Ordeal of Sigbjørn
    Wilderness," 1970.B28
Ortiz y Ortiz, Raúl, 1962.B37
"The Other Edge of Existential
    Awareness: Reading of Malcolm
    Lowry's Under the Volcano,"
    1973.B31
"The Outer Ring of Hell" (Anon.),
    1968.B2
"The Outer Ring of Hell"
    (Besterman), 1968.B6
"Outstanding Novels," 1947.B27
"Outward Bound," 1969.A5, See
    also October Ferry to
    Gabriola
"Outward Bound" (Grace), 1976.B8
"Ouvrages de Malcolm Lowry
    publiés en français,"
    1974.B67
The Oxford Companion to Canadian
    History and Literature,
    1967.B39

P. I. W., 1933.B5-6
Pacey, Desmond, 1961.B46
Pagnini, Marcello, 1952.B6
Pagnoulle, Christine, 1974.B72
"Paisaje y novela en México,"
    1967.B29
Palmer, Helen M., 1971.B4
"Paperbacks in Review: Malcolm
    Lowry," 1964.B22
"Paradigms of Hell: Symbolic
    Patterning In Under the
    Volcano," 1971.B2
"Par-delà les miroirs," 1974.B72
"Par l'eau et le feu: deux
    oeuvres de Malcolm Lowry,"
    1965.B15
Parsons, Ian, 1967.B12, B28
Pascal, R., 1930.B2
Patterns of Isolation in English
    Canadian Fiction, 1974.B65
Paul, Anthony, 1969.B33
"Pauline Johnson Honored - But
    What About Lowry?," 1963.B28
Paz, Octavio, 1967.B29
Pedagogy, 1962.B40; 1965.B24;
    1967.B30; 1976.B9
Pemberton, Nicholas, 1967.B30
Pépin, Robert, 1964.B27
"Perle Epstein," 1969.B34
Perrott, Roy, 1971.B23
Personne et personnage: le
    romanesque des années 1920
    aux années 1950, 1969.B45
Peter, John, 1962.B31
Petit, Marquel, 1964.B34
Phelan, Maurice, 1976.B16
"Phenomenology and Literary
    Criticism: A Definition and
    an Application," 1970.A2
Pidancet-Laude, Corinne, 1972.B31
"Pietà, Pelado, and 'The Ratifi-
    cation of Death': The Ten-
    Year Evolvement of Malcolm
    Lowry's Volcano," 1971.B8
Pilot, Marian, 1972.B32
"Piquefort's Column," 1968.B4
"Plaque Mounted on Big Boulder
    Sought to Mark Lowry's
    Beach," 1961.B53
Plomer, William, 1971.B13
"Plot, character, etc.,"
    1961.B55

Pocock, Robert, 1967.B12
"Pod Wulkanem" (Bieńkowski),
    1964.B7
"Pod Wulkanem" (Elektorowicz),
    1964.B19
"Pod wulkanem" (Rabinowicz),
    1967.B32
"Poetry and Legend," 1963.B13
"The Poetry of Malcolm Lowry in
    Relation to the Fiction,"
    1976.A2
Polac, Michel, 1971.B17
Politics, 1966.B14; 1967.B43;
    1968.A5, B50; 1969.B22;
    1972.B35; 1973.B15; 1974.B9,
    B24, B44, B83
Ponce, Juan García, 1964.B35
"Portrait-montage de Malcolm
    Lowry," 1974.B20
"A Portrait of Malcolm Lowry,"
    1967.B12
Porzio, Domenico, 1961.B47
"Posłowie," 1963.B20
"The Possessed Artist and the
    Ailing Soul," 1961.B36
Possibilities, 1973.B2
"Postface," 1950.B2
"Postface: Malcolm et les
    ambiguités," 1965.B4
"A Posthumous Publication from
    Author of Under the Volcano,"
    1961.B44
Post Man, 1962.B32; 1963.B26
"Post-Scriptum Malcolm Lowry,"
    1971.B17
Pottinger, Andrew, 1975.B28;
    1976.B17
Pownall, David E., 1974.B74
"Predgovor," 1966.B13
Pree, Barry, 1963.B27
"Préface," 1950.B7
"Preface to a Novel," 1961.B41
"Preface" to Dark as the Grave,
    1968.B17
Preface to Nine Poems, 1961.B20
"Prefacio" to "Oscuro como la
    tumba donde mi amigo yace,"
    1968.B19
"Prefazione," 1971.B9
Prescott, Orville, 1947.B27
"Prétentieux mais emouvant,"
    1968.B9

Preyer, Robert, 1973.B26
Price, R. G. G., 1968.B39
"Primitiveness in 'The Bravest
Boat,'" 1969.B10
Pritchett, V. S., 1933.B7
The Private Labyrinth of Malcolm
Lowry: "Under the Volcano"
and the Cabbala, 1969.A5
--reviews, 1969.B24-25, B34, B38,
B44; 1970.B6, B27
"The Private Volcano of Malcolm
Lowry," 1974.B47
"Prologo" to Lunar Caustic,
1970.B25
Pryce-Jones, David, 1967.B31
"Psychological Melodrama,"
1967.B27
"Psychology and Symbols,"
1947.B8
"Publisher's Notes," 1961.B14
Purdy, Al, 1962.B33; 1968.B40;
1969.B34; 1974.B75

"Quest for Eridanus: Malcolm
Lowry's Evolving Art in
Under the Volcano," 1968.A2
"The Quest for Love," 1965.B21
"The Quest Motif in Malcolm
Lowry's Novel, Hear Us O
Lord from Heaven Thy Dwelling
Place," 1975.A4

R., B., 1952.B7
Raab, Lawrence, 1972.B33
Rabinowicz, Włodzimierz, 1967.B32
"Radio in Review," 1947.B10
Raine, Kathleen, 1975.B29
"Rake in a Suit of Armour,"
1963.B2
Ramsay, Robin, 1970.A6
Rapin, René, 1966.B26
Read, Forrest, 1961.B48
Read, Michael, 1975.B30
Read Canadian, 1972.B29
"A Reader's Guide to Under the
Volcano," 1971.A4
"Realism and Creative Fable in
Nostromo and Under the Vol-
cano: An Approach to Tech-
nique and Structure,"
1974.B45

"Recapitulation of a Masterpiece,"
1968.B22
"Recent Fiction," 1971.B26
"Recollections of Malcolm Lowry,"
1960.B11
Redgrave, Michael, 1967.B33
"Réflexions sur Styron, ses
critiques et ses sources,"
1967.B6
Reger, Muriel, 1970.B29
"Reviews," 1963.B9
"Revisitation," 1969.B3
"Revival for Lowry," 1961.B34
Reynolds, Stanley, 1968.B41
A Rhetoric of Irony, 1974.B15
"Rich Boy as Deck Hand," 1927.B1
Richey, Clarence W., 1975.B31
Riddell, John A., 1970.A7
Ripatti, Aku-Kimmo, 1969.B35
Robertson, Anthony, 1966.A3;
1972.B34
Ronson, Robert, 1967.B34
Roper, Gordon, 1969.B36
Rose, Alexander, 1963.B28
Rosenlund, Jarkko, 1969.B37
Rotstein, Abraham, 1972.B29
"Rozmowy z Konsulem," 1967.B24
Rulfo, Juan, 1967.B29
Russell, John, 1974.B76
"Russian Views of Lowry,"
1974.B9
Rutherford, Malcolm, 1963.B29

S., M., 1973.B27
Sadkowski, Wacław, 1964.B36;
1968.B42
St. Pierre, Paul Matthew, 1975.A4
"Salmon Drowns Eagle," 1953.B1
Sampson, George, 1970.B7
Sandwell, B. K., 1947.B28
Savage, D. S., 1947.B29
Savage, Meredyth, 1974.B77
Scannell, Vernon, 1962.B34
"The Scene Is Bellevue, The Hero
a Drunk, the Structure
Melville's," 1969.B24
"Scenes from Suburban Life,"
1969.B42
Schaljkwijk, Bob, 1964.B37
Schieder, Rupert, 1966.B27
Schonauer, Franz, 1963.B30

Schorer, Mark, 1947.B30
Schroeder, Andreas, 1968.B43
Scott, Jack, 1961.B49-52;
    1971.B24-25; 1973.B28
Scott, Michael Maxwell, 1971.B27
Scott, Peter Dale, 1962.B35
"The Seamy Side," 1962.B16
"Second Encounter," 1975.B19
"A Second Novel," 1960.B4
"Second Supplement to Malcolm
    Lowry Bibliography," 1964.B9
"See Hell on 65 Double Rums a
    Day," 1966.B2
"Se Faustus' undergang," 1970.B20
Selected Letters of Malcolm
    Lowry,
--general studies, 1969.B15, B27
--reviews, 1965.B2, B9, B11, B16,
    B23; 1966.B7, B10, B12, B18,
    B32; 1967.B2-3, B5, B18;
    1968.B9; 1971.B32, See also
    Lowry, Malcolm
Selected Poems of Malcolm Lowry,
--general studies, 1962.B9
--reviews, 1962.B19, B30-31, B39;
    1963.B9, B13, B21, B23, B35;
    1968.B35, See also Lowry,
    Malcolm
"Selected Poems of Malcolm
    Lowry," 1962.B31
"A Self-Consuming Light:
    Nightwood and the Crisis of
    Modernism," 1974.B12
"Sense of Tragedy," 1969.B11
"The Sequel to Lowry's Under the
    Volcano," 1962.B12
Serreau, Geneviève, 1964.B27;
    1970.B30
Servotte, Herman, 1971.B11
Seymour-Smith, Martin, 1968.B44;
    1976.B18
"Shadows of the Con-Men,"
    1963.B29
"The Shaping of Time," 1968.B32
"She Broke Gin Bottle - Found
    Husband Dead," 1957.B1
Shedd, Margaret, 1962.B36-37
Sheppard, R. Z., 1970.B31;
    1973.B29
Sherry, Norman, 1976.B3
Shierbeek, Bert, 1966.B31

Shorter, Kingsley, 1969.B38
"The Short Fiction of Malcolm
    Lowry," 1967.B15
Shuttleworth, Martin, 1967.B35
Siedler, Wolf Jobst, 1957.B7
Sigaux, Gilbert, 1950.B8;
    1960.B15-16; 1962.B38
Silverman, Carl Mark, 1971.A4
Simonson, Harold P., 1965.B24
Simpson, R. G., 1947.B31
Simpson, W. G., 1963.B31
Six Contemporary British
    Novelists, 1976.B5
Skelton, Robin, 1962.B39
Skorodenko, V., 1972.B35
"Skorpion czyli jeszcze słówko o
    Konsulu," 1973.B8
Skwarnicki, Marek, 1964.B38
Slade, Carole, 1975.B32; 1976.B19
Slemon, Stephen Guy, 1976.A5
"Śmierć w Meksyku," 1964.B36
Smith, A. J. M.,
--as author, 1948.B1; 1973.B30
--as subject, 1962.B33
Snoj, Jože, 1965.B25
Snow, C. P., 1971.B27
Solotaroff, Theodore, 1970.B14
"Some Comments on the Editing of
    Canadian Texts," 1975.B23
Something or other, A1, See
    Purdy, Al
Sommerfield, John, 1967.B12
"Sophisticated Innocence Abroad,"
    1962.B18
"The Southwest: Truth and
    Poetry," 1947.B35
"Souvenir de Quauhnahuac,"
    1960.B2
"Souvenirs sur Malcolm Lowry,"
    1957.B5
Space, Time and Structure in the
    Modern Novel, 1971.B28
Spariosu, Mihai, 1975.B33
"Special Notices," 1963.B27
Spencer, Sharon, 1971.B28
Spender, Stephen, 1965.B26;
    1967.B36-37
Spettigue, D. O., 1963.B32;
    1968.B45
Spiller, Robert E., 1948.B2
Spriel, Stephen, 1950.B3, B7;
    1960.B17

"The Squatter's Plato," 1961.B8
SR, RE, See Spiller, Robert E.
Stade, George, 1976.B5, B20
Stainsby, Donald, 1961.B53
Stallman, R. W., 1962.B40
Stansfeld-Jones, Charles Robert, 1970.B27; 1973.A5
Stansky, Peter, 1966.B29
Starrs, Roy, 1971.B29
"Stations of the Cross," 1969.B8
Steiner, George, 1961.B54
Stern, James, 1967.B12, B38; 1968.B46
Stevenson, George and Greta, 1966.B4
Story, Norah, 1967.B39
"Strange Comfort Afforded by the Profession" (New and Rosengarten), 1975.B26
"Strange Comfort Afforded By the Profession" (Stallman and Watters), 1962.B40
Stream of Consciousness: A Study in Literary Method, 1955.B1
Stromberg, Kyra, 1957.B9
"A Structural Analysis of the Wheel Symbolism in Malcolm Lowry's Under the Volcano," 1970.A3
"Structural Organization in Under the Volcano," 1967.A2
Sturm, Terry, 1970.B32
"Sturz in die Tiefe: Ein Roman des Rausches," 1952.B7
Style, 1933.B1-2, B4-8; 1947.B1, B18; 1955.B1; 1956.B1; 1957.B3; 1959.B1; 1960.B12; 1962.B12; 1963.B25; 1964.B8, B21; 1965.A3-4; 1966.A2, B26; 1967.A8, B31, B44; 1968.A3; 1969.B28; 1970.B32, B34; 1974.A5, B3, B29, B83, B86; 1975.A2
"A Stylistic Study of the Fiction of Malcolm Lowry," 1974.A5
Styron, William, 1955.B1; 1960.B4; 1967.B6
"Suffering Terminal Genius," 1974.B84
"Suicide of Cambridge Freshman," 1929.B2

Summers, Eileen, 1968.B47
"Sunday Best," 1969.B6
Sundqvist, Harry, 1969.B39
Supplement to the Oxford Companion to Canadian History and Literature, 1973.B36
"Sur l'art de Malcolm Lowry dans Under the Volcano," 1966.B26
Survey: A Short History of Canadian Literature, 1973.B33
Suvioja, Mika, 1969.B40
"Świadomość zabójcza," 1964.B10
"Swinging the Maelstrom: Malcolm Lowry and Jazz," 1970.B13
"Swinging the Paradise Street Blues," 1966.B17
Sylvestre, Guy, 1967.B40
"Symbolic Pattern in Under the Volcano," 1976.B12
"Symbolism and the Novel," 1958.B1
Symons, Julian, 1971.B30

Tao, 1976.B23
Taylor, Chet, 1971.B31; 1973.B31
Taylor, Frank, 1976.B21
Tender Is the Night, 1976.B7, B21-22
Terrés, Jaime García, 1964.B39
"This Is Lowry at the Full Power of His Talent," 1971.B25
Thoel, Rolf, 1952.B8
Thomas, Hilda L., 1965.A4; 1966.B30; 1971.B32
Thompson, John, 1961.B55
Thoreau, Henry, 1974.B27
Thorpe, Day, 1965.B27
Three Little Dog-Gone Mice, 1966.B17
"Through the Panama," 1960.B3; 1962.B41; 1966.A3; 1970.B12; 1974.B86; 1975.B4; 1976.A5, See also Hear Us O Lord from Heaven Thy Dwelling Place; Lowry, Malcolm, short fiction
Tibbetts, Bruce Hamilton, 1975.A5
Tiessen, Paul G., 1968.A6; 1970.B33; 1974.B79; 1976.B21-22
Time, 1947.B32; 1950.B6; 1957.B6; 1967.B21; 1968.B32; 1970.A6; 1974.A3; 1976.A5

Tindall, William York, 1948.B3; 1955.B4; 1956.B2
"Tod in Mexico," 1963.B30
"'___': A Topography of the Typography of Under the Volcano," 1974.B36
"A Tortured Life is Key to a Masterwork," 1965.B7
"To the Editor," 1963.B15
"'To the Volcano': The Life and Work of Malcolm Lowry," 1961.B13
"Toujours la quête éperdue," 1972.B12
Toye, William, 1973.B36
Toynbee, Philip, 1967.B41; 1969.B41; 1974.B80
Tradition and Dream: The English and American Novel from the Twenties to Our Time, 1964.B5
"Tradition and the West Indian Novel," 1967.B21
"Tragic Novel Praised As a Modern Classic," 1962.B6
"The Transformations of 'Billy Budd,'" 1970.B24
Trask, Willard R., 1958.B1
Trevor, William, 1967.B42
"The Triumph of Humpty Dumpty: Shattered Art in Under the Volcano," 1974.B11
Trotzig, Birgitta, 1962.B41
Truth Will Out, 1949.B2
Tuohy, Frank, 1961.B56
"Turning New Leaves (1)," 1962.B35
"Turning New Leaves," 1968.B40
The Twentieth Century Mind, 1972.B5
"The Two Consuls: Under the Volcano," 1972.B33
"Two Letters," 1970.B22

U., S., 1952.B9
"UBC Buys Works of Late Writer-Poet," 1961.B4
"Ucieczka Malcolma Lowry," 1964.B11
Uhlig, Helmut, 1952.B10
"Ultramarina," 1971.B5

Ultramarine,
--general studies, 1947.B25; 1953.B2; 1961.B3, B60; 1962.B8, B19, B23, B26; 1964.B24; 1965.B4, B15; 1967.A9, B1, B28; 1968.B1, B52-53; 1973.A5; 1975.B2, B6-7, B9, B11; 1976.B8
--reviews, 1933.B1-8; 1962.B4, B14, B18, B22; 1963.B2-3, B5, B7, B25, B27, B29, B32, B36; 1964.B34; 1966.B5; 1971.B5
"Ultramarine," 1933.B6
"Ultra Writer," 1966.B10
"Ulysses, Lowry's Volcano, and The Voyage Between: A Study of an Unacknowledged Literary Kinship," 1967.B14
"Um Escritor Maldito - Malcolm Lowry," 1974.B62
"Under Malcolm Lowry," 1975.B17
"Under Seymour Mountain," 1961.B61
"Under the Volcano" (short story), 1965.B26
Under the Volcano,
--general studies, 1947.B20; 1949.B3; 1950.B6; 1952.B10; 1954.B1; 1956.B2; 1958.B1-2; 1959.B2; 1960.B5-6; 1961.B36. B41, B56, B60, 1962.B21, B26, B41; 1963.B4, B8, B16, B24; 1964.B3, B5-6, B18, B21; 1965.B17, B25-26; 1966.B2, B13-14, B19, B31; 1967.B16, B24; 1968.A2-3, B16, B20-21, B32; 1969.A5-6, B4, B20, B43, B45; 1970.A4, B1, B10, B14; 1971.A3-4, B13; 1972.A3, B6, B17, B31; 1973.A3, A5, B8, B15; 1974.B44; 1975.B33; 1976.A1, A3, A5
--adaptations of, 1947.B10, B33; 1976.A1
--allusions in, 1960.B2, B12, B17; 1964.B17; 1965.A3-4, B12; 1967.A4; 1969.A5, B32; 1970.A1, A3; 1972.B7; 1973.A5; 1975.B13, B31-32; 1976.A3, B16
--characterization in, 1947.B28; 1960.B17; 1964.B35; 1969.B45;

1971.B28, B31; 1972.B14;
1974.A2; 1975.B32; 1976.B2,
B17, B19
--film and, 1952.B8; 1965.B26;
1968.A6; 1969.A3; 1970.B33;
1972.A4; 1973.A5; 1974.B4;
1976.A1, B7, B22
--influences upon, 1947.B12;
1949.B3; 1952.B3; 1966.B21;
1967.B13-14; 1970.B22;
1976.B7, B16
--myth in, 1952.B8; 1960.B14;
1964.B29, B31; 1965.B13;
1967.B17, B44; 1969.B5;
1971.B34; 1972.A1; 1974.A2;
1976.B9
--reception of, 1966.A1, B8;
1967.B4, B20, B25; 1969.B44;
1974.B8, B61
--setting, 1954.B1; 1960.B2;
1964.B37; 1967.A5, B29, B32;
1970.B29; 1971.B21; 1972.A1;
1973.B22, B25; 1974.B44, B73,
B81-82; 1975.B3, B20; 1976.B2
--structural and stylistic devices in, 1947.B19, B30;
1955.B4; 1960.B6, B12;
1961.B59; 1964.B7; 1965.A1;
1966.B21, B26; 1967.A2, A9,
B17; 1968.A3, B8, B52;
1969.B14; 1970.B37; 1971.B2;
1973.B8, B12; 1974.B34, B36,
B45, B72; 1975.B32; 1976.B1,
B12, B16-17
--themes in, 1948.B3; 1950.B2;
1952.A2; 1957.B2, B7;
1959.B5; 1960.B1; 1963.B20;
1964.B7, B12, B18, B38;
1965.B5, B21; 1967.B17, B21;
1968.A5, B8, B50, B52;
1969.B14, B45; 1972.B13, B16,
B33, B35; 1973.B7, B29, B31;
1974.B11, B15, B30-31, B45-
46, B62, B72; 1976.A3, B9,
B12
--reviews, 1947.B1-6, B8-9, B11-
19, B21-24, B26-32, B34-35;
1948.B2; 1950.B1, B4-5, B8;
1951.B1; 1952.B1-2, B7, B9;
1957.B9-10; 1960.B15;
1961.B16, B24, B26, B32, B35,

B47, B58; 1962.B6; 1963.B17,
B30, B37; 1964.B1, B10, B14,
B19, B25, B36; 1965.B7, B25,
B27; 1967.B5, B35; 1968.B26,
B28, B33; 1969.B17, B21-23,
B28, B31, B35, B37, B39-40;
1970.B20; 1971.B21, See also
Cabbala; Humour; Lowry,
Malcolm; Style; Time
"'Under the Volcano'" (Kirk),
1961.B40
"Under the Volcano: A Book of
the Dead," 1974.B31
"Under the Volcano: A Considera-
tion of the Novel by Malcolm
Lowry," 1965.B5
"Under the Volcano and Dante's
Inferno I," 1975.B32
"Under the Volcano and October
Ferry to Gabriola: The
Weight of the Past," 1972.A3
"Under the Volcano: An Existen-
tialist Tragedy," 1959.B5
"Under the Volcano: A Reading of
the 'Immediate Level,'"
1968.B20
"Under the Volcano: A Study of
Malcolm Lowry's Novel,"
1972.B6
"Under the Volcano by Malcolm
Lowry: An Ergocentric
Approach," 1968.A3
"'Under the Volcano' by M. Lowry
Shows Style Also Symbolism,"
1947.B28
"Under the Volcano: Geoffrey's
Unposted Letter," 1968.B8
"Under the Volcano: Lowry and
the Cinema," 1968.A6
"Under the Volcano: Narrative
Mode and Technique," 1973.B12
"Under the Volcano: The Dantean
Design," 1976.B16
"'Under the Volcano': The Static
Art of Malcolm Lowry,"
1970.B37
"Under the Weather," 1969.B41
"Une rencontre avec Lowry,"
1959.B4
"University Buys Work of Late
Dollarton Poet," 1961.B5

Index

"The Unknown Poetry of Malcolm
Lowry," 1961.B21
"Un monument romanesque sans
précédent," 1961.B26
"Un nuovo Ulisse sotto il vulcano
di Lowry," 1961.B35
"Unpublished Manuscripts
Purchased," 1961.B6
"Un roman de l'ivresse mystique,"
1950.B1
"Un sommet de la littérature,"
1959.B1
"Unter dem Vulkan" (Baur),
1952.B1
"Unter dem Vulkan" (Braem),
1957.B3
"'Unter dem Vulkan'" (Thoel),
1952.B38
"The Use of Literary Sources for
Theme and Style in Lowry's
Under the Volcano," 1965.A3
"The Uses of Wilderness,"
1975.B1
Ushant, An Essay, 1952.A1
"Ushant's Malcolm Lowry,"
1964.B13

"Vancouver Was Eden," 1973.B34
Vandenburgh, John, 1966.B31
Van O'Connor, William, 1961.B57
Veitch, Douglas W., 1974.B81
"The Venture," 1930.B2
Veraldi, Attilio, 1971.B9
Verschoyle, Derek, 1933.B8
"Vetoinen kuolema joka tikitti
ja ähki," 1969.B23
"Viagem Através du Vulcão,"
1973.B11
Vigorelli, Giancarlo, 1961.B58
Villelaur, Anne, 1961.B59
Vinson, James, 1976.B14
"Volcanic Vagueness," 1975.B28
"Volcano," 1966.B8
"The Volcano and the Barranca,"
1974.B44
Volcano: An Inquiry into the
Life and Death of Malcolm
Lowry, 1976.A1, B10
"The Volcano Inside," 1947.B4
"The Volcano Revisited," 1966.B9
"Von der Weltläufigkeit zur
Weltangst," 1957.B9

Von Nostitz, Oswalt, 1957.B10
"The Voyage Begins: Toward an
Understanding of Malcolm
Lowry," 1974.B37
"The Voyages of Malcolm Lowry,"
1964.B23
"Voyage That Never Ended,"
1961.B9
"The Voyage That Never Ends,"
1962.B19
"The Voyage that Never Ends:
Time and Space in the Fiction
of Malcolm Lowry," 1974.A3
Vuilleumier, Jean, 1963.B33

W., G., 1963.B36
Wain, John, 1966.B32; 1968.B48
Walker, Gerald, 1967.B23
Walker, Ronald Gary, 1974.B82;
1976.B9
Walsh, William, 1973.B32
Warner, Rex, 1947.B8
Waterston, Elizabeth, 1973.B33
Watt, F. W., 1962.B42
Watters, R. E., 1955.B2; 1966.B40
Waugh, Auberon, 1971.B33
Waugh, Evelyn, 1974.B82
Webb, W. L., 1968.B49
Weeks, Edward, 1947.B32
Weintraub, Stanley, 1968.B50
"A Wellspring of Magma: Modern
Canadian Writing," 1968.B37
"Weltschmerz Refurbished,"
1947.B12
West, Nathanael, 1974.B11
West, Paul, 1963.B34
West, Rebecca, 1974.B83
"Western i symfonia," 1964.B14
"We Were Led to Hope for More,"
1965.B11
"'What About Female Readers?':
The Character of Yvonne in
Under the Volcano," 1976.B19
"What Is Really Under the Vol-
cano?," 1966.B27
White, John J., 1971.B34
White, Kayce, 1973.B34
White, Patrick, 1972.B23
Whitley, John, 1968.B30; 1969.B42
Who's Who in Twentieth Century
Literature, 1976.B18

161

"'Why has God given this to us?'
But What God gave, the city
took. The story of Malcolm
Lowry in Vancouver," 1968.B29
Widmer, Eleanor, 1969.B43
"Widow, Birney Present Unfinished
Lowry," 1968.B30
"Widow Gets Lowry Award," 1962.B3
Wilbur, Robert Hunter, 1968.B51
Wild, Sister Bernadette, 1967.A9;
1968.B52
Wild, Roland, 1947.B33; 1960.B19
"William Burroughs and the Liter-
ature of Addiction," 1967.B26
Williams, E. T., 1971.B4
Wilson, John Anthony Burgess,
1967.B43-44; 1974.B4
Wilson, Milton, 1963.B35
"Wolfe's Clothing," 1971.B27
Wood, Barry, 1976.B23
Woodburn, John, 1947.B34
Woodcock, George, 1954.B1;
1958.B2; 1960.B20-21;
1961.B41, B60-61; 1963.B36;
1969.B44; 1970.B34-36;

1971.A5; 1973.B35-36;
1974.B84-85; 1975.B16;
1976.B24
Woolmer, J. Howard, 1968.A7, B53
Wordsworth, William, 1976.B15
"Wrestling with Lowry," 1974.B14
Wright, Terence, 1970.B37
"Writer's Memorial Site Asked,"
1961.B10
"Writing the Biography of an Un-
known Genius," 1974.B32
"Wulkany," 1964.B38

Xirau, Ramón, 1962.B43; 1964.B40

Yacoubovitch, R. I., 1974.B86
"Year of Books: A Survey of the
Problems of Publishing and
Buying and a Look at the
Highlights of 1947," 1947.B21
Young, Vernon A., 1947.B35

Zeraffa, Michel, 1969.B45
Zimmer, Dieter E., 1963.B37